Ius Gentium: Comparative Perspectives on Law and Justice

Volume 85

Ius Gentium is a book series which discusses the central questions of law and justice from a comparative perspective. The books in this series collect the contrasting and overlapping perspectives of lawyers, judges, philosophers and scholars of law from the world's many different jurisdictions for the purposes of comparison, harmonisation, and the progressive development of law and legal institutions. Each volume makes a new comparative study of an important area of law. This book series continues the work of the well-known journal of the same name and provides the basis for a better understanding of all areas of legal science.

The *Ius Gentium* series provides a valuable resource for lawyers, judges, legislators, scholars, and both graduate students and researchers in globalisation, comparative law, legal theory and legal practice. The series has a special focus on the development of international legal standards and transnational legal cooperation.

More information about this series at http://www.springer.com/series/7888

Peter C. H. Chan · C. H. van Rhee
Editors

Civil Case Management in the Twenty-First Century: Court Structures Still Matter

Springer

Editors
Peter C. H. Chan
School of Law
City University of Hong Kong
Hong Kong, The People's Republic of China

C. H. van Rhee
Faculty of Law
Maastricht University
Maastricht, Limburg, The Netherlands

ISSN 1534-6781 ISSN 2214-9902 (electronic)
Ius Gentium: Comparative Perspectives on Law and Justice
ISBN 978-981-33-4511-9 ISBN 978-981-33-4512-6 (eBook)
https://doi.org/10.1007/978-981-33-4512-6

This Springer imprint is published by the registered company Springer Nature Singapore Pte Ltd.
The registered company address is: 152 Beach Road, #21-01/04 Gateway East, Singapore 189721, Singapore

Currency Exchange Rates Table

Currency	Exchange rates[a]	Date
USD	100.0000	October 16 2020
HKD	775.0366	October 16 2020
MOP	798.2877	October 16 2020
NTD	2880.7238	October 16 2020
GBP	77.5855	October 16 2020
Kuna	647.1650	October 16 2020
Euro	85.1716	October 16 2020

[a]https://www.imf.org/external/np/fin/data/rms_rep.aspx.

Contents

Introduction

Peter C. H. Chan and C. H. van Rhee

Abstract The information age provides novel tools for case management. While technology plays a crucial role, the way in which courts are structured still maintains a critical role in ensuring effective case management. The correlation between court structure and case management is a pivotal topic. The existing debate concentrates predominantly on the micro and case-specific aspects of case management, without further inquiry into the relationship between court structure, court management, and case management. The contributions within this volume fill this gap from a comparative perspective, undertaking a macro/structural and sub-macro perspective of procedure and case management.

Court structures and judicial case management are closely connected with one another. A well-structured court in terms of its horizontal and vertical structures, coupled with effective court management protocols, makes it easier for judges to manage cases. Good case management promotes the overall effectiveness of adjudication. Therefore, it is fair to say that a well-structured court enhances the quality of justice. As Professor Richard Marcus said, 'Any consideration of the case management approach of a nation's judicial system must begin with an appreciation of the architecture of the court system.'[1] Irrespective of jurisdiction, litigants as users of the courts are looking for a procedural experience that is efficient, cost-effective, proportionate and user-friendly. However, the judges can only do so much with the case management tools that are available to them. Take, for example, the overloaded dockets in Mainland China.[2] Despite the most effective case management tools, the

[1] See Marcus in this volume.

[2] See Chen in this volume.

P. C. H. Chan (✉)
City University of Hong Kong, Hong Kong, The People's Republic of China
e-mail: pchchan@cityu.edu.hk

C. H. van Rhee
Maastricht University, Maastricht, The Netherlands
e-mail: remco.vanrhee@maastrichtuniversity.nl

P. C. H. Chan and C. H. van Rhee (eds.), *Civil Case Management in the Twenty-First Century: Court Structures Still Matter*, Ius Gentium: Comparative Perspectives on Law and Justice 85, https://doi.org/10.1007/978-981-33-4512-6_1

Chinese judges would not be able to overcome the structural deficiencies in the system that allowed the uncontrollable influx of cases. Obviously, some kind of structural channelling or re-channelling of cases is necessary to alleviate the most overcrowded dockets.

This volume examines how court structure and the management of judicial institutions affect case management. The existing debate appears to focus predominantly on the micro and case specific aspects of case management (e.g. timetabling issues, setting and enforcing procedural deadlines, limiting certain procedural rights of parties) without a further enquiry into the relationship between court structure, court management and case management. This volume intends to fill this gap from a comparative perspective, taking a macro/structural and sub-macro[3] view of procedure and case management. For the purpose of this volume, case management has a broad interpretation. Case management refers to the use of available procedural tools by the court to enhance efficiency and effectiveness in the management of the case at every phase of litigation.[4] The use of such tools may not only affect procedural decisions, but also have a bearing on the substantive rights of the parties (e.g. the common law court exercising its powers to limit discovery has both procedural and substantive impact on the case).[5]

The court structure has horizontal and vertical dimensions. It can be argued that there is a third dimension, i.e. the variation in the composition of the court in response to the importance and/or the complexity of the case (the 'importance/complexity' dimension). On the horizontal plane, courts are able to achieve a form of 'structural proportionality' through the creation of different procedural tracks, as seen in the English system,[6] or the use of specialized courts, as witnessed in most jurisdictions. Having a specialized commercial court or division to handle commercial disputes and a small claims court for low-value cases are key components of the 'Court Structure and Proceedings Index' of the Enforcing Contracts Methodology (*Doing Business*) of the World Bank.[7] Specialized judges can focus their mind and time on a specific type of cases within their core competences. The specialized court can apply a set of procedures tailored for the needs of the cases, promote specialization and professionalization of the bench and adopt innovative remedies and reliefs (interlocutory or final) that are uniquely effective in disposing the particular type of cases it handles

[3] A sub-macro view would be, for instance, the use of procedural tracks in England: see Sorabji in this volume; or the use of court lists in Hong Kong: see Rehman in this volume.

[4] The court is responsible for active and effective case management, but always in cooperation with the parties. Such cooperation includes the duty to consult the parties, and wherever possible secure their agreement on the form, content and timing of particular steps in the proceedings. Throughout the proceedings the court monitors whether all those involved observe their obligations. The court's duty of active case management authorizes judges to encourage the parties to identify the real issues in dispute, and to openly discuss with them the appropriate steps and methods for dealing with these issues during a case management conference.

[5] van Rhee and Fu (2012, pp. 1–7).

[6] See Sorabji in this volume.

[7] World Bank (2020).

(e.g. reliefs that are uniquely applicable to matrimonial cases).[8] An obvious example of such a court is the small claims tribunal. Court resources would be inefficiently deployed if small claims are handled under the usual civil litigation process. The small claims procedure, which provides for an expedited and cheap resolution of low-value claims, contributes to efficient case management. As Rehman explains when commenting on the Hong Kong system, 'From a case management perspective, [specialized] courts and tribunals are effective in their operations because … the differentiation or channelling of cases according to the nature of the claim in the tribunals and courts allows the judges with specialist knowledge in that particular area to preside over the cases. The constant contact with one particular area of the law allows judges to accumulate jurisdictive experience in that distinct area of the law and not only enhances their judicial skills in that area but also allows them to become intimately familiar with the case management issues that may arise in those types of cases.'[9]

On the vertical plane, a well-structured appellate system will have lasting effects on case management. An example are small claims again. In some jurisdictions like Mainland China, the decisions made under small claims procedure are not amenable to appeal. This closes the floodgate of courts that otherwise would have to entertain an enormous volume of small-value appeals. In comparison to final appeals, most jurisdictions ensure only the most meritorious or significant cases reach final appeal. This helps the highest court to manage its docket better and focus its resources on the most relevant and meritorious appeals. These examples demonstrate an important principle in the structuring of the appellate system: while appeal may lay as of right for most cases, it should be discretionary for some. The discretionary mechanism of the appellate system is an important case management tool for courts. In some jurisdictions, the vertical structural implication goes beyond appeal. In Mainland China, for instance, the higher court plays a critical role in supervising the lower court. This supervisory function would inevitably impact the way cases are managed in lower courts.[10]

It is sometimes reasonable to expect, at least in some jurisdictions, the composition of the tribunal to be different depending on the complexity or the significance of the case. In Mainland China, less complex cases are usually heard before a single judge under the summary procedure. More complex cases are commonly heard by a collegiate bench consisting of three judges under the ordinary procedure. There is a possibility of extending the collegiate bench to five adjudicators if the case is very important or sensitive. The composition of the tribunal would inevitably affect the way cases are managed. Trial before a single judge is conducted in an expedited fashion, whereas trial before a collegiate bench is longer with more complex procedural issues. A complex case usually requires an extended fact-finding phase.

---

[8] See Chan in this volume.

[9] See Rehman in this volume.

[10] Chan (2014, pp. 161–210).

Having more than one judge can help share the workload. As such a case involving a wide range of issues and specialist areas, can benefit from the expertise of different judges.[11]

The contributors of this volume were asked three general questions at the outset: (1) What are the specialized courts according to the various types of litigation (family cases, commercial cases, labour cases, etc.) in their respective jurisdictions and what are their functions? How effective are they from a case management perspective? (question on horizontal arrangement); (2) How does the vertical arrangement of the court system in their respective jurisdictions, from first instance to final appeal, help achieve case management objectives? (articulation between the courts of the different levels; filtering of the recourses, etc.). Is the current vertical arrangement effective from a case management perspective? (question on vertical arrangement); and (3) How do their respective jurisdictions adapt the composition of the court to the importance and/or the complexity of the case (single judge, a panel of judges, etc.)? Is it effective from a case management perspective? (question on case importance/complexity arrangement). Subsequently the contributors were asked twelve specific questions: (a) describe the legal historical contexts of their court structures, procedural rules, and case management systems (in particular, if procedures were shaped by foreign procedural rules and practices); (b) to define 'case management' as a theoretical concept in their respective jurisdictions and what the key objectives of case management are; (c) to provide concrete examples of procedural mechanisms that have profoundly impacted case management in a positive manner and to supply the relevant statistics or evidence where necessary; (d) to conduct a critical review of the relevant literature on the structural issues of case management in their respective jurisdictions; (e) to discuss any recent reform in their respective jurisdictions that impacted on case management (in particular, to discuss how the reform changed the court structure with the view to promote case management); (f) to describe the structure and function of special procedures and tribunals, if any; (g) to explain the financial or other threshold for cases to appeal to the final appellate court and its effectiveness in keeping unmeritorious claims from reaching the final appellate court; (h) to discuss what institutional measures were adopted that helped shorten trials (e.g. a 'district/county court' that took on less complex and/or lower-value cases); (i) to comment on the role of ADR in case management (e.g. whether there were any costs incentives for settling cases); (j) to describe how the courts are financed and how the financing structure impacted the way courts manage cases; (k) to comment on how far the current court structure is the product of top-down policies from other branches of government (in other words, is the judiciary able to make independent decisions on structural changes for the purposes of promoting case management?); and (l) to assess the extent to which the current court system is structurally geared towards dealing with complex/difficult cases, as opposed to processing routine matters (mass case-processing versus 'hard cases' dilemma).

[11] See Chan in this volume.

Obviously, the above questions were to serve as a guide only. Contributors could deviate from those questions in addressing the general theme or focus solely on specialist topics.[12]

This volume includes thirteen contributions: two are comparative contributions and eleven are jurisdiction-specific contributions focusing on nine different jurisdictions: Mainland China, Taiwan, Hong Kong, Macau, Brazil, the United States of America, England and Wales, Hungary and Croatia.

The volume begins with two comparative studies of case management in the context of the horizontal and vertical structures of the court system. The first comparative contribution examines the interrelations between court structure (vertical, horizontal, and important and complex dimensions) and case management in four jurisdictions: Mainland China, Hong Kong, Macau and Taiwan. It appears that all four jurisdictions have employed similar horizontal structural designs to deal with case management needs, for example the use of specialized divisions and courts for the purpose of channelling cases.[13] The divergences are noticeable when it comes to vertical arrangements. Taiwan and Hong Kong have imposed different levels of restrictions regarding final appeal. Macau has retained the practice that appeals are 'as of right' (including final appeals, so long as a certain financial threshold is met). In Mainland China, the vertical structure is distinctly different from the other three jurisdictions as the appellate procedure looks more like a hearing de novo than an actual appellate review. It appears that for those jurisdictions that have a tradition of trial by a collegiate bench (usually with three adjudicators), the trend is that now more cases are being heard by a single judge under some form of summary procedure. Indeed, with limited judicial resources, courts must find a procedural arrangement that best optimizes resources.[14]

The second comparative contribution examines the theories of case management, the role of managerial judges, and the interrelations between court structure, court management and case management. In this contribution it is evident that case management is dependent on the structural arrangement of courts. In particular, the availability of specialized courts (e.g. family and labour tribunals), the flexible composition of the tribunal that corresponds to the complexity, and the importance of the case (single judge or a panel of judges), and the interplay between superior and inferior courts (access filters and the scope of review) are all critical in ensuring effective case management.[15] The author also discusses the use of artificial intelligence ('AI') in case management. AI can be used for 'basic administrative support' and 'online tracking systems', as well as assisting as an AI court clerk.[16]

The jurisdiction-specific contributions commence with an analysis of the 'unified system' of adjudication and administration of Mainland Chinese courts. It explains

---

[12] Two contributions focused completely on specialist themes: see F Wang in this volume on e-courts in China and Dos Santos in on the mandatory mediation regime in Macau.

[13] See Chan in this volume.

[14] *Ibidem.*

[15] See Pérez Ragone in this volume.

[16] *Ibidem.*

that judging is a collective exercise in China due to the intertwined relationship between adjudication and court administration. While collectivism may promote consistency and even quality, it undermines the independence of the tribunal. As such, Chen explains how reform measures since 2015 have attempted to weaken this collectivism and the bureaucratic nature of judicial decision-making.[17] For instance, the president, vice-presidents, and division heads that are not directly involved in the case are not allowed to examine and approve judgments. The jurisdiction of adjudication committees is now limited to truly difficult and complex cases. Chen also discusses the positive impact of the reform in transferring many of the powers previously vested in the president and the court leadership to the provincial high court.[18]

The contribution by Wu examines how the American concept of 'case-flow management' has helped improve the quality of civil justice in Taiwan; a jurisdiction that was heavily influenced by German and Japanese procedural law. It examines how specialized courts and procedures, in areas such as family and intellectual property, have helped improve case management in Taiwan.[19] Wu's contribution provides a comprehensive overview of Taiwan's court structure and how its structural makeup influenced case management.[20]

Rehman's contribution looks into how the Civil Justice Reform (CJR) in Hong Kong impacted case management. The CJR conferred considerable case management powers to the judge to deal with the adversarial excesses in the system. Judges are given procedural and substantive powers of case management (e.g. the power to limit discovery). Rehman also explains how horizontal and vertical dimensions of the Hong Kong court structure have helped improve case management.[21]

W Wang explains how the introduction of the formal adequacy principle transformed the case management landscape in Macau. The formal adequacy principle alleviated the procedural rigidity of the past and allowed the judge to 'determine the best procedural arrangements for the case' when the established procedure does not fit the specific details or needs of an individual case.[22]

Marcus' contribution begins with an introduction to the US court system, both federal and state, and an explanation of American exceptionalism in procedure. American civil justice is unique in many ways: jury trials, the wide extent of discovery and all-or-nothing type contingency fee arrangements. Marcus argues that these procedural attributes, while resulting in a 'litigation explosion', created the need for managerial judging.[23] It then discusses the historical background to American case management, the resistance to managerial judging, and the positive results of case management. In the latter part of Marcus' contribution, judicial settlement promotion

---

[17] See Chen in this volume.

[18] *Ibidem.*

[19] See Wu in this volume.

[20] *Ibidem.*

[21] *Ibidem.*

[22] See W Wang in this volume.

[23] See Marcus in this volume.

is explained, 'Putting judicial management together with settlement promotion and the idea that agreed outcomes might be preferable to litigated decisions could seem to invite untrammelled judicial control of the actual result of litigation.'[24] Indeed, judges command a special authority that, if used properly, could set parties on the right course in settlement negotiations.

Cabral's contribution discusses the main features of case management in Brazil within the context of international trends. It examines specifically case assignment management, court management and litigation agreements.[25] Case assignment management is an important topic; an even distribution of cases among judges not only improves efficiency, but also the quality of adjudication.[26] The use of litigation agreements is also important as it allows stakeholders (parties as well as judges) to play a role in case management. Litigation agreements also serve an additional purpose, as Cabral explains, '[L]itigation agreements have generated a major shift in the activity of procedural management. Case management always concerns a pending case whereas litigation agreements deal with cases that are yet to come before the courts and before the dispute even occurs. The goals differ: one manages pending disputes whereas the other aims at avoiding litigation. Preventing litigation has arguably created a 'no-case management system'.'[27]

In Sorabji's contribution, the development of case management in England and Wales since the Woolf and Jackson Reforms is discussed. Key to the analysis is how the principle of structural proportionality is implemented in English procedures through the use of procedural case tracks. There are three case tracks: the small claims track, the fast track, and the multi-track.[28] Each case track calls for a different case management approach. Sorabji explains, 'While all three tracks are available in the County Court, only the multi-track is available in the High Court. Allocation to track is primarily determined by claim value. Value is not, however, determinative. Other factors that go to determine allocation are: the remedy sought; the complexity of the issues; the amount of oral evidence required; the views and circumstances of the parties.'[29] The use of case track provides a sub-macro perspective in developing case management, in addition to the traditional macro (court structure) and micro (case-specific case and costs management) levels of case management.[30]

Harsági's contribution provides a succinct overview of case management in Hungary, looking at both the contemporary procedural framework and the legal historical origins of case management. Concrete examples are given as to how the court structure affects case management. For instance, in regards to the complexity dimension, the usual civil case is heard at first instance by one professional judge, but in 'cases relating to the protection of industrial property rights (which require

[24] *Ibidem.*

[25] See Cabral in this volume.

[26] *Ibidem.*

[27] *Ibidem.*

[28] See Sorabji in this volume.

[29] *Ibidem.*

[30] *Ibidem.*

more specialized expertise), the panel shall consist of three professional judges, two of whom shall have a higher level of education.'[31]

Bratković's contribution exposes the inefficiencies of the Croatian procedural system and proposes ways that could improve case management focusing on the court's users. An example of this is that first instance proceedings are frequently delayed due to long adjournments between 'multiple, usually short, hearings'.[32] The socialist tradition in Croatian procedure means that priority is given to the 'material truth over procedural efficiency' by courts. Bratković argues, '[T]he civil justice system should be refocused on citizens as users of the system … [I]t is paramount for the court to establish a sound classification of claims, not only in relation to their nature but also in respect of their value and complexity. One-size does not fit all. Dealing with a large number of simple cases requires different skills than dealing with juridically complex cases.'[33]

The volume ends with two short contributions, one from F Wang that discusses the use of information and communication technology in promoting case management in Mainland Chinese courts. The other from Dos Santos which highlights the need to introduce a mandatory mediation regime in Macau.[34]

This volume is significant in the following ways: (1) it offers a focused academic discussion on the interrelations between court structures and case management (the macro view) as well as the case management tools that work well in the specific case (the micro view); (2) it covers nine jurisdictions (in Europe, Asia and the Americas) that have different legal traditions; (3) it provides updates on the development of case management from international trends to local experiences; (4) it addresses the role of technology in case management, which is a pivotal topic in civil justice today; (5) it explains how the legal historical backgrounds of some jurisdictions covered influenced the contemporary landscapes of case management; and (6) it includes specific recommendations on improvements in case management that can be adopted in each jurisdiction and common suggestions that are applicable to all jurisdictions.

The information age provides novel tools for case management. While technology plays a crucial role in case management, the way that courts are structured still plays a critical role in ensuring effective case management. It is hoped that this volume will become the foundation of future studies in court structures and case management.

---

[31] See Harsági in this volume.

[32] See Bratković in this volume.

[33] *Ibidem.*

[34] See F Wang and Dos Santos in this volume.

References

Chan PCH (2014) Civil appeals and other means of recourse against judgments in China: A critical review of the procedural issues. In: Van Rhee CH, Uzelac A (eds) Nobody's perfect: Comparative essays on appeals and other means of recourse against judicial decisions in civil matters. Antwerp, pp 161–210

Van Rhee CH, Fu Y (2012) Introduction. In: Van Rhee CH, Fu Y (eds) Civil litigation in China and Europe: Essays on the role of the judge and the parties. Heidelberg, London, New York, Dordrecht, pp 1–7

World Bank (2020) Doing business. https://www.doingbusiness.org/Methodology/Enforcing-Contracts. Accessed 20 June 2020

Comparative Studies

Comparing the Civil Court Structures of Mainland China, Taiwan, Hong Kong and Macau from a Case Management Perspective

Peter C. H. Chan

Abstract This contribution examines the interrelations between court structure (vertical, horizontal, and important and complex dimensions) and case management in four jurisdictions: Mainland China, Hong Kong, Macau and Taiwan. It also examines the legal historical roots of each jurisdiction's civil procedure and explains how its legal tradition impacted on its contemporary case management system. It appears that all four jurisdictions have employed similar horizontal structural designs to deal with case management needs, for example the use of specialized divisions and courts for the purpose of channelling cases. The divergences are noticeable when it comes to vertical arrangements. It appears that for those jurisdictions that have a tradition of trial by a collegiate bench (usually with three adjudicators), the trend is that now more cases are being heard by a single judge under some form of summary procedure. Indeed, with limited judicial resources, courts must find a procedural arrangement that best optimizes resources.

1 Introduction

It is intriguing to explore how the court structures compare (in the context of case management) when the jurisdictions under review are from very different legal traditions. It is even more interesting if the jurisdictions all belong to a common cultural heritage. This contribution discusses the case management systems of four jurisdictions: Mainland China, Taiwan, Macau and Hong Kong. This is a rare attempt to compare the civil court structures of these four jurisdictions from a case management perspective. This contribution also highlights the legal historical roots of each

---

An earlier version of this contribution was published in 2018 Peking University Law Journal 6(1): 55–79 (in English).

P. C. H. Chan (✉)
City University of Hong Kong, Hong Kong, The People's Republic of China
e-mail: pchchan@cityu.edu.hk

P. C. H. Chan and C. H. van Rhee (eds.), *Civil Case Management in the Twenty-First Century: Court Structures Still Matter*, Ius Gentium: Comparative Perspectives on Law and Justice 85, https://doi.org/10.1007/978-981-33-4512-6_2

jurisdiction's civil procedure and explains how its legal tradition impacted on its contemporary civil procedure.

A proceduralist assessment of the case management structure of any jurisdiction must be premised on the understanding that litigants generally want (and expect) very similar things from their civil justice system, which include the following: (a) efficiency of the process (the avoidance of undue delay); (b) cost-effectiveness of the procedure; (c) appropriate avenues to negotiate and reach settlements; (d) fair distribution of costs; (e) proportionality of the procedure (procedural rules and practice calibrated in a way that balances the need of producing a fair outcome and other goals of civil justice); (f) user-friendliness of the civil procedural system; and (h) an enforcement system that is effective and simple to operate.

2 Horizontal Arrangement: Specialized Courts

Specialized courts have an important place in good case management. Having in place a specialized commercial court or division to handle commercial disputes and a small claims court for low-value cases are key components of the 'Court Structure and Proceedings Index' of the Enforcing Contracts Methodology (*Doing Business*) of the World Bank.[1] A specialized court produces positive case management results in the following aspects: (1) the judge can focus his mind and time on a specific type of case (which presumably is within his core competence) and is freed from the trouble of handling different types of disputes (some of which may not be within his core competence); (2) the specialized court can apply a set of procedures tailored for the type of cases that falls within its jurisdiction; (3) the specialized court performs the function of channeling disputes from the ordinary civil process, thereby releasing the pressure from the ordinary civil court; (4) a specialized court allows further specialization and professionalization of the bench, as judges are given more opportunities to be exposed to cases within their core competences; and (5) the specialized court may adopt innovative remedies and reliefs (interlocutory or final) that are uniquely effective in disposing the particular type of cases it handles (e.g. reliefs that are uniquely applicable to matrimonial cases).

Specialized courts in Hong Kong are generally effective from a case management perspective. '[The] differentiation or channeling of cases according to the nature of the claim in the tribunals and courts allows the judges with specialist knowledge in that particular area to preside over the cases. The accumulation of experience in a distinct area of the law not only enhances the substantive legal skills of the judges in that area but also allows them to become intimately familiar with the case management issues that may arise in those types of cases.'[2] The Judiciary's confidence in proposing to increase the Small Claims Tribunal's jurisdictional limit from HKD 50,000 to HKD 75,000 is evidence of the effectiveness of the tribunal.

[1] World Bank (2019).

[2] Rehman (2017, para. 1).

The Family Court (which operates within the District Court) received praise for operating a distinctly different (and highly effective) mediation regime tailored for matrimonial disputes.

In Mainland China, while there are no specialized courts as such (apart from, say, military courts), civil and commercial cases are handled by different 'civil divisions' of the court. Traditional civil cases (such as matrimonial cases and simple breach of contract cases) are usually handled by the First Civil Division. The Second Civil Division deals with commercial cases. The Third Civil Division usually deals with intellectual property cases. The Fourth Civil Division, if established, generally deals with cross-border disputes (e.g. cases involving foreign parties or with foreign elements). Some courts establish additional divisions to deal with different types of disputes: '[For example,] the intermediate court in Shenzhen has its own bankruptcy division. Some basic courts also set up labour dispute tribunal, environmental protection tribunal, financial dispute tribunal and other divisions in accordance with the economic characteristics of the region.'[3] The separation of the civil court into different divisions allows judges to specialize in a particular area of civil litigation. This is particularly relevant for specialist areas like intellectual property law and cross-border disputes where judges are expected to master highly complex legal principles and procedures.

In Taiwan, the trend is to establish more specialized courts to enhance the effectiveness of case management and promote judicial specialization. Existing specialized courts include the Intellectual Property Court based in New Taipei City and the Juvenile and Family Court based in Kaohsiung City. There is suggestion that a specialized commercial court should be established for Taiwan in the near future.[4]

In Macau, only the *Tribunal Judicial de Base* (court of first-instance) may form specialized tribunals. Existing specialized tribunals include *Juízo de Pequenas Causas Cíveis* (Small Claims Tribunal), *Juízo de Familia e de Menores* (Family and Juvenile Tribunal) and *Juízo Laboral* (Labour Tribunal).[5]

3 Vertical Arrangement

Since judicial resources are limited, appeal should only be available to those cases that are sufficiently meritorious and/or significant. The appellate procedure should not be only limited to correcting errors. The appellate courts (especially the final appeal courts) are in a unique position to declare fundamental norms and unify jurisprudence.

There is a welcoming change in Hong Kong's civil procedure that gives the Court of Final Appeal (CFA) (or the Court of Appeal (CA)) discretion in determining what cases are to be heard by the CFA. Rehman observed, '[The] new provisions state that

[3]Chen (2017, para. 1).

[4]Wu (2017, para. 1).

[5]Wang (2017, para. 1).

all civil appeals to the CFA are subject to discretionary leave from either the CA or the CFA, regardless of the amount involved. This change will theoretically allow the CFA to hear genuine and more meritorious appeals. It has also brought Hong Kong in line with other common law jurisdictions.' This new discretionary leave contrasts sharply with the old arrangement, where any appeal to the CFA from the CA lay 'as of right' so long as the monetary threshold was HKD 1 million or more. The revision of the procedural rules for appeal to the CFA was motivated by the argument '[that] the adoption of an arbitrary financial limit to determine the right of appeal enabled any claimant whose claim was above the financial threshold to obtain leave, regardless of the merits of the claim. This situation led to the court having to hear appeals that were unmeritorious.'[6]

In Mainland China, the vertical arrangement of the judiciary is geared towards the supervision of lower courts by the superior courts. Under the Chinese court hierarchy, the higher-level courts (the Supreme People's Court (SPC) at the apex of the hierarchy, followed by the provincial high courts) play a regulatory role within the Chinese court system. Higher level courts issue directional publications (in the form of notices or judicial interpretations) to give guidance to lower courts with regards to certain procedural matters. Sometimes where there is a gap in the statutory law, the higher-level courts will issue interpretations to give directions to lower courts on how the law should be interpreted and applied. Generally speaking, higher courts exercise supervisory powers over lower courts through the following formal channels: (a) exercising the usual powers of the appellate court; (b) the higher court may re-open a legally effective case decided by a lower court under the 'adjudication supervision procedure' (e.g. the higher level court may retry the case itself or remand the case to the lower level court ordering a retrial); (c) the higher court has the authority to assess the performance of the lower courts (the so-called 'case quality evaluation', which in fact is a number-crunching quantitative exercise)[7]; and (d) through issuing directional publications to direct the behaviour of lower courts. When it comes to informal channels, the avenues of 'supervision' (or intervention) are numerous: for example, 'in order to avoid a case remanded by a higher court for a new trial, lower courts may sometimes communicate with the superior court [outside of] the normal procedure or seek the superior court's opinion before making the judgment'.[8] This type of informal 'communication' (*qingshi*) was in fact common practice throughout China's legal history.[9]

In Taiwan, the judiciary (or the 'Judicial Yuan') is led and managed by the 'grand justices', who also sit as constitutional adjudicators in Taiwan's constitutional court. The civil jurisdiction has three levels of courts: the Supreme Court, Taiwan High Court (and its four Branch Courts) and 21 Taiwan District Courts.[10] A civil case

[6]Rehman (2017, para. 10).

[7]Chan (2016, pp. 14–23).

[8]Chen (2017, para. 2).

[9]Minzner (2011, pp. 58–90).

[10]In addition to the jurisdiction of these courts over the island of Taiwan, there is another system of courts with jurisdiction over regions not within the jurisdiction of the island of Taiwan: i.e. Fuchien

tried at the district court level can be appealed to the Taiwan High Court, which can then be further appealed to the Supreme Court (i.e. a three-tier system). The party appealing to the Taiwan High Court (or its Branch Courts) may seek to challege the factual findings of the district court. But any further appeal to the Supreme Court is a discretionary review appeal limited to only legal issues (i.e. a court of *Revision*).[11]

There are three levels of courts in Macau: *Tribunal Judicial de Base* (Basic Level Court), *Tribunal de Segunda Instância* (Intermediate Level Court) and *Tribunal de Última Instância* (Court of Final Appeal). A civil case heard at the *Tribunal Judicial de Base* may be appealed twice. An appellant is not allowed to lodge an appeal unless it is shown that the value of the case meets a certain dollar threshold. Under certain circumstances (e.g. when the appeal is essentially a jurisdictional challenge), the appellant is not required to meet the dollar threshold. A special recourse is available for parties to challenge a legally effective judgment under a re-adjudication procedure if it is shown that there was dereliction of duty on the part of the judge or where there was a serious procedural error (e.g. where the evidence was proved to be falsified). A third party recourse is available to third parties (whose interests are detrimentally affected) to challenge a legally effective judgment if it is shown that the original lawsuit was a sham. Currently, the appellate system in Macau does not allow an appellant to lodge a direct appeal to the *Tribunal de Última Instância* against a decision by the *Tribunal Judicial de Base*. Macau's judiciary should consider introducing this direct appeal mechanism as it will speed up (and simplify) the appeal procedure and save costs.[12]

4 Case Importance/Complexity Arrangement

The complexity and/or importance of the case should have a bearing on the composition of the tribunal. Complex and/or important cases sometimes call for a different composition of tribunal (usually meaning having more than one judge to hear the case). For instance, a complex case in China is usually heard by the collegiate bench (comprising three adjudicators) under the normal procedure. There is a possibility of extending the collegiate bench to five adjudicators if the case is very important or sensitive.

The rationale for a different composition of tribunal for hearing complex and/or important cases is that (a) complex and/or important cases usually involve more fact-finding, hence justifying the need for more adjudicators to share the work; (b) such cases are likely to involve difficult legal issues, so a decision made by a majority (at least 2 to 1) of a panel of judges command greater legitimacy than one single judge;

High Court Kinmen Branch Court, which oversees two district courts (Fuchien Kinmen District Court and Fuchien Lianjiang District Court).

[11] Murray and Stürner (2004, p. 386).

[12] Wang (2017, para. 2).

(c) such cases may involve a wide range of issues and specialist areas, so the case can benefit from the expertise of different judges.

When compared to civil law systems, the common law trial court is always composed of a single judge. Only in appellate courts will there be multiple judges. From the common law perspective, 'The adjudication of most cases by a single judge is preferable, effective and constructive from a case management perspective,'[13] as there is usually a shortage of judges in common law courts. The situation in Hong Kong is a classic example of this phenomenon:

> The increasing number of cases being brought before the courts and the surge in the claims being instigated by litigants in person have not only caused a serious strain on judicial resources but also placed time constraints on the judges who must preside over these cases. Unlike civil law countries where judges are often recruited at a relatively young age and go through extensive on the job training, judges in Hong Kong who are appointed to the High Court are often very experienced and distinguished practitioners who may already be in their late 40's or early 50's when they are appointed. This tradition coupled with the disinclination of some qualified and successful practitioners to accept appointments to the bench have led to a shortage of judges in the upper levels of the judiciary. Faced with an already limited number of judges, it is prudent from a case management standpoint to continue to have cases in the DC [District Court] and CFI [Court of First Instance] be adjudicated by single judges.[14]

In Mainland China, most civil and commercial cases (over 80%) are heard by a single judge under the summary procedure. This is partly due to 'the heavy caseloads, limited [number of] judges and overworked local courts.'[15] Obviously, the shorter timeframe in the summary procedure (three months, as opposed to six months in the ordinary procedure) is another reason for its 'popularity'.

In Macau, a civil claim with a value of MOP 50,000 or below is heard by a single judge, while a claim with a value over MOP 50,000 is heard by a collegiate bench comprising three judges. Insisting on a collegiate bench to hear civil cases ignores the problem of lack of judicial manpower. Possible reform includes raising the dollar threshold to MOP 100,000 for trial by collegiate bench or eliminating collegiate bench hearings altogether unless there are special circumstances meriting it.

In Taiwan, all civil cases at the district courts are heard by a single judge. But the district court may form a collegiate bench of three judges under special circumstances (e.g. if the case is particularly complex). Proceedings at the High Court (whether Taiwan High Court or Fuchien High Court) are heard by a three-judge collegiate bench. Proceedings at the Supreme Court are handled by a five-judge collegiate bench.

---

[13] Rehman (2017, para. 3).

[14] *Ibidem.*

[15] Chen (2017, para. 3).

5 To What Extent is the Current Court System of Case Management Shaped by the Procedural Principles and Rules of Other Legal Systems ('Jurisdictions of Origin')

Law, in its contemporary form, is the result of decades (if not centuries) of metamorphism. Ignorance of the legal history of a jurisdiction runs the danger of taking law at its face value. The four jurisdictions selected in this contribution all inherited traditional Chinese culture, but more importantly, the jurisdictions were shaped by different foreign legal traditions, either due to colonization (Hong Kong inheriting the English legal tradition; Macau inheriting the Portuguese legal tradition) or legal transplant (Mainland China transplanting the Soviet model of legality; Taiwan transplanting the Japanese and German models).

In the realm of procedural law, the influence of foreign law is sometimes difficult to assess. For instance, in Mainland China, the drafting of the 1982 Civil Procedure Law was not said to be modeled on Soviet procedural law, but since the drafters at that time were predominantly exposed to the 'Russian legal heritage', key Soviet procedural principles (such as the supervision system of the procuratorate and the two-instance system) influenced the ultimate Chinese procedural code.[16] The Soviet state's interventionist approach in civil procedure fitted well in China's political system where the judiciary traditionally played a subservient role. While the interventionist approach has weakened over time, state control of the civil process has always been a question of degree and never a question of whether there should be control or not.

Comparatively, Hong Kong's situation pre-2009 was an outright adoption of the old English civil procedural rules (pre-Woolf procedural system). While there were some fine differences, the procedural framework was almost identical. However, problems arose when the old English procedural rules proved to be too adversarial and too lax when it came to non-compliance. As one learned author observed, 'However, Hong Kong's civil litigation system was not immune from the inherent deficiencies (especially in relation to case management issues) that can result from an adversarial system in which too much of the discretion and initiative is left in the hands of the litigants. By the turn of the century, the judiciary and the other stakeholders in the civil litigation system were acutely aware of the inefficiency, delay and the spiralling costs associated with conducting civil litigation in Hong Kong.'[17]

Macau's Civil Procedure Code of 1999 was the product of a considered adoption of the modern Portuguese procedural law (more precisely, the procedures in force in Portugal between 1995 and 1996). While Macau adopted the various case management features from Portugal during that period, Macau did not seek to update itself when Portugal's procedures underwent further reform after that period. As such, two key case management features are still absent in Macau's civil procedure today: (1)

[16]Chen (2017, para. 3a).

[17]Rehman (2017, para. 3a).

the pre-trial review procedure; and (2) the separation of the judge from enforcement proceedings (enforcement proceedings are to be handled predominantly by private enforcement agents).

Taiwan's civil procedural law relating to case management was inherited from the German procedural tradition.[18] The Taiwanese case management model focused on the powers of the judge in directing the course of the litigation in a way that ensures procedural efficacy and compliance with procedural deadlines. This tradition is now watered down by Taiwan's adoption of American methods of case-flow management. Judges in Taiwan today are less involved in case management as they now focus more on the actual adjudication work. Case management and procedural matters at the pre-trial stage are now handled by judicial assistants and designated procedural judges.

6 (Wholesale) Adoption of Foreign Procedural Law, or Not?

A jurisdiction may choose to adopt a foreign procedural code in a wholesale fashion (perhaps with only minor amendments to cater for local situations). This is likely to happen with colonization. When Hong Kong was colonized by Britain, the English civil procedural framework was transplanted to Hong Kong in its entirety. While certain aspects of indigenous substantive law were retained (e.g. Qing land and matrimonial customs), Hong Kong civil procedural law was completely imported from England. Obviously, Hong Kong's procedural framework departed from England after the Civil Justice Reform in 2009, when Hong Kong decided to selectively adopt the Woolf Reforms and not to adopt the CPR. The current procedural system of Hong Kong is unique, which is what the judiciary wants: a framework that suits the particular circumstances of the region.

The same can be said about Macau. The Macau's Civil Procedure Code of 1999 adopted the modern procedural code of Portugal (predominantly based on the procedural code effective between 1995 and 1996 in Portugal) with such amendments that cater for the local circumstances in Macau. The Civil Procedure Code of 1999 did not adopt the principle of party presentation. The judge in Macau may direct fact-finding beyond the ambit of the facts established by the parties. The judge was also given extensive powers of investigation. The judge may go beyond certain procedural rules and impose his own procedural directions if there is an overwhelming need to do so in the particular case. These extensive powers are consistent with their principle of active judicial case management.

The wholesale adoption of foreign procedural law is contrasted with the situation where a jurisdiction is simply using the procedural framework of another jurisdiction for reference. During the Qing and Republican periods, the drafters of the Chinese civil procedural codes referred to both the German and Japanese procedural laws. The

[18] In particular, the Code of Civil Procedure (or *Zivilprozessordnung* (ZPO)) of 1877.

contemporary Chinese Civil Procedure Law is not based on any foreign procedural law, although earlier versions of the law were influenced by Soviet procedural principles. There are no clear structural resemblances between the current Chinese Civil Procedure Law and the Soviet Code of Civil Procedure. Chen made the following remark regarding Soviet influence:

> As mentioned above, the Soviet Code of Civil Procedure has a significant impact on China's civil litigation system and legal procedure theory. However, when the 1982 Civil Procedure Law was adopted, the Sino-Soviet relations had not been repaired from the rupture in the early 1960s and remained politically hostile. Therefore, the Act [1982 Civil Procedure Law] does not directly refer to the Soviet Code of Civil Procedure as a model. In fact, the latter still had an indirect influence on the former by the legal scholars who had educational background of the Soviet law and [were] familiar with the concept of Soviet civil procedure law. By 1991, [when] the Civil Procedure Law was formally implemented, the Soviet Union was already disintegrated. The Soviet Civil Procedure Code also no longer existed. As a result, it is difficult to tell which procedural rules were being transplanted and which were abandoned. To be precise, the Chinese Civil Procedure Law has never directly 'transplanted' the specific provisions of the Soviet Union. Therefore, it is difficult to compare the difference in terms of the structure of law between the two laws.[19]

The contemporary procedural law of Taiwan is the result of multiple revisions of the procedural code promulgated by the Republican government as early as 1930. The Republican procedural law of 1930 was very much a substantial replica of the German Code of Civil Procedure (or *Zivilprozessordnung* (ZPO)) of 1877. In 1999, 2000 and 2003, major revisions were made to Taiwan's civil procedure law. These revisions introduced a number of novel features to the Taiwanese civil procedural system, including the establishment of the small claims procedure, the reform of the civil evidence regime and the strengthening of assets/property preservation procedures. As a result of these changes, Taiwanese civil procedure is now more adapted to local conditions and has entrenched the principle of party disposition in day-to-day civil processes.

7 Definition of 'Case Management'

The concept of 'case management' may diverge with different legal traditions and judicial practices. For instance, from the common law perspective, case management means the handling of proceedings in a way consistent with relevant principles such as efficiency and cost-effectiveness. This is contrasted with procedural systems where case management is equated to 'judicature management', i.e. the administration of the court organization. With different definitions of 'case management', the objectives of case management are bound to be different. For instance, if case management is focused simply on making proceedings more efficient, then other non-proceedings related objectives are irrelevant. But if case management is defined to include a

---

[19] Chen (2017, paras. 3b–3c).

broader administrative objective, then non-proceedings related functions must also be assessed and managed.

In Mainland China, case management is taken to an extreme. The term commonly used is 'trial management' or 'judicature management' (*shenpan guanli*). 'Trial management' is categorically different from the Western concept of 'case management'. Apart from considering the efficiency of handling cases, the concept of 'trial management' embraces an administrative perspective of managing the court institution, the individual judge (including disciplinary matters) and the implementation of policy objectives in civil adjudication. From the Chinese legal perspective, the court's main function is dispute resolution. The Chinese contemporary concept of 'dispute resolution' is about the pursuit of a state where 'the case is closed and the dispute is [truly] resolved' (*Anjie shiliao*). *Anjie shiliao* is not a purely procedural concept but rather a socio-legal phenomenon. Trial management measures the procedural efficacy and social effect of court work by meticulously collecting and analyzing data on case processing. Among other benchmarks, trial management takes indices such as 'mediation settlement rate', 'withdrawal rate', 'actual enforcement rate' and 'the rate of reversal and new trial by remittal of first instance decisions (decisions in error)' into account in its assessment of judicial merit. These benchmarks feature in a scoring matrix that measures the level of fairness (*gongzheng zhibiao*), efficiency (*xiaolü zhibiao*) and effectiveness (*xiaoguo zhibiao*) in the handling of cases by the court under review. Some academics in Mainland China have questioned the appropriateness of using indices like 'mediation settlement rate' as points of reference for the evaluation of judicial work, because overemphasizing settlement rates may result in the proliferation of abusive practices in court mediation.[20] Essentially, trial management is a mass case-processing system designed for a social policy agenda.

In Hong Kong, case management is given a narrow meaning: the management of proceedings in a way consistent with principles such as efficiency and cost-effectiveness.[21] Under the notion of 'justice on the merits' in the pre-2009 era (i.e. before the Civil Justice Reform), effective case management was never a fundamental goal of civil justice. Under this notion, courts are reluctant to strike out a claim so long as there is still substantive merit, despite the party in question had already breached numerous procedural deadlines. As a result of the lax in enforcement (or non-enforcement) of procedural deadlines, undue delay became almost a pandemic of civil litigation. Other problems arising from the neglect of case management is that parties were given a free hand to do whatever procedurally is not prohibited, but may not be conducive to the resolution of the case. Even the judiciary itself has admitted that the excessively adversarial nature of civil litigation led to immoderations such as delay and complexity.[22] The underlying objectives of the revised

---

[20]Cai (2014, p. 46).

[21]Rehman (2017, para. 5): 'Whilst there is no definition of 'case management' in Rules of the High Court (RHC), active case management is commonly understood to be the means by which the courts have been directed to achieve the underlying objectives of increasing cost effectiveness and warranting that cases are dealt with in an expeditious and feasible manner.'.

[22]Final Report (2004, p. 10, para. 31).

Rules of the High Court (RHC) and the Rules of the District Court (RDC) (which came into force following the Civil Justice Reform in 2009) were introduced into the rules to not only increase cost-effectiveness and procedural expediency but also ensure fairness between parties and facilitate settlement of disputes.[23] The grant of control to the judges to exercise their case management powers either on application or of their own motion[24] is an aspirational undertaking to achieve the imperatives of effectiveness, efficiency and fairness in the civil litigation system.

Despite the term 'case management' never appeared in Macau's civil procedure law, the *Código de Processo Civil* explicitly states that the judge has the authority (and obligation) to impose measures to ensure that the case is dealt with in an efficient manner and avoid undue delay.[25] The judge is expected to act proactively in managing cases, including finding ways to save costs, simplifying the procedure where possible and reducing delay.[26]

In Taiwan, 'case management' is understood as 'case-flow management', i.e. how can the case-flow model be simplified and expedited in a way that allows cases to be disposed of efficiently. A large part of Taiwan's case management reform was to free judges (as much as possible) from pretrial matters, which allows them to focus purely on adjudication. Pretrial matters are handled by judicial assistants and 'procedural judges'. Parties are encouraged to take proactive steps to prepare their cases at the pretrial stage, so as to save time and costs.

8 Reforms

Civil justice reforms were carried out in all four jurisdictions (in one form or another) in the past decade or so. These reforms had huge impact on case management.

The Civil Justice Reform (CJR) in Hong Kong has completely changed the case management landscape in that judges (who used to be passive) were given explicit mandate to play a proactive role in case management. The introduction of the underlying objectives stated in the amended RHC[27] was a landmark development in the

---

[23] RHC and RDC O. 1A, r. 1.

[24] RHC O. 1B, r. 2.

[25] Art. 6(1) of the *Código de Processo Civil.*

[26] Wang (2017, para. 5).

[27] RHC O.1A, r.1 reads:

'The underlying objectives of these rules are–

(a) to increase the cost-effectiveness of any practice and procedure to be followed in relation to proceedings before the Court;

(b) to ensure that a case is dealt with as expeditiously as is reasonably practicable;

(c) to promote a sense of reasonable proportion and procedural economy in the conduct of proceedings;

(d) to ensure fairness between the parties;

(e) to facilitate the settlement of disputes; and

(f) to ensure that the resources of the Court are distributed fairly.'

history of Hong Kong's civil case management. From then on, all civil procedural rules must be interpreted in a way that is consistent with the underlying objectives. In other words, no party can take advantage on a specific rule with the view to delay proceedings or for the tactical purpose of running up the costs of the other side. Rehman provided a succinct summary of what the CJR has achieved since its implementation in 2009:

> Since its implementation, the aim of the CJR has been to cure undue delay and excessive complexity and cost in the civil litigation system. However, unlike the English approach that was adopted in the Woolf Reforms, the Hong Kong judiciary adopted a more cautious approach by selectively amending the existing civil [procedural] code rather than introducing a whole new code. The aim of introducing changes such as the underlying objectives, active case management, timetabling and the use of milestone dates, the new system of sanctioned offers and payments and provisional assessment of costs in the new code has been to enhance the cost-effectiveness of the system, reduce its complexity and reduce delays in litigation.[28]

The Supreme People's Court's Opinions on the Comprehensive Entrenchment of Reforms in the People's Courts (Fourth Five-Year Reform Outline of the People's Courts)[29] (SPC 2015 Reform Opinion) outlines in detail China's judicial reform package, setting out 65 points of reform. Article 1 of the SPC 2015 Reform Opinion sets the tone of the reform: i.e. the construction of a judicial system where 'the people feel that justice is done in every single court case'. This tone marks a clear departure from previous emphasis on the social impact of court decisions and the dispute resolution function of the court. Article 1 also touches on the importance of ensuring that courts adjudicate independently (which, in fact, is a constitutional guarantee) free from outside interference. Article 2 then outlines five key principles that underscore the reform: (1) upholding the political leadership of the Chinese Communist Party in judicial reforms; (2) respecting that the judiciary is a unique organ of the state in that the adjudication process must be afforded such procedural protections for it to function independently and impartially; (3) propelling the reform efforts in a stable and progressive manner based on the law (e.g. entrenching reform measures through timely legislation); (4) focusing on the key problems first, i.e. tackling structural problems such as external interference with adjudication; and (5) strengthening top-down supervision and high-level planning, but at the same time allowing sufficient room for local innovation (e.g. pilot programmes on the local level should be encouraged). There are seven key aspects of the reform: (i) reforming the administrative structure of the court system; (ii) constructing an 'adjudication-centred' judiciary; (iii) formalizing and strengthening the functional systems within courts with clear 'terms of reference' (e.g. docketing system); (iv) improving and calibrating the operational mechanisms of the adjudicative process; (v) constructing an 'open, dynamic, transparent and people-centred' judicial system; (vi) formalizing and professionalizing court personnel appointment and management; and (vii) guaranteeing the independent exercise of adjudicative powers by the courts.[30]

---

[28] Rehman (2017, para. 8).

[29] Effective since 4 February 2015 (Judicial Notification [2015], No. 3).

[30] Chan (2017).

In Taiwan, since October 2016 (when the new president of the Judicial Yuan was appointed), six areas of reform have been identified: (1) emphasis on adjudicatory independence and the protection of human rights in court procedures; (2) professionalization of adjudicators; (3) strengthening the principle of party presentation in adjudication; (4) unifying jurisprudence by avoiding conflicting judgments; (5) reducing the workloads of judges to a reasonable level; and (6) reform relating to constitutional adjudication. Among these six areas, the goal of reducing judicial workload (thereby increasing efficiency and effectiveness of the procedural system) became the most important reform objective. To achieve this objective, the Judicial Yuan approached the problem of backlogs from a case management perspective. Simplifying procedure, restructuring the court organization, reducing unmeritorious cases entering the system, increasing the role of judicial assistants in handling pre-trial matters (thereby easing the workloads of judges, so judges can focus on trials) have all become important items on the reform agenda.[31]

Macau's judicial system went through reform in 2004, including the restructuring of its *Tribunal Judicial de Base* by creating specialized tribunals. As mentioned above, these tribunals are: *Juízo de Pequenas Causas Cíveis* (Small Claims Tribunal), *Juízo de Familia e de Menores* (Family and Juvenile Tribunal) and *Juízo Laboral* (Labour Tribunal).

9 Small Claims Procedure

A common characteristic among all four jurisdictions is the existence of structural design to channel less complex and/or low-value disputes to summary/speedy procedures (usually known as small claims procedures). Small claims are either heard by a separate tribunal (e.g. Hong Kong's Small Claims Tribunal) or by the ordinary civil court (e.g. in Mainland China, small claims are heard by the civil division of the court). Jurisdictions employ different standards in determining what constitutes a small claim, some applying a straightjacket dollar threshold, while others apply a more complicated formula. In Hong Kong, subject to certain exceptions, the Small Claims Tribunal has exclusive jurisdiction over monetary claims founded in contract or tort where the claim is HK $75,000 or less. In Mainland China, only if a case has three characteristics would it be considered a small claim case: (a) a simple case with clear facts and unambiguous rights and obligations; (b) relating to minor dispute; and (c) the amount of the subject matter is lower than 30% of the previous year's average annual wages of workers in that particular province.[32] The availability of recourse is also divergent among the four jurisdictions.

The effectiveness of the small claims procedure received mixed reviews in the four jurisdictions. Chen noted, 'Judging from the statistical data of local courts, the application rate of small-claim litigation procedure is generally not high, and its effect

[31] Wu (2017, para. 8).

[32] Article 162 of the PRC Civil Procedure Law.

of improving the efficiency of trial is not significant.' This may be due to the fact that there is already a summary procedure under the usual civil process that performs the function of channelling less complex disputes from the ordinary procedure, leaving the Chinese small claims procedure playing only an ancillary role. It may also be due to the fact that the threshold for qualifying as a small claim under the Chinese procedure is paradoxically complex.

The position in Mainland China stands in stark contrast to Hong Kong's small claims procedure, which worked extremely well.

The small claims procedure was introduced in Macau in 2004. Any monetary claim within MOP 50,000 may be heard at the *Juízo de Pequenas Causas Cíveis* (Small Claims Tribunal). The procedure is very user friendly. The claimant is not required to follow the usual formalities of a 'statement of claim' and simply needs to file a standardized MA1 form (which is much more simple than the usual statement of claim). The claimant is not required to make a 'security deposit' (i.e. security for costs) for his claim (which is a requirement for usual civil claims). A decision by the small claims tribunal is not subject to appeal.

In Taiwan, a monetary claim below NT$ 100,000 must be referred to the Small Claims Tribunal. If both parties agree, a monetary claim below NT$500,000 may be referred to the Small Claims Tribunal from the District Court (but subject to the court's discretion to move the case back to the District Court). The decision of the Small Claims Tribunal is subject to appeal, once, to the District Court with jurisdiction over the matter. The appeal is heard by a panel of three judges at the District Court. The appeal must be on the basis of any legal error in the decision of the Small Claims Tribunal.

10 Final Appeals

The availability of final appeal allows the highest court of the land to review important or controversial legal issues with the view of unifying jurisprudence. It follows that not all cases are suitable for final appeal.

The position in Hong Kong is succinctly summarised as follows:

> In Hong Kong, the appeal mechanism for cases to be heard in the Court of Final Appeal (CFA) was considered highly unsatisfactory before the Administration of Justice (Miscellaneous Provisions) Ordinance 2014 came into effect in December 2014. Previously, an appeal lay to the CFA 'as of right' from a final judgement of the CA where the matter in dispute amounted to HKD 1 million or more or the appeal involved a question which, by reason of its great general or public importance, or otherwise, ought to be submitted to the CFA for decision. The main point of objection was in relation to the former provision as it was argued that the adoption of an arbitrary financial limit to determine the right of appeal enabled any claimant whose claim was above the financial threshold to obtain leave, regardless of the merits of the claim. This situation led to the court having to hear appeals that were unmeritorious. The new provisions state that all civil appeals to the CFA are subject to discretionary leave from either the CA or the CFA, regardless of the amount involved. This change will theoretically

> allow the CFA to hear genuine and more meritorious appeals. It has also brought Hong Kong in line with other common law jurisdictions.[33]

The mandatory requirement (in Hong Kong) to seek discretionary leave from the CA or the CFA has made it much harder for a case to reach the final appellate stage. Any case that successfully obtains leave is almost guaranteed to be a case of great significance, either due to its public importance or because of the fundamentally critical legal issue(s) involved.

In Mainland China, a second instance decision is said to be 'final'.[34] However, the Chinese concept of 'finality' is nebulous. A second instance decision may be reopened under the adjudication supervision procedure. The adjudication supervision procedure allows a legally effective judgment or ruling (or mediation statement)[35] to be reopened for re-adjudication[36] on the basis that the decision has been tainted by error.[37] Adjudication supervision is a discretionary procedure and should only be used sparingly (i.e. only when a definite error has been identified in the final judgment).[38] The notion that uniformity of the law can be achieved through adjudication supervision may be sound in theory. In practice, however, retrial decisions (especially retrial decisions of lower-level courts) can be just as inconsistent as first or second instance decisions. The rules of adjudication supervision are primarily catered for correcting errors identified in effective judgments, not for achieving consistency in jurisprudence. To achieve uniformity, the highest level of courts must be in a position to declare universal norms. Some Chinese academics are in favour of revoking the current two-instance system[39] in the long run, to be replaced by a three-tier system with a third level *Revision* to the SPC.[40]

In Macau, final appeal comes as of right so long as a certain dollar threshold is met (i.e. the claim is over MOP 1,000,000). It is expected that final appeal would

---

[33]Rehman (2017, para. 10).

[34]Article 175 of the PRC Civil Procedure Law; Article 12 of the PRC Organic Law of the People's Courts.

[35]A 'mediation statement' (*tiaojie shu*) is a written court-sanctioned settlement agreement reached through court mediation. It has the same legal effect as a civil court judgment and can be enforced directly by the parties.

[36]'Re-adjudication' (*zaishen*) (sometimes translated as 'retrial'), is a key component of the adjudication supervision procedure. A 're-adjudication' must be distinguished from a 'new trial' (*chongshen*) triggered by the remittal of a case from the appellate court to the first instance court in the appellate procedure.

[37]The threshold for reopening a legally effective decision varies with the entity initiating the adjudication supervision process. For instance, if a party applies for re-adjudication, the legally effective decision must fall under any of the circumstances set out in Article 200 of the PRC Civil Procedure Law. If the adjudicative committee of the court that rendered the legally effective judgment sought to reopen the case, a finding of 'definite error' in the judgment is required (see Article 198 of the PRC Civil Procedure Law).

[38]Adjudication supervision is a special procedure, which should be distinguished from the day-to-day adjudicatory work of the courts.

[39]Under the current Chinese appellate system, a second instance decision is said to be 'final': Article 175 of the PRC Civil Procedure Law and Article 12 of the PRC Organic Law of the People's Courts.

[40]Murray and Stürner (2004, pp. 386–399).

remain as of right going forward, but no strong argument is presented to support its continuation.[41] The need to weed out unmeritorious appeals allows the *Tribunal de Última Instância* (Court of Final Appeal) to focus on cases that are significant, either in the sense that the cases are of public importance or the cases involve a very important legal point. It is submitted that Macau could look to Hong Kong for inspiration in reforming its final appellate system.

Final appeal in Taiwan is discretionary in the sense that '[No] appeal may be taken to the court of third instance except on the ground that the original judgment is in contravention of the laws and regulations'.[42] A certain dollar threshold must also be met (i.e. the claim is over NT$1,000,000 for ordinary proceedings). The court has the discretion to increase or deduce the dollar threshold in the appropriate case.[43]

11 Shortening First Instance Proceedings

First instance proceedings form the bulk of civil litigation. Whether or not the parties eventually reach the trial stage, first instance proceedings (given the need to conduct fact-finding) are usually the most costly and time-consuming. Shortening first instance proceedings, both in terms of streamlining the pre-trial procedure and simplifying trial, is critically important if one were to make the civil process more efficient.

In Hong Kong, less complex cases involving monetary claims at or under HK $75,000 are dealt with by the Small Claims Tribunal. Parties appearing in the Small Claims Tribunal cannot be represented by lawyers.[44] For first instance proceedings at the District Court and the Court of First Instance, the availability of summary judgment (where the defendant has no defence) and default judgment (where the defendant failed to file the defence or the intention to defend) helped shorten the overall time of proceedings.

Most civil cases in China at first instance are heard under the summary proceedings. Summary proceedings are handled by single-judge tribunals. Litigation must be concluded within three months from commencement to the conclusion of proceedings.

In Taiwan, first instance proceedings are shortened through the restructuring of the pre-trial procedures and the active management of trial. These changes have expedited first instance proceedings significantly.[45]

---

41 Wang (2017, para. 10).

42 Article 467 of the Taiwan Code of Civil Procedure.

43 Article 466 of the Taiwan Code of Civil Procedure.

44 However, if they can provide valid reasons, they may be allowed to have a representative appear for them. The litigants or their representatives have to prepare all the witness statements and other documents that are to be used during the trial and they also have to conduct the examination of witnesses during the trial.

45 Wu (2017, para. 11).

12 The Use of ADR

From a proceduralist perspective, mediation occupies a unique position in any civil justice system in that it (if appropriately deployed) provides an alternative to litigation while preserving the parties' right of access to court.

An extremely successful procedural measure in Hong Kong was Practice Direction 31 (PD 31). Under PD 31, procedures are in place to encourage settlement of disputes through mediation. The court may impose an adverse costs order on the successful party that had unreasonably refused to participate in the mediation. In exercising this discretion, the court will consider, among other things, the nature of the case, the merits of the case, the extent to which other settlement methods have been attempted, and whether the ADR has a reasonable prospect of success.[46] The following passage best summarizes how effective PD 31 was in promoting settlement in Hong Kong:

> Stakeholders generally regard the PD 31 regime as effective. An experienced mediator is of the view that the use of mediation does not prolong delays, especially if the case is suitable for mediation. He is also of the view that the mediators are generally skilful and the parties are willing and committed to resolving their disputes by mediation. A leading litigation practitioner commented that, after the CJR, the court is more successful than before in facilitating settlement. Under the new environment, parties are much more active in considering settlement (usually through mediation) at an early stage of proceedings. This increases the likelihood of settlement.[47]

In Mainland China, the use of mediation reached its height during Wang Shengjun's tenure as president of the Supreme People's Court (March 2008–March 2013). Courts acted very much like state-sponsored mediation centres where special preference was given to mediation. Some courts even competed with one another to reach the so-called 'zero judgment' mark, which was considered a great achievement back then. The judicial policy that favoured mediation has technically been abandoned since the change in SPC leadership in March 2013. However, there is literature that suggests the innate preference for mediation by Chinese judges had not changed.[48]

In Taiwan, certain causes of action are subject to the mandatory mediation regime, including ownership disputes between joint tenants of property, medical disputes, employment disputes (disputes directly arising from an employment contract), matrimonial disputes relating to property entitlement, land disputes involving neighbours and disputes relating to the common area of a condominium.[49] Outside of the mandatory mediation regime, courts may attempt conciliation at any point in the civil process whenever there is an opportunity for settlement (provided that both

---

[46] *Halsey v Milton Keynes General NHS Trust* [2004] 1 WLR 3002, at 3009.

[47] Chan et al. (2014, pp. 71–125).

[48] Chan (2017).

[49] Article 403 of the Taiwan Code of Civil Procedure.

parties consent to conciliate). The mediation is conducted by a designated 'conciliation judge'. Third parties may be invited to participate in the conciliation if their participation is deemed conducive to reaching a settlement.[50]

In Macau, under the ordinary procedure, mediation occurs at two separate stages: (a) mediation may be attempted within 15 days after the close of pleadings (voluntary mediation); and (b) the parties are required to go through mediation right before the court hearing (mandatory mediation). It is pointed out that no incentives are given to parties to mediation under the voluntary mediation procedure. The mandatory mediation procedure is also not very successful in reaching settlement.[51]

13 Financing of Courts

The fiscal arrangement of the judiciary impacts immensely on the autonomy of courts. A judiciary that lacks any real say regarding its own budget (and relies heavily on arbitrary fiscal decisions of the government) tends to be dependent and plays a subservient role to the administration. Studying the budgeting and financing models of courts therefore provides very useful indicators for judicial independence.

The courts in Hong Kong are financed predominantly by the government as the annual budget of the judiciary is part of the overall budget of the government of Hong Kong. The annual budget of the government is approved on an annual basis by the Legislative Council through appropriation legislation. Over the last decade or so, the Hong Kong government has been able to accumulate significant fiscal reserves through land sales and through the adoption of a conservative monetary policy. Thus, the judiciary has not faced any significant difficulties in securing the necessary financing for the administration of the judiciary.[52] The judiciary also has unrestrained autonomy in deciding its own budget.

The judiciary in Macau receives funding from two sources: (a) government appropriation; and (b) its own income. The Court of Final Appeal President's Office (*O Gabinete do Presidente do Tribunal de Última Instância*) (Office) comes up with the budget, which is approved internally by the Administrative Committee of the Office. The Administrative Committee is chaired by the President of the Court of Final Appeal. Its members are the presidents of the *Tribunal Judicial de Base* (Basic Level Court), and *Tribunal de Segunda Instância* (Intermediate Level Court).[53]

The budget of courts in Taiwan is prepared by the Judicial Yuan. The Executive Yuan has no authority to add or subtract from the budget, but may comment on it. The budget is then passed on to the Legislative Yuan for approval. The relative autonomy of the Judicial Yuan to determine the budget allows it to pursue bold

---

[50] Article 377 of the Taiwan Code of Civil Procedure.

[51] Wang (2017, para. 12).

[52] Rehman (2017, para. 13).

[53] Wang (2017, para. 13).

reform objectives. Much of the reform relating to case-flow management involved significant appropriations from the Legislative Yuan.[54]

In Mainland China, courts used to be financed by local governments (with some financial support from the central government in certain regions). Since 2015, China's judiciary introduced a reform programme, which among other things, sought to change the old financing model. The reform objective is to centralize fiscal powers at the provincial high court. Under the reform, the provincial high court now formulates the budget, the provincial people's congress approves the budget, and the provincial people's congress standing committee approves any final revisions to the budget. This is the first time the provincial high courts are put in charge of such a colossal financial task. It is too early to tell whether the fiscal reform is successfully implemented or not.

14 Policy-Making and Case Management Structure

Government policies play a significant role in shaping court procedures in some jurisdictions. The questions to ask are: (a) how much of the current case management structure is the product of top-down policies from other branches of government?; and (b) is the judiciary able to make independent decisions to change its structure for the purposes of promoting case management?

The Hong Kong judiciary is completely independent from other branches of government. No government policy can change the structure of Hong Kong's courts. The judiciary is at complete liberty to make independent decisions to promote case management: 'In the period before the implementation of the CJR, the judiciary received the recommendations from the Working Party to improve efficiency and reduce delay and all subsequent decisions it made to apply the recommendations were made independently and without any interference from the other branches of the government.'[55]

The judiciary of Macau is (in principle) independent from other branches of government. The judiciary is basically able to make independent decisions to modify procedures with the view to promote case management.[56] The same can be said about the Judicial Yuan of Taiwan.[57]

In Mainland China, policies of the administration play a critical role in the development of the judiciary. Case management in China, as mentioned above, takes the form of 'Trial Management'. The 'Trial Management' system in China is the product of policy. Apart from considering the efficiency of handling cases, the concept of 'trial

---

[54]Wu (2017, para. 13).

[55]Rehman (2017, para. 14).

[56]Wang (2017, para. 14).

[57]Wu (2017, para. 14).

management' embraces an administrative perspective of managing the court institution, the individual judge (including disciplinary matters) and the implementation of policy objectives in civil adjudication.

15 Routine Case-Processing v 'Hard Cases'

Complex cases (especially cases involving an important legal question) deserve the deployment of greater court resources given their potential significance. It follows that routine cases (particularly cases with considerably lower value) should be disposed by a routine case-processing system that best optimizes court resources. The distinction between the methods of handling routine cases and 'hard cases' underscores the notion that court resources are scarce and therefore must be utilized in a way that maximizes outcome.

In Hong Kong, the civil process is designed in such a way that routine cases and 'hard cases' are differentiated with reference to the monetary value of the claim.[58] This differentiation obviously fails to take into account cases that involve important points of law (but not necessarily of high value). But such differentiation already allows some form of channelling under which more resources will be allocated to higher value cases. Aside monetary value, cases are also differentiated in accordance with the nature of the claim. This differentiation, while not aimed at separating routine cases from 'hard cases', helps the judiciary to establish groups of judges specializing in a particular area of law at different levels of courts:

> For example, the DC [District Court] enjoys matrimonial jurisdiction in its capacity as the Family Court. In the CFI [Court of First Instance], several lists have been established to enable judges supervising those lists to deal with the proceedings. Currently, in the CFI, there is a Personal Injuries List, a Commercial List, a Construction and Arbitration List, a Constitutional and Administrative Law List, an Admiralty List and an Employees Compensation List. Each list is presided over by a specialist judge in that particular area and the judge has control of the cases in his list. Any party wishing to have its case transferred to a particular list may apply by summons to the judge in charge of the list.[59]

In Mainland China, 'hard cases' refer to those cases that are complex, sensitive and/or socially significant. Hard cases are handled by the Adjudication Committee, which is the most powerful organ within every court in China. The committee's decision on a case is final. Legally effective judgments may be reopened by the committee for re-adjudication.[60]

---

[58] Jurisdiction up to HKD 75,000 for the Small Claims Tribunal; HKD 3 million for the District Court and unlimited civil jurisdiction for the Court of First Instance.

[59] Rehman (2017, para. 15).

[60] Chen (2017, para. 15).

16 Concluding Remarks

Case management is a practical matter that concerns every civil court. The problems surrounding the management of civil proceedings are strikingly similar. These are highly technical questions. Procedural efficiency, cost effectiveness of the system, proportionality of the process and the effectiveness of the ADR regime are all common questions that every case manager needs to address.

This contribution surveyed four jurisdictions: Mainland China, Hong Kong, Macau and Taiwan. Each of these jurisdictions has developed unique structures to deal with case management problems. These structures are the result of the jurisdiction's rich legal tradition as well as practical institutional needs.

It appears that all four jurisdictions have employed similar horizontal structural designs to deal with case management needs, e.g. the use of specialized divisions and courts for the purpose of channelling cases. It also appears that the small claims procedure proves to be very effective (with the exception of Mainland China, as the usual summary procedure is already quite efficient in dealing with cases of lower values).

The divergences are more noticeable when it comes to vertical arrangements. Taiwan and Hong Kong have imposed different degrees of restrictions when it comes to final appeal. Macau seems to have retained the practice that appeals are 'as of right' (including final appeals, so long as a certain dollar threshold is met). In Mainland China, the vertical structure is distinctly different from the other three jurisdictions in that the appellate procedure looks more like a hearing de novo than an actual appellate review. Also, the Supreme People's Court is not a court of *Revision* or Court of Cassation.

It appears that for those jurisdictions that have a tradition of trial by a collegiate bench (usually with three adjudicators), the trend now is that more cases are being heard by a single judge under some form of summary procedure. Indeed, with limited judicial resources, courts must find a procedural arrangement that best optimizes resources.

ADR plays a key role in case management. All four jurisdictions encourage mediation to a different degree. In Taiwan and Macau, some lawsuits must go through mediation. In Hong Kong, while mediation is voluntary, the potential negative costs consequence in refusing to mediate effectively makes mediation a quasi-mandatory requirement. In Mainland China, it remains to be seen whether the contemporary policy of mediation (one that seeks to give mediation its full ADR effect) is being implemented in practice.

For court financing, it appears that all jurisdictions understand the importance of allowing the judiciary to independently make decisions on budgetary matters. While some form of scrutiny is unavoidable (and, to a certain extent, necessary), the judiciary of each jurisdiction is minded to retain as much fiscal power as possible. The most fiscally dependent judiciary out of the four is the judiciary of Mainland China. But that too is changing with the judicial reform since 2015.

All four jurisdictions have implemented positive reform measures that help enhance case management. To say the least, each jurisdiction has employed practical measures to reduce the caseload pressure of judges. These measures have been generally effective.

References

Cai YM (2014) Case management in China's civil justice system. In: Van Rhee CH, Fu YL (eds) Civil litigation in China and Europe: Essays on the role of the judge and the parties. Dordrecht, pp 39–58
Chan PCH (2016) An uphill battle: How China's obsession with social stability is blocking judicial reform. Judicature 100(3):14–23
Chan PCH (2017) Mediation in contemporary Chinese civil justice: A proceduralist diachronic perspective. Leiden, Boston
Chan PCH, Chan D, Chen L (2014) Hong Kong. Selective adoption of the English Woolf reforms. In: Van Rhee CH, Fu YL (eds) Civil litigation in China and Europe: Essays on the role of the judge and the parties. Dordrecht, pp 71–125
Chen H (2017) Mainland report. IAPL Conference 2017 (unpublished)
Final Report (2004) The final report of the Chief Justice's Working Party on Civil Justice Reform. 3 March 2004. https://www.civiljustice.hk/fr/documents/cjr_final_report.pdf. Accessed July 2020
Minzner CF (2011) Judicial disciplinary systems for incorrectly decided cases: The imperial Chinese heritage lives on. In: Woo MYK, Gallagher ME (eds) Chinese justice: Civil dispute resolution in contemporary China. New York, pp 58–90
Murray PL, Stürner R (2004) German Civil Justice. Durham, NC
Rehman UU (2017) Hong Kong Report. IAPL Conference 2017 (unpublished)
Wang W (2017) Macau Report. IAPL Conference 2017 (unpublished)
World Bank (2019) Enforcing contracts methodology. https://www.doingbusiness.org/Methodology/Enforcing-Contracts. Accessed June 2020
Wu J (2017) Taiwan Report. IAPL Conference 2017 (unpublished)

Case Management from a Comparative Perspective: Horizontal and Vertical Court Arrangements

Álvaro Pérez Ragone

Abstract The demand for judicial attention will continue to exceed the supply of judicial time. Various solutions have been suggested to counter the rising caseload. Examples are a reduction of the number of court applications, an increase in the number of judges, and improving the efficiency of the courts with the introduction of appropriate case and court management instruments. Court management and case management are critical components within an efficient judicial system. They depend on the court structure and arrangements within and between the courts both from a horizontal and from a vertical point of view. The structural design of a judicial system depends on multiple factors, including legal culture and policy. This contribution explores, from a comparative perspective, the theories of case management, the role of managerial judges, and the interrelations between court structure, court management and case management. It is evident that case management is dependent on the structural arrangement of courts. In particular, the availability of specialized courts, the flexible composition of the tribunal that corresponds to the complexity and the importance of the case, and the interplay between superior and inferior courts are all critical in ensuring effective case management.

1 Introduction

Current judicial systems are enthusiastically embracing case management. Improving the case management skills of the judiciary and magistrates is one avenue to reduce delay and costs. In this respect, it is important to realize that judicial training to implement reforms has traditionally been jurisdiction-specific and knowledge-based rather than skills-based.[1]

[1] Benvenuti (2015).

Á. Pérez Ragone (✉)
Universidad del Norte, Antofagasta, Chile
e-mail: alvaro.perez01@ucn.cl

Institute for Social, Political and Cultural Studies - Universidad San Pablo, Tucumán, Argentina

P. C. H. Chan and C. H. van Rhee (eds.), *Civil Case Management in the Twenty-First Century: Court Structures Still Matter*, Ius Gentium: Comparative Perspectives on Law and Justice 85, https://doi.org/10.1007/978-981-33-4512-6_3

A reference to the efficiency of judicial systems is necessary, because efficiency may be seen as a facet of the wider claim to the effectiveness of the judicial protection of rights.[2] With this key observation, I do not mean to reduce the discussion to market ideology, where the judicial protection of rights depends only on a profit-maximizing and cost-minimizing approach. As Professor Caponi remarks, if one maintains that judicial protection of rights and efficiency are incompatible, one would be bound to believe that individuals do not care about the judicial protection of rights.[3] Efficiency is different from effectiveness, as the former is connected to the purposes and arrangements of the whole civil justice system, while effectiveness is linked to the purpose(s) of a single proceeding(s).[4]

For a better administration of justice,[5] a combined micro and macro view of case management is necessary. The relationship between the rule of law and economic growth has been one of the more dynamic areas of theoretical and empirical work in political science, economics and law, in addition to an interest in institutions and fundamental economic processes.[6] The effective protection of rights should be provided in a fair process and in an efficient manner. One may ask how this should be done. In my opinion, the answer is by appropriate allocation of the court's resources to each case taking into consideration the need of other cases as well.[7] We live in a world where resources for litigation are scarce,[8] but at the same time this is combined with the idea that every person is entitled to his or her day in court.[9] The problem and challenge is, as Professor Caponi remarks, finding a way to determine how much individuals value judicial protection of rights in comparison with other goods and services they want to obtain and, accordingly, how many resources they wish to devote to the judicial system in comparison with other sectors of public administration.[10] In this regard, the final decision is a result of political processes.[11] The management of justice thus can be seen as involving a tension between the market and human rights. It is necessary to manage the case-flow without breaching the guarantees of a fair trial.[12] The principle of case management is that the courts, rather than the litigants, control the pace of litigation. It is a modern approach to dispute resolution

---

[2]Tronson (2016, pp. 21–23).

[3]Caponi (2016, pp. 139–164).

[4]*Ibidem*. See for the difference between efficiency and procedural economy: Brändli (2013, pp. 46–62).

[5]Cf. Alt and Le Theule (2011); La Porta et al. (2004).

[6]Cf. Brändli (2013, pp. 62–70); Calabresi (2016, pp. 15–25); Stürner (2014, p. 271).

[7]Caponi (2010, p. 389), and (2016). Prof. Caponi states: 'The pursuit of efficiency shall not be detrimental to the right of access to court and the effective protection of rights.'

[8]Bone (1993, p. 561).

[9]Lahav (2015, p. 536).

[10]Caponi (2016).

[11]Alt and Le Theule (2011), Carrington (2010), Klöpfer (2016, pp. 13–20). Cf. Dondi et al. (2015, pp. 27–30).

[12]Uzelac and Van Rhee (2017, pp. 3–13), cf. Amrani-Mekki (2010), Stürner (2007, pp. 128, 130, 140).

which seeks to move away from the old bitter adversarial arguments and encourage cooperation and partnership between the parties.[13]

Access to justice is a key factor in many justice systems around the world. As in other fields, technology is considered as the way forward to guarantee access to justice. Apart from deciding cases, work in court is mainly concerned with registration, indexing and the follow up of individual cases. A systematic and efficient case management system can provide important information for courts and thus guarantees unbiased decision-making.

Apart from the Introduction (Sect. 1), this essay is divided into four sections: in Sect. 2, I will discuss the complex connection between efficiency, effectiveness and judicial independence from the perspective of case management and judicial performance requirements; in Sect. 3, I will consider some key points concerning case- and court management; in Sect. 4, I will examine procedural arrangements relating to case- and court management; and in Sect. 5, I will discuss artificial intelligence and case management. In the conclusion, some of the key findings of this article will be summarized.

2 Efficiency, Effectiveness, Courts and Rights Protection

Judicial 'attention' is a scarce resource: the number of cases per judge has grown drastically. Various proposals have been made in response to the rising caseload, including ways to reduce the number of court applications, increasing the number of judges, and improving efficiency with appropriate case and court management, which is to be discussed here. Additionally, access to the court and effective protection of rights should be on the top of the agenda. One should realize that the demand for judicial time will continue to exceed the supply of it.[14] Therefore, the adaptation of proceedings and court structures should be a priority.[15]

Applying judicial 'managerial' theories, it must be assured that proportionality in devoting court time to cases is considered a top priority according to constitutional

[13]Turner (1997).

[14]Prof. Andrews mentions the following problems in the English civil justice system: lack of economic access to courts; delay during appeals; inefficiency within the system of enforcing judgments; slow movement towards superior forms of information technology within the court system; disparities of judicial provision between London and the regions, the capital being better served, see Andrews (2017), cf. Briggs (2016).

[15]Da Fonseca Gajardoni (2017).

standards. Both constitutional and procedural law need to be considered. Constitutional limitations certainly apply also in the sub-constitutional law sphere.[16] Limitations to fundamental rights resulting from case management may be challenged.[17] The constitutionality of case and court management should be tested within the framework of the rule of law. The introduction of vigorous case management in the US has caused resistance, particularly among American academics. Professor Resnik questioned its effectiveness more than 36 years ago.[18] Others worry that the judges are given too much unconstrained power.[19] As Professor Wolff remarks, the explosion of the interest in the role of judges over the last thirty years has produced valuable insights into the institutional responsibilities and limitations of the judiciary.[20]

According to Professor Marcus, a significant part of the culture shift in the US as regards case management is related to the enhanced judicial management of cases by judges. This is, for example, visible in amendments to the rules concerning discovery, especially where it concerns proportionality. Most recently, the 2015 amendments to Rule 26(b)(1) of the Federal Rules of Civil Procedure stressed the need to limit discovery according to the proportionality principle, thus highlighting the courts' responsibility to ensure that litigation is cost effective.[21] Professor Marcus states:

> Actually, this concept [i.e. proportionality] had been in the rules since 1983, but in the 2015 amendments it was made more prominent and drew much attention. The idea is that the parties should scale their litigation efforts and expenditures to what is at stake. One hope was that the lawyers themselves would implement proportionality. But realism requires us to recognize that judges will have to play a role in achieving proportionality.[22]

Critical components of an efficient judicial system are court and case management. These deal with the courts' structure and the imperative arrangements within and between the courts, both from a horizontal and vertical point of view (courts at the same level of the court hierarchy and courts at different levels respectively). The structural design of a judicial system depends on multiple factors, but culture may be the main one.[23] As explained by Professors Cappelletti and Garth 30 years ago, the idea of courts and the system of civil justice were derived largely from the characteristics of civil litigation at first instance (trial level).[24] These characteristics include horizontal arrangements within the courts beginning at the base of the

---

[16] Ferreres Comella (2009, pp. 10–25), cf. Zucca (2008), cf. Baer (2009); also see Petersen (2017, pp. 38–63). On the relationship between proportionality and constitutional rights as necessity or contingent connexion, see Alexy (2014), cf. Terhechte (2011, pp. 1–9).

[17] See in general, Caponi (2010), cf. Emiliou (1998), Webber (2009, pp. 25–50), Barak (2012, pp. 1–12), Klatt and Meiste (2012, pp. 13–35), Tronson (2016).

[18] Resnik (1982, p. 374), cf. Flanders (1984, pp. 519–520).

[19] Marcus (2017).

[20] Wolff (2013), cf. Turner (2004).

[21] *Ibidem.*

[22] *Ibidem.*

[23] Cf. Dondi et al. (2015, pp. 27–30).

[24] Cappelletti and Garth (1984, p. 250).

pyramid, but also vertical ones and an adequate interaction between the superior and lower courts.[25]

Professor Bovend'Eert mentions the construction of a court management organization in the judiciary and its possible effects as regards judicial independence and the separation of powers. He states:

> It is vitally important to have sufficient safeguards against outside pressures from executive branch authorities, to maintain the independence of the judiciary and respect separation of powers.[26]

Providing effective judicial protection of rights can include responding to the risk of unequal bargaining power between the parties which can give rise to unjust settlements. Also, in the dialogue between lower and appellate courts, it is important to consider the volume of appellate cases.[27] Taking into account key features of a judicial system such as independence (and specialization) of courts (as well as overall performance indicators) could help understand the real and effective role of mediation in the system.[28]

Professor Caponi remarks that one of the tasks of scholars is to recognize that the study of procedural law can only make sense if one is aware of the fact that every technical choice should fit, almost always, into a broader context. It has become a commonplace that some judicial systems are inefficient, demonstrated by the huge backlog of cases and also the delay in the hearing of ordinary civil cases.[29] To assess the current state of affairs, indicators concerning the flow of cases through the courts are used which include clearance rates, disposition time, numbers of judges, numbers of lawyers, litigation rates, and so on.[30] Although the use of statistical indicators is important, it is also risky to compare the data unless the user of the statistics takes into account the methodological techniques used in compiling these indicators.[31]

Judicial independence is a major and pivotal principle of civil procedure.[32] It has both institutional and procedural aspects: there should be bodies and proceedings ensuring its implementation and the necessary action against its violation by other (public and private) entities. To achieve independence requires an interplay between recruitment of judges, tenure, salaries, sanctions, immunity, physical security, administrative autonomy and training.[33] Paradoxically, the courts must manage

---

[25]Cf. Damaška (1986, 2010).

[26]Bovend'Eert (2016).

[27]Caponi (2015, p. 117), cf. Shany (2012, pp. 251–267).

[28]Guinchard (2015).

[29]Cf. Shany (2012).

[30]*Ibidem.*

[31]Cf. Kern (2007, *passim*), Davis et al. (2012, *passim*), Lindquist and Cross (2009, Rottenburg (2015, *passim*). I would also like to mention the EU Justice Scoreboard, published annually by the European Commission.

[32]Seibert-Fohr (2012, pp. 5–20), Burbank and Friedman (2002, *passim*), Bovend'Eert (2016).

[33]Cf. Shetreet and Turenne (2013, p. 4–20), Guinchard (2015), Jackson (2012, pp. 19–25).

proceedings to avoid abuse, but at the same time this produces additional workload that, given the current demand for justice, may paralyze the justice system.[34]

In 2011, the European Network of Councils for the Judiciary (ENCJ) adopted the Vilnius Declaration with recommendations for the judiciaries of Europe. The recommendations are as follows:

> The development of long-term policies must include necessary reforms of the judiciary. Courts should improve their efficiency, alternative dispute resolution should be promoted, and the judiciary should develop stronger relations with civil society to reinforce public confidence and gain support for the necessary reforms. Councils for the judiciary should take the lead in the reform process involving judges and courts.[35]

Justice should be accessible to the citizens. To this end, access to justice in cross-border proceedings should also be facilitated.[36] Additional reforms may be brought about by the economic crisis that currently affects most jurisdictions.[37] The impact of the economic crisis on the judiciary is significant. It results in an increase in the number of cases and a decrease in budgets. In some countries, the poor performance of the judiciary, for instance with respect to timeliness, is a factor that hinders economic development.[38] The organization of the judiciary should balance between respect for the internal independence of judges in their adjudicative activities, and improvement of the timeliness and quality of the administration of justice.[39]

3 Court and Case Management

Court and case management are intertwined. Case management is a judicial process aimed at providing an effective, efficient and a purposeful treatment of cases so as to achieve a timely and high-quality resolution of the dispute. The early identification of disputed issues of fact and law, the establishment of a procedural calendar for the case and the exploration of possible resolution of disputes through methods other than adjudication by the courts (ADR) can be defined as the main goals of case management.[40] This requires the early assignment of a case to a judge who then exercises judicial control and decides on how to proceed. The judge applies the rules of procedure to ensure the active participation and communication amongst the parties and their lawyers.[41] The court assists the parties and their lawyers[42] in identifying the real controversies, seeking early responses from the opponent party

---

[34] Lienhard and Kettiger (2017).

[35] Cf. Fleck (2014).

[36] ENCJ (2012).

[37] Cf. Caponi (2016).

[38] Caponi (2015, p. 117).

[39] Cf. Shany (2012).

[40] Cf. Zuckerman (2009, p. 105).

[41] Cf. Salas (1998, p. 119).

[42] Zuckerman (2005), Jeuland (2018).

to questions of fact and law, thus minimizing or narrowing down the controversies. The court may also refer the case to alternative dispute resolution.[43]

Since the end of the nineteenth century, a discussion on the role of the judge within the civil lawsuit has been taking place in Europe. The European debate also spread to Latin America. In general terms, it may be said that the Continental European judicial systems after the French Revolution and well into the twentieth century, were characterized by a private and individualistic understanding of the civil process. Only the protection of private and individual rights was considered to be the main objective of civil litigation.[44] The parties could control their claims freely and therefore directly control the purpose, nature and speed of civil proceedings.[45]

The new doctrine underlines the 'public' character of civil litigation.[46] The new approach emphasizes the need to put the management power of civil litigation in the hands of the courts.[47] Thus, the norms of civil procedure were adopted (although not without hesitation and setbacks throughout the twentieth century) as rules of public law. In a similar way, the role of the judge was gradually changed, not as a passive spectator of the activities of the parties, but as a proactive participant who sought to direct the realization of the public purposes of the process.[48] These purposes can be categorized as two types: on the one hand, the social objective concerns the equal position of the parties since social or economic superiority can translate into procedural superiority; at the same time, the management of the process aims to avoid delays or obstructive behaviour of the parties.[49] As Professor Andrews remarks:

> Case management has three main functions: to encourage the parties to pursue mediation, where this is practicable; secondly, to prevent the case from progressing too slowly and inefficiently; finally, to ensure that judicial resources are allocated proportionately, as required by 'the Overriding Objective' in CPR Part 1 (reformulated in 2013 to highlight the need for cases to be dealt with justly and 'at proportionate cost').[50]

Between civil and common law traditions, there are striking similarities and differences that need to be emphasized. The European notion of 'the direction of the process' was developed alongside the emergence of the managerial judge in the United States. The following expressions can be found: in German there is the 'Prozessleitung des Richters', and in the Romanic languages we find 'dirección judicial del proceso' (Spanish), 'direzione del proceso' (Italian), 'direction (or maîtrise) du procès' (French), and finally 'Gerenciamiento, condução, direcção' (Portuguese).

The general trend is an increasingly broad judicial management of litigation in the US. To illustrate, in January 2017, the federal court in San Francisco issued

[43]Cf. Caponi (2016).

[44]Cf. Langbroek (2017, pp. 1–2).

[45]Andrews (2012), cf. Dondi et al. (2015).

[46]Cf. Bettinger (2016, pp. 3–8).

[47]Tronson (2016).

[48]Turner (2004).

[49]Langbroek (2017, pp. 1–2).

[50]Andrews (2017), quoting CPR 1.1(1): These Rules are a new procedural code with the overriding objective of enabling the court to deal with cases justly and at proportionate cost.

a Standing Order for Joint Case Management Statements in all civil cases.[51] For Germany, Professors Stürner and Wendelstein remark:

> [C]ase management is not a technical term used in German procedural law, nor is there a direct German translation. The closest would be the judicial power to direct the course of the proceedings. While it is up to the parties to initiate proceedings, to determine its scope and to state the material facts, the ultimate responsibility for the progress of the proceedings lies with the court.[52]

These remarks apply to most continental civil procedure systems. The court is responsible for the direction of the proceedings. This concerns formal aspects of the proceedings, for example the power to open the hearing and direct its course (e.g. Section 136(1) ZPO), and to close the hearing and issue a judgment (e.g. Section 136(4) ZPO).[53] The court is to discuss with the parties questions of substance and procedure.[54]

While the Europeans speak of 'judicial direction of the process', the Americans use the term 'case management'. In accordance with the principle of moderation of the pure adversarial system, case management (in criminal and civil matters) is a process oriented towards the courts (and not the parties) controlling the progress of the proceedings.[55] Just as the Europeans have criticized the adversarial system (without turning the civil process into an inquisitorial process), the Americans have discovered the limitations of the adversarial principle.[56] Legal journal articles show that, in fact, there may be excesses of 'adversarialism'. The Americans have observed that the purely adversarial model with the judge as a neutral arbitrator does not avoid the possible excesses of adversariality.[57] As Professor Marcus states:

> [T]he way in which case management can operate depends significantly on the structure and orientation of the court system in which it is to operate. The American system is, of course, a common law system. Iberoamerica, on the other hand, is mainly or entirely dominated by civil law systems modeled on Continental Europe. In a way, that means that judges may regularly be called upon to take a more active role in controlling the cases and lawyers.[58]

Techniques of case management also include mechanisms to allow collaboration between the courts and the introduction of minimum standards of organization within the courts.[59] The power to direct the process requires a careful management of the case, the hearings and the record, as well as discretionary powers on the part of the judges.[60] Case management is exercised, first, by persuasive methods and techniques, and by consensus and party agreements. This approach is variously called

---

[51] Marcus (2017).

[52] Stürner and Wendelstein (2017).

[53] *Ibidem.*

[54] *Ibidem.*

[55] Ormazabal (2017).

[56] Marcus (2017), cf. Guinchard (2015, pp. 807–810).

[57] Cf. Jolowicz (1996, p. 198), cf. Dondi et al. (2015, pp. 157–177), cf. Amrani-Mekki (2010).

[58] Marcus (2017).

[59] Cf. Kramer (2014).

[60] Cf. Turner (2004).

'process management', 'litigation management', or simply 'procedural control'. The 'management of the process' is accompanied by parallel techniques of 'management of the office' (court management) and 'management of judicial staff'. Assistance to the judge is crucial. As an American author holds:

> Although largely invisible to the public, behind the scenes, judicial assistants/law clerks frequently play a vital role in the process of adjudication. Yet, especially outside of the U.S., little is known about their role and duties in the judicial decision-making process.[61]

When discussing case and court management, it is important to mention ADR. ADR can serve as an indicator for the quality of a legal system. The increased use of ADR may result in a reduction of the case-load of the courts, but it is not guaranteed that litigants are better off if they opt for ADR.

In Germany, as a general rule, conciliation attempts precede any oral hearing unless efforts to reach an agreement have already been made at an earlier stage or conciliation does not have any real prospect of success. Should a party fail to appear at a conciliation hearing or should conciliation be unsuccessful, a formal court hearing is to be held immediately afterwards.[62] In Germany, according to the 2012 rules on 'Internal-Court Mediation' (Section 278a ZPO), the judge may refer the parties to a mediation judge. If this happens, litigation comes to a stand-still and will only be continued after mediation has failed.[63] In France, recent law reforms support and incentivize the use of ADR.[64] In England & Wales, mediation is voluntary, but the court encourages parties to consider out-of-court mediation.[65] In Poland, according to Article 10 of the Code of Civil Procedure, in cases where a settlement is admissible, the court will invite parties to settle throughout the proceedings, particularly by inducing parties to mediate.[66] And in Chile, judicial conciliation is an essential stage of the proceedings.[67] It should be noted here that in many jurisdictions there are no qualitative indicators about the popularity of ADR among lawyers and civil justice system users.[68]

---

[61] Holvast (2016).

[62] Stürner and Wendelstein (2017).

[63] See also Von Bargen (2008, pp. 25–50).

[64] Amrani-Mekki (2010).

[65] Andrews (2012).

[66] Tronson (2016).

[67] Cf. Kern (2007, *passim*); Davis et al. (2012, *passim*); Lindquist and Cross (2009), Rottenburg (2015, *passim*).

[68] *Ibidem*.

4 Procedural Arrangements

Civil procedure generally consists of three stages: the written introductory stage (drafting statements of claim and defense), the fact-finding stage, and the stage leading up to the judgment. The fact-finding stage often requires several hearings or written proceedings after evidence has been collected.[69]

As is now generally accepted, case-flow management denotes the supervision or management of the time involved in processing a case through the court system, through the different stages, from the point of initiation of the procedure to the point of disposition.[70] To make the sequence and timing of these events more predictable is one of the goals of active case-flow management. The management of the intervals between various procedural steps clearly affects the overall case disposition time. Also, effective case-flow management involves attorneys preparing cases well.[71] Judges need to ensure that the planned dates are realistic and that the parties agree to abide by them.[72] As remarked by Professor Fleck, transparency in the division of authority and the separation of powers are decisive factors in the operation of the judicial administration as a whole.[73]

There are two important components related to case management that need to be taken into consideration: (i) the specialization of the courts,[74] and (ii) flexibility to adapt the composition of the courts based on the importance and/or complexity of the case (a single judge or a panel of judges). As regards the first point, one should distinguish between ordinary and specialized courts (examples are courts dealing with family, labour and social welfare disputes and administrative courts).[75]

Additionally, it is important to take note of the interplay between superior and lower courts. Professor Stürner states for Germany:

> The reform of 2001 is maybe not the result of great comparative work. However, the explanatory memorandum of the draft reform bill refers to examples of 'good practice' from England, Austria, Switzerland (Zurich), France, and Italy to show that the envisaged changes were already implemented in other jurisdictions. The major development of the 2001 reform was the abolition of the full-blown first appeal where ordinarily a full rehearing of fact and of law was undertaken. References were made to Austrian and to English law to demonstrate that the focus should rather be on the first instance proceedings.[76]

---

[69] See Bettinger (2016, pp. 41–49), cf. Andrews (2017).

[70] Cf. Shany (2012, pp. 251–267).

[71] Uzelac and Van Rhee (2011, *passim*).

[72] Steelman (2004, pp. 10–53).

[73] Cf. Fleck (2014, p. 11).

[74] Comoglio (2014, p. 16).

[75] Badó (2014).

[76] Stürner (2017).

The court is unlikely to provide good leadership when its workload is excessive and increasing. That is why the judicial management of cases takes place by dejudicialization.[77] Five key points should be mentioned in this context: (i) rationalization and (re)organization of courts and public prosecutor offices; (ii) reduction in the volume of court cases; (iii) simplification of judicial proceedings, improvement in case management and introduction of new technologies; (iv) financing of the judicial system; and (v) court and case management and the distribution of cases within and between the courts and out-of-court (ADR).[78]

5 Artificial Intelligence

The number of courts and their geographical distribution have important effects on the quality of justice and case management. The introduction of IT and artificial intelligence creates a virtual space for the hearing of cases.[79] Specialization helps to reduce costs. Costs reductions my be achieved through closing underused courts and shifting cases to nearby courts. Finally, several small courts could be brought together within one main court in order to reduce costs and overhead in general.[80] Although such reorganizations may result in longer travel time for parties and thus in a deterioration of geographical access to justice, IT may help to solve this problem since the physical presence of the parties and witnesses is becoming less important. Video conferencing is becoming the norm in large jurisdictions. In other jurisdictions, however, it is believed that parties and witnesses should be physically present in specific types of cases. The combination of IT and physical court rooms may be the solution for these jurisdictions.

The utility of artficial intelligence (AI) for case and judicial management is obvious.[81] First, it can be used for basic administrative support (digital or electronic files and digital signatures) and online tracking systems. Technology could also replace mechanical tasks by way of algorithms. It could even replace human beings. Finally, AI can be used for deciding cases. Officially, it is still the judge who decides the case, but he/she is assisted by a qualified artificial (electronic) 'clerk'.

With the COVID-19 pandemic, the use of technology in court proceedings has become more important than ever. In fact, many jurisdictions have allowed court hearings to take place online (it is, for example, allowed in Hong Kong on a discretionary basis). Some procedural steps that used to be executed in person may now be done using technology. For instance, it was possible to register for the filing of cases online in Mainland China even before the pandemic. In the US, Congress has directed the lawmakers to consider whether changes to the procedure rules should

[77] Cf. Amrani-Mekki (2010).

[78] Stürner (2017).

[79] With critical remarks: Zeleznikow (2017).

[80] Stürner (2017).

[81] Sourdin (2018), Amofah (2017, pp. 1–56).

be adopted to address emergencies. It is not at all clear whether any rule changes for civil cases will result.

6 Conclusions

Judicial time has become a scarce resource since the number of cases handled per judge has grown dramatically. Various solutions have been suggested to counter the rising caseload. Examples are a reduction of the number of court applications, an increase in the number of judges and improving the efficiency of the courts with the introduction of appropriate case and court managment instruments. Court and case management are critical components of an efficient justice system. They are central to court structure and arrangements within and between the courts.

Three important components of court and case management should be mentioned here: (i) the specialization of courts; (ii) the distribution of cases within the courts; and (iii) the implementation of IT and artificial intelligence. Additionally, the aims of appeals to superior courts is relevant, as well as access filters, caseload and the scope of review.

The reforms of the justice systems and the judiciary must be based on sound principles that will improve the quality of justice for the citizens. They should improve access to justice and the image of the judiciary, as well as enhancing public confidence in the judicial system, and they should neither compromise the quality of justice nor access to court. It is hoped that this contribution has shown the way forward in this respect.

References

Alexy R (2014) Constitutional rights and proportionality. Revus—J Const Theory Philos Law 2:51–65

Alt E, Le Theule M-A (2011) La justice aux prises avec l'éthique et la performance. Pyramides. Revue du Centre d'études et de recherches en adm publique 22:137–159

Amofah L (2017) Electronic court case management system. Working Paper Ghana Technology University College (GTUC)

Amrani-Mekki S (2010) The future of the categories, the categories of the future. In: Walker J, Chase OG (eds) Common law, civil law and the future of categories. Markham, Ontario, pp 247–266

Andrews N (2012) A fresh start: The four pillars of civil justice. In: Shetreet S, Forsyth C (eds) The culture of judicial independence. Leiden, Boston, pp 97–109

Andrews N (2017) English case management system. General report, IAPL conference 2017 (unpublished)

Badó A (2014) 'Fair' selection of judges in a modern democracy. In: Badó A (ed) Fair trial and judicial independence—Hungarian perspectives. Cham, pp 27–58

Baer S (2009) Dignity, liberty, equality: A fundamental rights triangle of constitutionalism. Univ Toronto Law J 59(4):417–468

Barak A (2012) Proportionality. Constitutional rights and their limitations, Cambridge

Benvenuti S (2015) The European judicial training network and its role in the strategy for the Europeanization of national judges. Int J Court Adm 7(1):59–67
Bettinger N (2016) Prozessmodelle im Zivilverfahrensrecht: Erfolg des Hauptverhandlungsmodells. Tübingen
Bone R (1993) Statistical adjudication: Rights, justice, and utility in a world of process scarcity. Vanderbilt Law Rev 46:561–663
Bovend'Eert P (2016) Judicial independence and separation of powers: A case study in modern court management. European Public Law 22(2):333–353
Brändli B (2013) Prozessökonomie im schweizerischen Recht. Bern
Briggs LJ (2016) Civil courts structure review: Final report. https://www.judiciary.gov.uk/wp-content/uploads/2016/07/civil-courts-structure-review-final-report-jul-16-final-1.pdf. Accessed June 2020
Burbank SB and Friedman B (eds) (2002) Judicial independence at the crossroads, an interdisciplinary approach. Thousand Oaks
Calabresi G (2016) The future of law and economics. Essays in reform and recollection, New Haven
Caponi R (2010) Il principio di proporzíonalitá nella giustizia civile: Prime note sistematiche. Rivista Trimestrale Di Diritto E Procedura Civile 65(2):389–406
Caponi R (2015) 'Just settlement' or 'just about settlement'? Mediated agreements: A comparative overview of the basics. Rabels Zeitschrift Für Ausländisches und Internationales Privatrecht 79:117–141
Caponi R (2016) European minimum standards for courts. Independence, specialization, efficiency. A glance from Italy. In: Festschrift für Nikolaos K. Klamaris, vol II. Athens, Thessaloniki, pp 151–172
Cappelletti M and Garth B (1984) A comparative conclusion. In: Cappelletti M (ed) Ordinary proceedings in first instance—International encyclopedia of comparative law. Tübingen, pp 250–252
Carrington PD (2010) Politics and civil procedure rulemaking: Reflections on experience. Duke Law J 60(597):617–618
Comoglio P (2014) Il giudice specializzato in materia di impresa. Torino
Da Fonseca Gajardoni F (2017) Procedimentos, déficit procedimental e condução ativa dos procedimentos civis pelo juiz no Brasil. National report, IAPL Conference 2017 (unpublished)
Damaška M (1986) The faces of justice and state authority. New Haven
Damaška (2010) The common law/civil law divide: Residual truth of a misleading distinction. In: Walker J, Chase OG (eds) Common law, civil law and the future of categories. Markham, Ontario, pp 3–22
Davis K, Fisher A, Kingsbury B (2012) Governance by indicators. Global power through classification and rankings, Oxford
Dondi A, Ansanelli V, Comoglio P (2015) Processi civili in Evoluzione. Una Prospettiva Comparata, Milano
Emiliou N (1998) The principle of proportionality in European law: A comparative study. London
ENCJ (2012) Vilnius Recommendation. https://www.encj.eu/images/stories/pdf/GA/Dublin/encj_report_judicial_reform_def.pdf. Accessed June 2020
Ferreres Comella V (2009) Constitutional courts and democratic values: A European perspective. New Haven
Flanders S (1984) Blind umpires: A response to professor Resnik. Hastings Law J 35:505–522
Fleck Z (2014) A comparative analysis of judicial power, organisational issues in judicature and the administration of courts. In: Badó A (ed) Fair trial and judicial independence—Hungarian perspectives. Cham, pp 3–25
Guinchard S (2015) Les garanties institutionelles du droit à un bon judge. In: Guinchard S et al, Droit Processuel—Droits fondamentaux du procès. Paris, pp 843–852
Holvast N (2016) The power of the judicial assistant/law clerk: Looking behind the scenes at courts in the United States, England and Wales, and the Netherlands. Int J Court Adm 7(2):10–28

Jackson VC (2012) Judicial independence: Structure, context, attitude. In: Seibert-Fohr A (ed) Judicial independence in transition. Heidelberg, pp 19–86
Jeuland E (2018) Towards a new court management? General report (Research Report) Université Paris 1—Panthéon Sorbonne. Paris
Jolowicz JA (1996) The Woolf report and the adversary system. CJQ 15:198–210
Kern C (2007) Justice between simplification and formalism. Tübingen
Klatt M, Meiste M (2012) The constitutional structure of proportionality. Oxford
Klöpfer M (2016) Missbrauch im europäischen Zivilverfahrensrecht. Tübingen
Kramer XE (2014) The structure of civil proceedings and why it matters: Exploratory observations on future ELI-UNIDROIT European rules of civil procedure. Uniform Law Rev 12(2):218–238
La Porta R, Lopez-de-Silanes F, Pop-Eleches C, Shleifer A (2004) Judicial checks and balances. J Polit Econ 112:445–470
Lahav A (2015) Participation and procedure. DePaul Law Rev 64:513–536
Langbroek PM (2017) From the managing editor: Court administration in Europe—Management in a different context. Int J Court Adm 8(3):1–20
Lienhard A, Kettiger D (2017) Between management and the rule of law: On the move towards a management model for the judiciary—Results from the project 'Basic research into court management in Switzerland.' Int J Court Adm 8(2):7–19
Lindquist S, Cross F (2009) Measuring judicial activism. Oxford
Lupoi MA (2015) Appellate procedures in Italy. https://www.academia.edu/34400455/Appellate_procedures_in_Italy. Accessed 11 July 2020
Marcus R (2017) Controlling the cowboy lawyers: How American judges are managing American cases. National Report, IAPL Conference 2017 (unpublished)
Ormazabal SG (2017) Las facultades judiciales de dirección material de los procesos civiles en la legislación y experiencia españolas (unpublished)
Petersen N (2017) Proportionality and judicial activism. Cambridge
Resnik J (1982) Managerial judges. Harvard Law Rev 96(2):374–448
Rottenburg R (2015) The world of indicators. The making of governmental knowledge through quantification, Cambridge
Salas D (1998) Le tiers pouvoir. Paris
Seibert-Fohr A (ed) (2012) Judicial independence in transition. Heidelberg
Shany Y (2012) Judicial independence as an indicator of international court effectiveness: A goal-based approach. In: Shetreet S, Forsyth C (eds) The culture of judicial independence. Leiden-Boston, pp 251–269
Shetreet S, Turenne S (2013) Judges on trial. The independence and accountability of the English judiciary, 2nd edn. Cambridge
Sourdin T (2018) Judge v robot? Artificial intelligence and judicial decision-making. The Univ New South Wales Law J 41(4):1114–1133
Steelman DC (2004) Case-flow management: The heart of court management in the new millennium. National Center for State Courts, United States of America
Stürner M (forthcoming) Sharing responsibility: The German federal court of justice and the civil appellate system. In Bravo-Hurtado P, Van Rhee CH (eds) Supreme Courts under pressure: Controlling caseload in the administration of civil justice
Stürner M, Wendelstein C (2017) Case management in civil proceedings in Germany. National Report, IAPL Conference 2017 (unpublished)
Stürner R (2007) Markt und Wettbewerb über Alles? München
Stürner R (2014) Die Rolle des dogmatischen Denkens im Zivilprozessrecht. Zeitschrift Für Zivilprozess 127(3):271–332
Terhechte JP (2011) Konstitutionalisierung und Normativität der europäischen Grundrechte. Tübingen
Tronson B (2016) Towards proportionality—The 'quick, cheap and just' balance in civil litigation. In: Picker C, Seidman G (eds) The dynamism of civil procedure—global trends and developments. Cham, pp 183–202

Turner R (1997) Some thoughts on the multi-track inside track. Law Society Civil Litigation Newsletter December (2).

Turner R (2004) The proactive judge and the provision of a single transnational case management system and its associated procedures. In: Andenas M, Andrews N, Nazzini R (eds) The future of transnational civil litigation. London, pp 73–88

Uzelac A, Van Rhee CH (eds) (2011) The landscape of the legal professions in Europe and the USA: Continuity and change. Antwerp

Uzelac A, Van Rhee CH (2017) Revisiting procedural human rights. Fundamentals of civil procedure and the changing face of civil justice. In: Uzelac A, Van Rhee CH (eds) Revisiting procedural human rights. Cambridge, pp 3–13

Von Bargen JM (2008) Gerichtsinterne mediation. Tübingen

Wallace A (2017) The impact of technology on courts. Int J Court Admin 8(2):1ff

Webber G (2009) The negotiable constitution: On the limitations of rights. Cambridge

Wolff TB (2013) Managerial judging and substantive law. Washington Univ Law Re 90:1027–1069

Zeleznikow J (2017) Can artificial intelligence and online dispute resolution enhance efficiency and effectiveness in courts? Int J Court Admin 8(2):30–45

Zucca L (2008) Conflicts of fundamental rights as constitutional dilemmas. In: Brems E (ed) Conflicts between fundamental rights. Antwerp, pp 19–37

Zuckerman A (2005) Court control and party compliance. The quests for effective litigation management. In: Trocker N, Varano V (eds) The reforms of civil procedure in comparative perspective. Torino, pp 143–161

Zuckerman A (2009) Litigation management under the CPR: A poorly-used management infrastructure. In: Dwyer D (ed) The civil procedure rules ten years on, London, pp 89–107

Jurisdictional Contributions

The Unified System of Adjudication and Administration of Chinese Courts

Hang-ping Chen

Abstract After a long period of historical evolution, Chinese courts established a unique, organizational structure known as the 'Unified System of Jurisdiction and Administration' in the early 1980s. The system combines adjudication and judicial administration under the full authority of the President of the Court. Although the Unified System once played a positive role in China's rapid economic growth, it has negatively impacted judicial independence and justice. This negative impact has gradually outweighed the positive effects. Ongoing judicial reform in China is changing the judicial system.

1 Introduction

From the mid to late 1950s, China created a unique social structure. This structure enabled the ruling Chinese Communist Party to strengthen their powers within society through the State and its various organs. The strong influence exerted by the State on society still exists and has even been aggravated in the last few decades, albeit the social changes stemming from the implementation of the economic reforms and the Opening-Up Policy in the late 1970s have mitigated this situation marginally.

The Chinese court system has evolved over a significant period of time. In the early 1980s, the Unified System of Adjudication and Administration (hereinafter referred to as 'the Unified System') was created. The Unified System incorporated both the adjudication and judicial administration of courts into one organizational unit. This entailed that judges and judicial administrative staff are governed by the same unit in terms of personnel organization (编制), remuneration (待遇), performance appraisal (考核) and promotion. Also, under the hierarchical structure of the Unified System, the appointment and dismissal of staff and the distribution of economic and political resources are controlled by the President of the Court. This role is monopolized by

H. Chen (✉)
School of Law, Tsinghua University, Beijing, The People's Republic of China
e-mail: chenhp@tsinghua.edu.cn

P. C. H. Chan and C. H. van Rhee (eds.), *Civil Case Management in the Twenty-First Century: Court Structures Still Matter*, Ius Gentium: Comparative Perspectives on Law and Justice 85, https://doi.org/10.1007/978-981-33-4512-6_4

the leading Party Group (党组). The organizational system is centralized, managerial and bureaucratic and introduces authoritarianism into the judiciary. Thus, this inevitably blurs the line between adjudication and administration, therefore resulting in the so-called phenomena of 'judicial politicization' (审判政治化) and 'judicial bureaucratization' (审判行政化). These phenomena constitute a unique institutional background and shape the practice of judicial case management in China.

In recent years, the Chinese Communist Party has accelerated the reform of the judicial system. The reform of the court's case management system is one of its focal points. The examination of the evolution of the Unified System allows an understanding of the many factors affecting the administration of justice in China and the urgency of judicial reforms.

2 The Historical Formation of the Unified System

After the establishment of the People's Republic of China in 1949, the Central People's Government created the Supreme People's Court and the Ministry of Justice. According to the original organizational framework stipulated in the 'Organization Regulations', promulgated by the Supreme People's Court and the Ministry of Justice, the former was to be the court of law while the latter was mainly responsible for handling judicial administrative affairs of the court.[1] At the central government level, there had been a separation of adjudication and judicial administration of courts until the Ministry of Justice was abolished in 1959. However, at the provincial level, adjudication and judicial administration only separated for a very short period of time from 1954 to 1959; at the district level, the two never separated.[2]

In April 1959, as a result of the Anti-Rightist Campaign in China, the Ministry of Justice was abolished and the Supreme People's Court became responsible for the judicial administrative affairs.[3] Local justice bureaus were also abolished. Without these events, adjudication would probably have been separated from judicial administration at the lower courts as well. In reality, Chinese courts have developed the Unified System, causing a series of problems arising out of the operation, management and supervision of court cases.

Since the outset of the Cultural Revolution in 1966, courts at all levels had been taken over by military commissions, affecting the court system gravely. After the end of military domination in 1972, the organizational structure of courts was restored to the structure before the Cultural Revolution. For example, internal judicial administrative departments and adjudication divisions were re-established. The new Organic

[1]See Regulations on the Trial Implementation of the Ministry of Justice of the Central People's Government, and Regulations on Trial Implementation of the Supreme People's Court. The two organizational regulations were approved by the Central People's Government Committee on 20 December 1949.

[2]See Article 17 of the 1951 Provisional Regulations of Court Organization, and Article 19 of the 1954 Organic Law of the People's Courts of the People's Republic of China.

[3]Lan (1995, pp. 50–53).

Law of the People's Courts passed in July 1979 ('1979 Organic Law') also preserved the 1954 provisions, which provided that the courts at the district level were responsible for their own judicial administrative affairs. The Ministry of Justice and the justice bureaus were responsible for the administrative affairs of the courts above the district level (Articles 17 and 22 of the 1979 Organic Law).

In May 1982, the Ministry of Justice recommended to the Central Committee of the Chinese Communist Party that the judicial administrative affairs of the courts should be administered by the courts themselves. In September 1983, the 1979 Organic Law was amended ('1983 Organic Law') and the Unified System was thereby inaugurated. However, the 1983 Organic Law did not contain any provisions governing the administration of the courts but only covered adjudication by the courts. Subsequently, the 'Judges Law of the People's Republic of China' (法官法) was passed in 1995.[4] It introduced assessment of judges by the Judicial Evaluation and Review Committees, but again, there were no further provisions governing the judicial administration of the courts. Therefore, the court's Unified System was not formally confirmed by legislation for a period of time. It remained, to some extent, an informal system. Thus, it is difficult for outsiders to obtain sufficient information on the courts' organizational structure by way of official documents.

Beyond legislation, the administration of the courts in practice has shaped the organizational structure of courts and court trials. This brought subtle and complex consequences. In July 2017, the Internal and Judicial Affairs Committee of the National People's Congress submitted a revised draft of the Organic Law to the Standing Committee of the National People's Congress for consideration. Articles 26 and 49 of the draft proposed the setting up of judicial assistant departments and judicial administrative organs, and to appoint the necessary staff correspondingly. The Organic Law was eventually revised in October 2018.

3 The Unified System

The Unified System is a unique phenomenon in the Chinese court system. The most important features of the Unified System are that, first, the definition of 'judicial administration' in this context is not the same as in Western societies, and second, adjudication and judicial administration are intertwined. The combination of adjudication and judicial administration in the organizational system of the courts is not a pivotal feature due to the fact that courts have always dealt with administrative affairs to a certain extent.

The current 'judicial administration' within the Chinese courts generally consists of three levels. The first level is 'embedded' in the trial process, which includes providing basic judicial assistance and facilitating the judicial process (through example guidelines provided to the parties, acceptance and delivery of case materials, distribution of cases, maintenance of office space and facilities, and document

[4]The latest revision of the Judges Law was in 2019.

management). This is not equivalent to the Western approach where courts take full responsibility to manage their own affairs. The second level falls within the scope of the Chinese-style 'trial management', which aims to ensure the quality, efficiency and effectiveness of trials through time limits (审限), evaluation and appraisal of cases, judicial supervision and so on.[5] The third level is a fairly 'unique' management system of staff. The President of the Court and the leading Party Group are in charge of the staff and are entitled to assess, reward and sanction the judges, the judicial assistants and the administrative staff of the court. Unless otherwise stated, the concept of 'judicial administration' used in this context only refers to the second and third levels.

3.1 No Clear Distinction of Staff Between Different Departments

After the establishment of the Unified System, the adjudication divisions, the judicial assistant divisions, and the administrative departments coexisted within the courts. The practical functions of these departments overlapped with blurred boundaries. In fact, judges had been involved in various administrative affairs such as case evaluation, appraisal and the management of judicial statistics. In the 1980s and 1990s, when judges were in short supply, it was not uncommon for administrative staff to hear cases on behalf of the judges.

From November 1982, together with other staff members of the court, judges are to be managed in accordance with the 'Special Establishment of Politics and Law' (政法专项编制).[6] The Civil Servant Law promulgated in 1995 also governs the recruitment, assessment, promotion, appointment, dismissal, reward and sanctioning of judges.[7] Although the Judges Law divides judges into four classes and twelve grades, this hierarchy has never been put into operation.

Qualified judges could be transferred from the adjudication divisions of the court to the judicial administrative departments. For the purpose of training, judges would also be transferred from one internal department to another. This was done to help

[5] Although trial management has always existed within the courts, it has started to gain attention only in recent years. All of the four Five-year Reform Outlines promulgated by the Supreme People's Court clearly show the continuous development of trial management. See also the Opinions of the Supreme People's Court on Strengthening the Trial Management of the People's Courts, No. 2 [2011] Supreme People's Court.

[6] Joint Notice of the Political and Legal Committee of the Central Committee of the Communist Party of China, the Organization Department of the Central Committee of the Communist Party of China, the Ministry of Labour and Personnel and the Ministry of Finance on Several Issues Concerning the Preparation and Funding of Public Security, Procuratorate, Court and Judicial Administrative Systems, No. 7 [1982]. The Special Establishment of Politics and Law entrusted judges with the task of special management.

[7] Notice of the General Office of the Central Committee of the Communist Party of China on Strengthening the Provision of Local Courts and Procuratorate Cadres, CPC Center Committee, No. 47 [1985].

familiarize the judges with different aspects of court work.[8] However, as a result, there were often too many judges in the administrative departments with a lack of work available to them. This weakened the function of the judiciary and further blurred boundaries between adjudication and administration.

Since then, the situation has changed. According to the Judges Law (as early as the 2001 Amendment), a judge must possess a diploma in law or equivalent legal knowledge and have passed the national judicial examination. The examination implemented since 2018 has improved the quality of the judges. Moreover, except for law students enrolled before 2017, candidates should have, at least, a bachelor's degree or an undergraduate degree in law, or a bachelor's degree in another subject but with legal experience for at least three years.[9] Additionally, since 2013, the courts have intensified the reform such that there is now a clear distinction between judges, judicial assistants, and judicial administrative staff.[10]

Under the 'Judge Quota System' (员额制), all judges will usually be sent to the 'front-line' of adjudication to handle court cases first. They are governed by a management system which is different from the system governing ordinary civil servants and are subject to a specialized system of promotion and wage growth. In July 2017, the reform of the judge quota system of the national courts became final, and a total of 120,138 'quota judges' (including 367 'quota judges' of the Supreme People's Court) were nominated and selected. Subsequently, the reform of the rules on judicial hierarchy established ranks for a total of 106,000 judges. Serving judges have been ranked according to the new classification system.[11]

3.2 Organizational Structure

In the early days after the founding of the People's Republic of China, a hierarchical framework of court positions was set up. The positions in court include the President, the Vice-President, the Chief Judge of a division, the Associate Chief Judge of

---

[8] An empirical survey shows that this kind of movement is quite frequent. See Ai (2006). Of course, the situation in local courts cannot be generalized. In some local courts, especially higher-level courts, transfer of staff between the adjudication divisions and the administrative departments is not common.

[9] Implementation Measures for the National Uniform Legal Profession Qualification Examination, Order No. 140 of the Ministry of Justice, 28–04-2018, Art. 9.22.

[10] Organization Department of the CPC Central Committee and the Supreme Court's Suggestions on the reform of the classification management system for the staff of the People's Court, No. 2 [2013] Organization Department of the CPC Central Committee, 01–03-2013. Judicial assistants are the staff who assist the judges in performing their judicial duties, including executives, assistant judges, clerks, judicial police and judicial technicians. They are responsible for enforcement of civil judgments, attending the court and conducting security work. Judicial administrative personnel are the staff members who engage in administrative affairs. They are responsible for Party affairs, administrative matters and logistics of the courts at all levels.

[11] See He (2017).

a division and the Ordinary Judge.[12] These positions, together with the leadership of the Party Group based on the principle of combining collective leadership with individual responsibility through a division of work, are the characteristics of the Unified System. As a result of the combination of judicial administration and adjudication, the amount of judicial administrative work, and the number of departments and staff in court have substantially increased. Heads of the major judicial administrative organs have joined the Party Group and become leaders of the courts.[13] With the increasing amount of judicial administrative affairs, the court's responsibility in adjudication and administration has also been strengthened. An example is that the Chief Judges of the adjudication division are now responsible for ensuring the quality of court hearings in their division and approving judgments submitted by their subordinates.

The President of the Court, who is the highest-ranking court member, is also the Secretary of the leading Party Group. The President presides over the meeting of the Judicial Committee and is responsible for summarizing complicated cases and rendering final decisions (even if none of the committee members attended the hearing of the case).[14] In summary, the President supervises both the adjudication and judicial administration of the court. The President has a strong decision-making power given his status in the Party Group and administrative ranking. As the principal person responsible for implementing the rule of law (执法责任制的第一责任人), the President should resign or be dismissed in cases of seriously wrongful judgment, grave violation of regulations or the laws, major incidents in administrative work, or major economic losses.[15]

The court has a bureaucratic structure which is under the full responsibility of the President.[16] This structure is shaped similar to a pyramid. Within the court, there are several small management units under the control of the Chief Judge. Both the President and the Chief Judge of the division do not handle cases, but mainly act as organizational managers or the executives of the court.

There is a large number of civil servants within the court and thus, many deputy and additional positions, including the Presidents, Vice-Presidents, Assistants to the

[12]Position management assigns tasks, powers, and resources according to rank (or administrative grade) and departments, while grade management involves issues such as remuneration, rights, status and security of people engaged in official duties. The two types of classification and management are highly relevant yet independent of each other. See Yan (2010, pp. 10–14).

[13]The President of the court acts as the Secretary of the Party and leads a fixed Party Group with the Vice-President, the leader of the disciplinary team and the political department director. In addition, other responsible persons may join the Party Group based on criteria such as status, personal qualifications and their personal relationship with the President. Currently, the most common new member of the Party Group is the director of the executive division of the court.

[14]Notice of the Supreme People's Court on Printing and Distributing the Implementation Opinions on Reforming and Perfecting the Judicial Committee System of the People's Courts, No. 3 [2010] Supreme People's Court.

[15]Notice of the Supreme People's Court on Printing and Distributing the Provisions on the Resignation of the Dean of the Local People's Courts and the Deputies of the People's Courts (for trial implementation), No. 21 [2001] Supreme People's Court.

[16]Wang (2010).

President, Chief Judges of the division, and so on. However, the recent reform of the judicial system has to a certain extent shaken the bureaucratic hierarchy of the court. For example, the President and the Chief Judge of the division are now required to hear a certain number of cases.[17] Under the reform of the judicial accountability system, single judges and collegial panels are required to sign judgments independently and assume their own responsibilities. There is little room for the President or the Chief Judge to review judgments given by other judges. The latest version of the Organic Law of the People's Courts (2018) also removes specific provisions governing the Chief Judge and the Deputy Chief Judge in order to reduce bureaucracy.

3.3 *Centralized Management of Court Staff*

The most important aspect of the Unified System is that the President and the leading Party Group of the Court have the authority to appoint and dismiss nearly all of the court staff, including judges. In practice, the Party Group has been given the power to manage the court's leadership and to appoint, dismiss and sanction staff members. The function of the Party Group in the court resembles ordinary, corporate human resource management, including recruitment of staff, training and development. Similarly, higher-ranking staff have a higher salary than lower-ranking staff.[18] As a result, there is a strong incentive for judges to get promoted.

In order to measure the capability of judges objectively, the court has relied on 'quantifiable data' to assess judges such as the number of cases handled, the number of mediated settlements, and the number of successful appeals against judgments issued by a particular judge. The opinion of the President of the Court will also influence the appointment and dismissal of court staff.

The latest judicial reform changed the above system to some extent. First, judges are now selected by the Judicial Selection Committee at the provincial level. However, in reality, candidates are actually recommended and ranked by the Party Group of the court based on separate assessment and their examination results. The Judicial Selection Committee will only be provided with written documents such as the resume of the candidate. The Committee is mainly composed of government officials, legal scholars and lawyers. Notably, it rarely refuses candidates recommended

[17] The number of cases to be handled by chief judges of the primary and intermediate people's courts on a yearly basis is ca. 50–70% of the average number of cases handled by ordinary judges in the same department. The number of cases to be handled by the President of the primary people's court is ca. 5–10% of the average number of cases handled by the ordinary judges of the same court. Other leaders of the court are to handle 30–40% of the average number of cases handled by the ordinary judges of the court. The number of cases to be handled by the President of the Intermediate People's Court is ca. 5% of the average amount of cases handled by the ordinary judges of the court. The leaders of the court are to handle 20–30% of the average number of cases handled by the ordinary judges of the court. See Opinion of the Supreme People's Court on Strengthening the Work of Cases by the Presidents of People's Courts at All Levels (Trial Implementation), No. 10 [2017] Supreme Court.

[18] See Lin (2005, p. 173).

by the court.[19] Secondly, following the implementation of the Provincial Unified Management Reform of Staff, Budget and Property (省级人财物统管改革), certain management powers over court staff have been transferred to the local level, namely the party committees at the district and municipal levels (组织部). Although such management powers are limited, the authority of the Party Group of the Court has indeed been increased.

3.4 *Critical Reflections on the Unified System*

The direct effect of the Unified System on adjudication is that the court's decision-making power is vested in the judges, and that the leaders of the court are now responsible for both adjudication and its efficiency. The Chief Judges of divisions, the Vice-Presidents, the President and the Judicial Committee exercise their powers according to the nature of the case, the amount of the claim and the magnitude of the penalty.

Judgments, in regards to important or difficult cases and specific types of judgments (such as probation and parole), must be submitted to the administrative superiors for examination and approval. The most important, difficult, and complicated cases must be submitted to the Judicial Committee for further discussion and consideration. It is unlikely for judges to disobey the instructions and orders from their superiors. Meanwhile, the Examination and Approval System (审批制) transcends the organizational boundaries of general courts and applies also to the lower courts. Through continuous enhancement of supervision and management of staff, finances and assets, higher courts have turned the lower courts into their administrative subordinates.[20] Cases are placed on the 'assembly line' and are passed from the lower courts to the higher courts. Since first-instance judgments only have temporary effect, lower courts often decide cases through 'requests' (请示) and 'reports' (汇报), i.e. through informal channels in order to obtain prior confirmation from the higher courts.

The institutional arrangement for approval of cases in stages has positive effects. It helps maintain the quality of adjudication despite the occasional low quality of judges, many of whom are veterans without legal education background. It also allows judges to spread the risk of wrongful adjudication to all superiors involved in

---

[19]For example, after the Supreme People's Court Selection Committee for Judges reviewed the first batch of 387 candidates, the Committee refused 17 candidates due to limited quota. The number of candidates being refused was said to be the highest in the country. See Luo (2017).

[20]The upper-level court's party group and its internal organs under the Unified System do not only assist the local party committees in managing the lower court's leadership team, but also take charge of the lower court's administrative equipment management, case quality and efficiency evaluation, and other work. With the recent reforms, the influence of provincial courts on lower courts has been further strengthened. Of course, there are exceptions. For example, the relationships between the Supreme People's Court and the provincial courts, and between the intermediate courts of the municipality directly under the Central Government and the grassroots courts, are relatively loose.

the process of examination and adjudication. In this way, judges may avoid disproportionate personal responsibility, though, at the expense of judicial independence. More importantly, this approach ensures the obedience of the courts to political and economic policies of the local party committee and government organs. In fact, the courts' active engagement in protecting and developing the local economy is indispensable to the local governments when participating in interregional competition under Chinese-style federalism.[21] For example, through the setting of time limits for the disposition of cases, judicial efficiency has been greatly improved and a larger number of cases have been adjudicated in China. This probably explains the 'mystery' of the economic take-off in China.[22] Although, under the Unified System the courts have encountered many adverse consequences such as the erosion of judicial independence, these consequences have contributed to China's unique economic development with sufficient social legitimacy.

By promoting political and economic development, the courts have acquired sufficient resources in return. Historically, Chinese courts were weak as political and legal organs and had been ignored in the early days after the founding of the People's Republic of China. Even until the 1980s, problems such as the appointment of judges without the necessary qualifications, serious shortage of funding and inadequate offices and equipment still existed. According to Hu Yaobang, the General Secretary of the Central Committee of the Chinese Communist Party, '[t]he court has long been a branch that [the] Party does not pay much attention to. Office buildings, funding and staffing are not better than that of other state organs.'[23] In 1985, the Supreme People's Court and the Ministry of Finance issued a notice, emphasizing that the financial departments at all levels should separately list out the funding for the judiciary in the budget with sufficient support. However, until 1988, 48% of Chinese courts still did not have formal courtrooms,[24] and only 75% of the necessary courtrooms had been built or were under construction at the end of 1992.[25]

Simultaneously, the court has gradually become a very important part of the 'comprehensive governance project' in helping to maintain economic development and social stability. This is not only due to the increase in funding, but also closely

---

[21] So-called 'Chinese-style federalism' refers to the extensive and profound economic and fiscal decentralization under the Chinese unitary government structure, thus effectively stimulating local governments to maintain the market and competition. Montinola et al. (1995). Qian and Roland (1998).

[22] This so-called 'mystery' refers to the fact that China has achieved unprecedented long-term and high-speed economic growth despite adverse conditions such as unclear property rights, unsound justice and corruption. A basic consensus in the world of economics is that the mystery of China is mainly attributable to effective interregional competition. See Zhang and Zhou (2008); Zhang (2009).

[23] Jiang (1989).

[24] Opinion of the Supreme People's Court and the State Planning Commission on the Construction of Trial Courts at People's Courts at Various Levels (30–08–1988).

[25] Jiang (2008).

related to the Unified System.[26] The unification between adjudication and judicial administration has not only expanded the size of the court organization, but also improved the courts' bargaining power with the Party and the government regarding allocation of resources. For example, the court president's status in the Party and administrative ranking has provided a role for the court president in politics. The establishment of an internal organization department has also facilitated the connection between the court and the corresponding functional departments of the Party and government organs.

As the gross domestic product continued to grow, China began to initiate reforms and blindly pursue economic development. Consequently, with the widening of the gap between the rich and the poor caused by long-term unfair distribution of resources, social conflicts have increased and social cohesion has partially collapsed. At present, the public's tolerance for social injustice has significantly reduced. The judiciary is theoretically the 'last line of defense' for social order and justice, and therefore, the demands for justice and judicial independence have grown stronger. Meanwhile, the courts have been pushed to resolve disputes and maintain social order.[27]

Following the comprehensive judicial reforms passed by the 18th National Congress of the Chinese Communist Party in 2012, the organizational structure of the court under the Unified System has been loosened and the trial management system began to change. First of all, the court has implemented the staff management system and the judge quota system in order to determine promotion of judges in a more informal manner. Judicial assistant staff and judicial administrative staff are subject to the rules governing civil servants. A judicial administrative affairs management department is also to be set up for handling all administrative affairs in the court. Furthermore, on the basis of a strict division of labor, the judicial accountability system is introduced to ensure the efficiency of judges in rendering judgments.

Consequently, judicial independence has been strengthened whereby single judges and collegial panels can now decide cases independently and are accountable for their own judgments. The President, Vice-Presidents and Chief Judges of the divisions that are not directly involved in the trials are forbidden to examine and approve judgments.[28] At the same time, the authority of the Judicial Committee is now limited. In principle, only serious cases relating to national diplomacy, national security and social stability, as well as difficult and complex cases can be submitted to the Judicial Committee.[29] Judges will remain accountable for the cases they adjudicated for their

[26]According to organizational sociology, an organization is not a closed system but is affected by the surrounding environment. Zhou (2003, pp.70–73).

[27]For example, in the early 1980s, the People's Mediation Committee resolved ten times as many civil and minor criminal disputes as the courts received. However, the number of cases brought before the courts is now exceeding that at the People's Mediation Committee. See Chen (2018).

[28]Several Opinions of the Supreme People's Court on Improving the Judicial Accountability System of the People's Courts, No. 13 [2015] Supreme People's Court, Art. 6.

[29]Several Opinions of the Supreme People's Court on Improving the Judicial Accountability System of People's Courts, No. 13 [2015] Supreme People's Court, Art. 9. However, there has been important progress in the newly revised Judicial Committee Working Rules of the local courts. For example,

lifetime. Finally, the divisions within the court will be abolished in stages, and the power of the Chief Judges of the divisions will be reduced gradually. A fixed trial team should be formed to replace the hierarchical management model with a flat management structure.

4 The Future of the Unified System

The Unified System proved to be necessary during a particular period in Chinese history. The old traditions of administrative and judicial integration of Yamen (衙门), as well as the relevant resources, in the first sixty years after the founding of the People's Republic of China, were insufficient to support the operation of a modern and neutral court system. However, as China enters a new era, the judiciary has become the backbone of social order and one of the main institutions in modern Chinese society. Therefore, further reforms of the court system are imperative to release the court from political duties, thus, shaping the court into a pure judicial organ akin to the Western model. However, since separating adjudication and administration involves adjustment of the political system and reallocation of political powers, such a reform is unlikely to happen in the near future.

Considering the political system, the social situation and the quality of judges in China, the author suggests that a reform of the Chinese court system may be carried out in the following steps. First, an Administration of Judicial Affairs Department shall be established within the court, which will take charge of judicial administrative work including the set-up of court divisions, financial management, buildings and courtrooms management, document management, enforcement of judgments and handling of judicial statistics. This department will be a specialized administrative agency headed by a 'Secretary-General'. The Secretary-General will only report to the President of the Court and follow the President's instructions. In other words, judges other than the President should not handle judicial administrative matters, which will be handled by full-time administrative staff instead. As such, the judicial administrative powers of the district courts and the intermediate courts can be concentrated in the hands of the Supreme People's Court and the provincial High Courts.

Second, 'trial management' should be strengthened and then gradually weakened. The judicial reform in Taiwan demonstrates that it can take a long time for the judicial system to be separated from the political system and be transformed into an autonomous institution. To achieve so, a substantial period of time coupled with the stringent training of judges, examination and approval of judgments and other

Article 9 of the Working Rules of the Judicial Committee of the Shenzhen Intermediate People's Court (amended on 31 August 2017) stipulates that the procuratorate may file a protest indicating a conflict with the judgment of a higher court. Cases reported to the higher court are to be decided by the Judicial Committee.

measures for improving judicial quality are required.[30] It is also necessary for the courts to implement standardized process management and judicial quality evaluation systems, which will help improve judicial efficiency and promote justice through reasonable allocation of resources. This will influence judges to perform better.

However, adjudication is different from the operation of a mechanized assembly line. Although stringent management can ensure the quality of judgments, it does not necessarily enhance the social legitimacy of the judiciary. Therefore, after the courts have obtained basic public trust or have improved their social credibility, trial management may be gradually weakened in order to safeguard the discretion of judges and judicial independence.

Finally, the court staff system should be adjusted according to the principle of the Party assuming the responsibility for cadres affairs (党管干部原则). Self-governance of the judicial profession should be achieved step by step. Specifically, a professional committee composed of judges should be established at the national and provincial levels. This committee should be responsible for assessing and appraising the ability of judicial candidates and conducting reviews on their professional accomplishments and skills. Such reviews could be used as reference by the Party's organizational department, which together with the leading Party Group of the court would remain responsible for examining the candidates' 'moral' (i.e. political) character. Based on the appraisal, the relevant party organization or group would determine whether the candidate is qualified for the position or not, followed by the submission of its opinion to the selection committee of judges for judicial nomination. According to the Judges Law, all nominees are to be appointed by the National People's Congress. The Administration of Judicial Affairs Department should keep detailed records of the judges' conduct, ability and performance in order to prepare relevant materials for staff management.

Accordingly, this kind of institutional arrangement would separate adjudication from judicial administration, judicial assistance from administrative affairs, staff management from other administrative powers and the President of the Court from ordinary judges, thus breaking down the highly centralized bureaucratic structure of courts under the Unified System. The President would still be fully responsible for adjudication and judicial administration of the court and could decide on the appointment and removal of administrative staff (including the Secretary-General). However, the President would no longer have the authority to decide on the appointment, promotion and remuneration of judges. Only judges would be responsible for adjudication with the help of judicial assistants. Judicial administrative staff would be responsible for ensuring the smooth and effective operation of the court and for providing services to the judiciary in terms of, amongst other things, funding, facilities, infrastructure and statistics. Trial management must be developed for improving the quality of trials, but it cannot interfere with the independence of the judiciary.

---

[30] According to Professor Su Yeong-Chin, judicial reform in Taiwan has gone through the stages of professionalization, specialization, independence and socialization since the late 1940s. The first stage ended in 1979. See Su (2001).

The above demonstrates that such a new institutional arrangement of the courts could guarantee due operation of the courts, without sacrificing judicial independence, and prevent erosion of powers of the court by the President and the judicial administrative departments. Consequently, it could avoid any improper outside interference by the Party, government organs or higher courts. In other words, judges would be able to refrain from 'absolute obedience to superior orders' under the examination, approval and performance appraisal system. They could rely on factual evidence and legal opinions to handle cases according to professional principles rather than political principles. This could also improve the authority and credibility of the judiciary. Lower courts would be more able to make final determinations on case facts, while higher courts could continue to confirm, interpret and develop new legal rules. Such institutional arrangement may not be able to draw a completely clear line between adjudication and judicial administration, but it could at least clarify what belongs to adjudication and what belongs to administration respectively.

References

Ai JH (2006) Judicial knowledge and movement of judges—An empirical analysis. Legal Soc Dev 4:95–112 (in Chinese)

Chen H (2018) Strengthening the team of people's mediators and promoting the modernization of state governance. People's Daily (overseas version) 28–04–2018. https://news.tsinghua.edu.cn/info/1011/58669.htm. Accessed July 2020 (in Chinese)

He F (2017) The effectiveness and improvement of the judicial personnel classification reform. 12th China Youth Law Forum. https://www.chinalaw.org.cn/portal/article/index/id/20330/cid/208.html. Accessed July 2020 (in Chinese)

Jiang FK (2008) Recollections of the material security work of the people's court in the 1980s. People's Court Newspaper, 9 Aug 2008 (in Chinese)

Jiang H (1989) Report on the serious difficulties of People's Courts in human resources, finance, and related matters. In: Jianghua judicial collection, 1st edn. Beijing, pp 305–312 (in Chinese)

Lan QP (1995) Judicial administration in contemporary China. Beijing (in Chinese)

Lin N (2005) Social capital—Theory of social structure and behaviour. Shanghai (in Chinese)

Luo SZ (2017) Work of the supreme people's court judge selection committee. People's Court Organization. https://www.chinacourt.org/article/detail/2017/07/id/2910349.shtml. Accessed July 2020 (in Chinese)

Montinola G, Qian Y, Weingast BR (1995) Federalism, Chinese style: The political basis for economic success. World Polit 48(1):50–81

Qian Y, Roland G (1998) Federalism and the soft budget constraint. Am Econ Rev 88(5):1143–1162

Su YC, (2001) Rethinking the experience of Taiwan's judicial reform. Seminar on Judicial Reform and Legal Development. School of Law, University of Hong Kong, Hong Kong

Wang YX (2010) Judicial costs and judicial efficiency: Financial security and incentives for judges in Chinese courts. The Jurist 4:132–137 (in Chinese)

Yan BK (2010) Introduction to the ancient Chinese official system. Beijing (in Chinese)

Zhang WC (2009) China's economic system. Beijing (in Chinese)

Zhang J, Zhou LA (2008) Competition for growth: Political economics of China's growth. Shanghai (in Chinese)

Zhou XG (2003) Ten lectures on organizational sociology. Beijing (in Chinese)

Taiwan's Court Structure from a Case Management Perspective

Jun Wu

Abstract This contribution provides a comprehensive overview of Taiwan's court structure and how its structural make-up influenced case management. It examines how the American concept of 'case-flow management' has helped improve the quality of civil justice in Taiwan; a jurisdiction that was heavily influenced by German and Japanese procedural law. Case-flow management can be regarded as an independent system which can enhance the performance of the judicial system, improve the allocation of resources and reduce the workload of judges. It aims to draw a distinction between auxiliary matters handled by junior court staff and judicial work handled by judges. This contribution also examines how specialized courts and procedures, in areas such as family and intellectual property, have helped improve case management in Taiwan.

1 Introduction

The judicial system of present-day Taiwan has its roots in the reforms of the Qing Dynasty (1644–1912) and was shaped by the judicial reform implemented by the Kuomintang government before it moved to Taiwan. In 1906, the Qing government changed the criminal department into a legal department, which then took charge of the judicial administration of the whole country. The Qing government also transformed the Dali Temple into the Dali Academy specializing in the highest-level judicial work, with the procuratorate (检察厅) as one of its main organs. A system of four levels of courts of which three are appeals courts (四级三审制) was introduced, which continued under the subsequent government of the Republic of China. In 1927, the government of Nanjing established the Executive Yuan (行政院), the Legislative Yuan (立法院), the Judicial Yuan (司法院), the Examination Yuan (考试院) and the Supervision Yuan (检察院) based on the concept of separation of

J. Wu (✉)
Soochow University, Suzhou, The People's Republic of China
e-mail: lawyerwujun@vip.163.com

P. C. H. Chan and C. H. van Rhee (eds.), *Civil Case Management in the Twenty-First Century: Court Structures Still Matter*, Ius Gentium: Comparative Perspectives on Law and Justice 85, https://doi.org/10.1007/978-981-33-4512-6_5

powers. The Judicial Administrative Department under the Executive Yuan was in charge of judicial administrative matters and consisted of, amongst others, civil, criminal and general affairs departments. The Judicial Yuan was the highest judicial organ, which consisted of the Supreme Court, the Administrative Court and the Civil Service Disciplinary Commission (公务员惩戒委员会).[1]

In October 1945, Japan ended its occupation of Taiwan and the Kuomintang government took over and reconstructed the legal system.[2] After 1949, Taiwan continued to promote legal and judicial reform, aiming to establish a just, independent and efficient judicial system. However, Taiwan's judiciary has been heavily criticized, especially for its delay in deciding cases and its lack of public trust. In light of the worldwide judicial reform in case management, it is important for Taiwan to further improve its judicial system by strengthening court organization and streamlining judicial procedures to maximize efficiency.

2 Current Court System and Types of Civil Procedure in Taiwan

2.1 *Court System*

The government of Taiwan is divided into the Executive Yuan, the Legislative Yuan, the Judicial Yuan, the Examination Yuan and the Supervision Yuan, which are referred to as the 'Five Yuan' (五院). The Judicial Yuan is the highest judicial body in Taiwan with the power to interpret law, the highest administrative court with disciplinary power over civil servants. The Judicial Yuan is composed of 15 Grand Justices (including one president and one vice-president) nominated by the President and appointed by the Legislative Yuan. The jurisdiction of the Judicial Yuan includes impeachment of the President and Vice-President and the power of the Grand Justices of the Constitutional Court to dissolve unconstitutional political parties. For civil and criminal litigation, the Supreme Court, the High Court and its branches and the District Courts (including Juvenile and Family Courts) constitute a 'three-level and three-instance system' (三级三审制) with the exception of a 'three-level and two-instance system' (三级两审制) in special circumstances. Issues of fact are heard at first and second instances (事实审) while issues of law are decided at third instance (法律审). For administrative litigation, the Supreme Administrative Court, the Higher Administrative Court and the Administrative Litigation Division (地方法院行政诉讼庭) constitute two instances of appeal and three levels of court. Again, issues of fact are heard at the first and second instances while issues of law are decided at third instance (Fig. 1).

---

[1] Liang (2007, p. 31).

[2] Chu (2003, pp. 139–156).

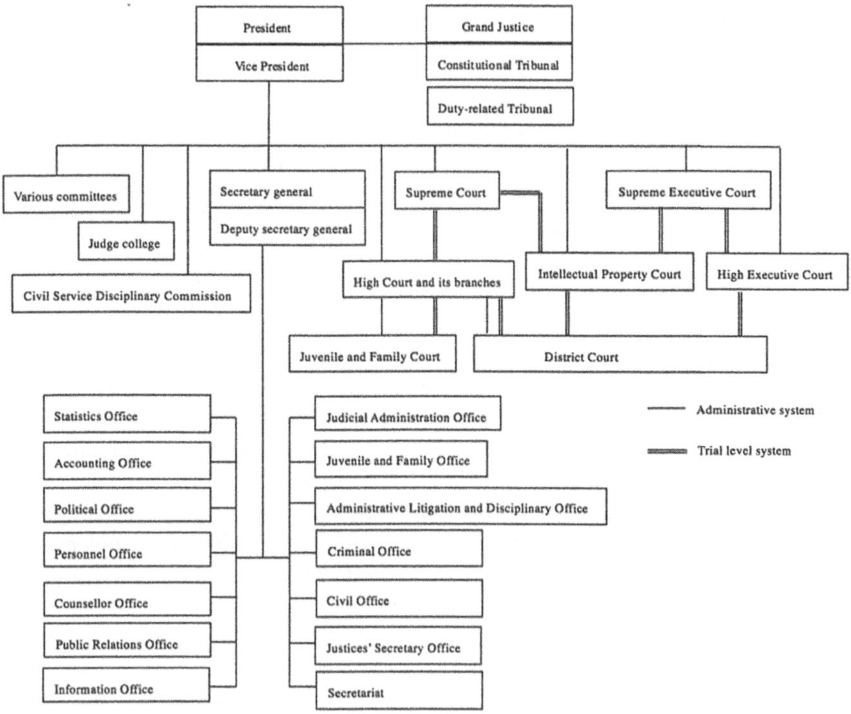

Fig. 1 Organizational chart of the court system of Taiwan. *Source* Judicial Yuan (2019b, p. 3)

The President exclusively manages the affairs of the Judicial Yuan, supervises various affiliated agencies and exercises different functions according to the law in order to improve and perfect the quality and performance of the judiciary. The Judicial Yuan has the right to draft bills and submit them to the Legislative Yuan on matters concerning the organization of the judiciary and the exercise of jurisdiction. The annual judicial budget prepared by the Judicial Yuan cannot be amended by the Executive Yuan, but has to be incorporated into the draft budget of the government and submitted to the Legislative Yuan for deliberation.[3] The judicial system of Taiwan guarantees the independence of courts given the judicial administrative role of the Judicial Yuan.

[3]Judicial Yuan (2019a).

2.2 Procedure

The main influence on civil procedure in Taiwan is German and Japanese law. In the last two decades, Taiwan's civil procedural law has been revised. Taiwan has set up professional and specialized courts for different types of cases. The main sources of Taiwan's current civil procedural law are the Code of Civil Procedure, the Family Act and the Intellectual Property Case Adjudication Act (智慧财产案件审理法).

Taiwan enacted the Juvenile and Family Court Organization Act (少年及家事法院组织法) and the Family Act in 2010 and 2012 respectively. According to the Juvenile and Family Court Organization Act, except as otherwise provided by law, the Juvenile and Family Court has jurisdiction in (1) cases that are within the scope of the Juvenile Delinquency Act, (2) cases that are within the scope of the Family Act, and (3) other cases stipulated by law that are within the scope of the Juvenile and Family Court, the Juvenile Court and the juvenile court divisions or family court divisions of the District Court (地方法院少年法庭或家事法庭). In the absence of a Juvenile and Family Court, cases are to be handled by the juvenile or family court division of the District Court. At present, only Kaohsiung City has a Juvenile and Family Court; other regions have set up a Juvenile Tribunal and Family Tribunal in the District Court to handle relevant matters.

In 2007, Taiwan enacted the Intellectual Property Court Organization Act and the Intellectual Property Case Adjudication Act (智慧财产案件审理法). In July 2008, the Intellectual Property Court was established to handle civil, criminal and administrative litigation concerning intellectual property matters. It is currently located in Banqiao District of New Taipei City. The Intellectual Property Court does not have exclusive jurisdiction in civil and administrative cases but only in criminal appeals. Therefore, civil and administrative cases concerning intellectual property matters are in principle tried by the Intellectual Property Court. However, under the doctrine of jurisdictional priority, if an ordinary court decides such a case, the judgment will also be valid even in the absence of jurisdiction. The reason for adopting jurisdictional priority rather than exclusive jurisdiction is that an exclusive jurisdiction enjoyed by the Intellectual Property Court would give rise to disputes regarding the legality of judgments.[4]

Taiwan is deeply influenced by the German legal system. Collective actions (*Verbandsklage*) have been used to compensate for damages (损害赔偿诉讼) in Germany. Taiwan first introduced collective actions under the Consumer Protection Act (消费者保护法) promulgated in January 1994. Consumer groups can either be asked by consumers to start an action or they can start an action directly based on provisions of the Consumer Protection Act. In July 2002, Taiwan promulgated the Securities Investor and Futures Trader Protection Act (证券投资人及期货交易人保护法) and established a securities collective action system for securities groups of plaintiffs based on the claims of securities investors and futures traders.[5]

---

[4] Li (2015, pp. 64–65).

[5] Xue (2016).

Judicial specialization has been a major topic of judicial reform in Taiwan. In May 2007, the National Conference on Judicial Reform (司改国是会议) in one of its sessions held a discussion about 'establishing specialized courts to hear relevant specialized cases'. The session passed a resolution to set up specialized Commercial Courts, Labour Courts and Tax Tribunals (税务法院), to develop procedural law for labour cases and to adjust legal fees and charges in favour of laborers.[6]

2.3 *Case Distribution (案件分流)*

Taiwan has not established a special court to handle summary cases, but the Code of Civil Procedure has introduced special procedures for handling such cases. Examples of the special procedures can be found in Part II Chap. 2 on mediation, Part II Chap. 3 on summary proceedings (简易诉讼程序) and Part II Chap. 4 on small claims procedure (小额诉讼程序).

According to Article 427 of the Code of Civil Procedure, summary procedures are applicable to actions concerning property rights where the value of claim (标的之金额或价额) does not exceed NT$500,000. However, there are 10 types of cases to which summary proceedings apply irrespective of the value of the claim, such as disputes over a fixed-term lease of a building or other object of work, or disputes arising from a fixed-term lender-borrower relationship (定期借贷关系). In addition, both parties may apply in writing for a summary procedure. Since the trial period of summary procedure is relatively short, the parties are in theory not obliged to prepare pleadings. Therefore, the court shall conclude oral arguments within one session (一次期日辩论终结/一次开庭审结) and may give a simplified judgment (判决书) or simply record the main points of the judgment and its reasoning in the transcript of the hearing without issuing a written judgment. First instance judgments (第一审裁判) under summary procedure are subject to appeal (抗诉) at the District Court and are heard by a collegiate bench. As for second instance judgments under summary procedure, if the awarded value exceeds the amount specified in Article 466 of the Code of Civil Procedure, the parties may appeal to the Supreme Court on the ground of wrongful application of law. Permission to appeal is required. Judgments of the Supreme Court become guiding judgments for future application of the relevant law.[7]

In actions for payment of money or securities, if the value of claim does not exceed NT$100,000, the small claims procedure will be applicable. If the value is not more than NT$500,000, the parties may apply for the small claims procedure only if they reach a consensus evidenced in writing. If the court considers the application for the small claims procedure inappropriate, it may decide *ex officio* that the original judge shall continue with the hearing of the case. The judgment of first instance in a

[6]Zhang (2017).

[7]Articles 427 and 466 of the Civil Procedure Law.

small-claims procedure may be appealed (抗诉) to the District Court and heard by a collegiate bench (合议庭).

2.4 *Alternative Dispute Resolution*

In order to alleviate the explosive increase in the number of cases in Taiwan, the Judicial Yuan has been actively promoting mediation since 2006. One of the goals is to enhance the professionalism and quality of mediators by increasing the use of mediation (调解使用率) and organizing regular discussions and workshops at the High Court and the District Courts.[8]

Taiwan's laws on mediation are very detailed—not only do they take into account the needs of the administration but also the needs of the industry. Agreement of the parties is at the core of mediation.

The Code of Civil Procedure provides for reconciliation (和解). Article 377 stipulates that the court, a commissioned judge or an assigned judge may seek settlement at any time of the proceedings. A third person may participate in the settlement with the permission of the court, or if the court deems it necessary, the court may take the initiative to instruct a third person to participate in the settlement.

Lawyers have an ethical obligation to promote reconciliation. Article 29 of the Code of Ethics for Lawyers provides that if a lawyer in the course of performing his duties discovers that a settlement, cessation of litigation (息讼) or admission of guilt is in line with his client's interests and justice, he should encourage such settlement, cessation of litigation or admission of guilt accordingly.

The Code of Civil Procedure also provides that the parties should try, through mediation, to resolve the cost of the settlement and litigation. Article 84 stipulates that in cases of settlement, the parties shall bear their own expenses except as otherwise agreed upon. When a settlement is reached, the parties may apply for reimbursement of two-thirds of the court fees within three months after the settlement date (see also Articles 420–421 of the Code of Civil Procedure).

3 The Meaning and Role of Case Management

In Taiwan, in line with the German approach, the exercise of case management powers by the judge is one element of efforts to improve case management. Another element is case-flow management based on the American model. Professor Kuan-Ling Shen from National Taiwan University College of Law points out that case management can be considered from different perspectives. The first is case management in a

[8] Gu and Zhang (2015).

specific case (or case management in the narrow sense), that is, management with regard to the subject matter of the case and its complexity and difficulty. From this perspective, the court may select the appropriate method to handle the dispute, adopt various methods to prepare and hear the case, tailor procedure to cater for the needs of the case and make the most appropriate and fair judgement in an efficient manner. The second perspective is management of the administration and organization of the judiciary (i.e. court management). In the United States, the central idea of court management is case-flow management, which requires the court to take a series of steps to facilitate the proceedings, including case allocation, setting of dates and case preparation. There is no clear boundary between court management and handling of cases (i.e. general court management).[9]

Judges in Continental European legal systems have a substantive responsibility for case management. Theoretically, there is a difference between adversarial (当事人进行主义) and inquisitorial (职权进行主义) systems in terms of the division of labour between the judges and the parties in case management. The adversarial system is driven by the wishes of the parties, whereas the inquisitorial system operates independent of the wishes of the parties. In Taiwan, the adversarial system (当事人进行主义) was adopted to respect the wishes of the parties and protect their private rights and duties. But the inquisitorial system was also partly adopted in order to prevent delay in the proceedings. The balance between the two systems has been a subject of reform in Taiwan.

Before the introduction of case-flow management, Taiwan's civil procedure rules had already adopted the system of concentrated trial (集中审理制度), which has two significant benefits. First, the parties are obligated to facilitate the proceedings—the system urges the parties to submit relevant procedural documents concerning known facts, evidence and other materials as soon as possible, sometimes even before commencement of proceedings. Second, the system entails a greater obligation on the justices. Both the justices and the parties can gain a better understanding of the cases by identifying and simplifying the issues at stake. This has promoted settlement of cases and facilitated the examination of evidence.[10] The major procedural technique for concentrated trial is the preparatory procedure. Article 270 of the Code of Civil Procedure provides that, if necessary, the court may appoint one of the judges as the commissioned judge to conduct the preparatory proceedings in cases heard by a panel of judges.

However, the establishment of concentrated trial has not solved the problem of case overload. The heavy workload of judges has led to complaints of delayed justice. The Judicial Yuan suggested to solve this matter by encouraging the parties to actively participate in pre-trial proceedings. The relevant pre-trial preparations are to be handled by court staff or judicial assistants, so that judges can focus on court hearings and the writing of judgments. Besides, information technology now allows the use of on-line procedures so that the progress of cases is easily accessible to the public. This has enhanced the transparency of trial proceedings. Consequently,

---

[9] Shen (2010, pp. 305–306).

[10] Judicial Yuan (2000, p. 1).

the system of case-flow management has effectively improved the efficiency of the court.[11]

Case-flow management was developed to reduce undue delay. The basic idea is that judges will only be involved in a case when it is ready for hearing. Prior to the introduction of this system, the preparatory work of cases was handled by the judges and their assistants. Because of this, only a limited number of judges could fully focus on court hearings and the writing of judgments. The new system has reduced such pressure for such preparatory work on the judges. In 2016, the Judicial Yuan sent its staff over to countries that have been successful in implementing case-flow management, like the United States, the United Kingdom, Singapore and Australia.[12]

The introduction of case-flow management is a reform of the concentrated trial system in Taiwan from the perspective of court organization and management. Case-flow management comprises two stages—the preparatory stage and the hearing stage. The preparatory stage involves the exchange of pleadings, sorting out of preliminary disputes and other non-judgmental affairs, while the hearing stage involves examination of evidence and establishment of facts. Under case-flow management, a large number of judicial assistants are assigned to assist the court (审查庭) to such an extent that most judges are no longer involved in the preparatory stage and court resources can be distributed more effectively.[13]

The Judicial Yuan selected the Civil Division of Kaohsiung District Court and the Criminal Division of Taoyuan District Court for a pilot program on case-flow management starting 1 May 2007 and 1 June 2007 respectively. The results of the pilot program were used to decide whether the system should be fully implemented across Taiwan. Since 2007, the pilot program has been extended to other courts, such as to the Criminal Division of Hsinchu District Court since 7 January 2009.

In a letter from the Judicial Yuan dated 30 December 2013 (No. 1020034802), it was held feasible to informally implement the case-flow management system in courts. The Judicial Yuan, in a letter dated 30 December 2013 (No. 1020034802), indicated it was feasible to informally implement the case-flow management system in courts. The evaluation of the pilot program demonstrated that the system had resulted in the disposition of a majority of cases by a small number of judges, thus remarkably reducing the backlog of cases. Besides, the number of cases being overturned on appeal had been reduced and the success rate of reconciliation and mediation had increased. Therefore, the Judicial Yuan issued the Points of Implementation of the Case-flow Management System for District Courts in Civil and Criminal Cases, which came into effect on 4 September 2014 and was revised on 30 June 2015 (hereinafter referred to as 'Points of Implementation'). The purpose of the Points of Implementation is to improve the quality of judgments and protect the rights and interests of litigants through enhancing the effectiveness of human

[11]Xu (2009, pp. 341–342).

[12]Judicial Weekly (2007).

[13]Xu (2009, p. 351).

resource utilization and the efficiency of case disposition. The case-flow management system provided in the Points of Implementation concerns matters that can be handled at the District Courts during the preparatory stage.

4 Case-Flow Management

Panels of judges in the District Courts are responsible for handling issues relating to case-flow management. Case-flow management should apply to civil and criminal cases preferably in larger courts with larger caseload. Therefore, the Judicial Yuan selected the District Courts to implement case-flow management under the Points of Implementation. Given the differences between different courts, whether or not to implement case-flow management in a particular court is subject to the decision of the council of judges. The most relevant parts of the Points of Implementation on case-flow management to base their decision on are the definition of case-flow management, the type and scope of cases subject to case-flow management, the time limits for handling cases, the review procedure, the number and distribution of cases, the reporting and closing of procedures and the examination of cases.[14]

Although larger courts are required to implement case-flow management, they may refuse to do so if they believe implementation to be difficult or unnecessary and they should report the specific reasons to the Judicial Yuan for approval. Small courts may also choose to implement case-flow management. When a court decides to implement case-flow management, that decision should be submitted to the Judicial Yuan for approval.

5 Judicial Reform and the Future of Case Management

In the early 1980s, Taiwan decided to set up a research institution on civil procedure law which would hold seminars every three months. In 1999, 2000 and 2003, the Code of Civil Procedure (first introduced in 1930) was subject to three major revisions. The first revision concerned a comprehensive revision of mediation and summary proceedings and the creation of a small claims procedure. The second revision involved the reform of evidence law and the implementation of concentrated trial. The third revision concerned the enhancement of supervisory proceedings (督促程序), the procedure of service by publication (substituted service) (公告催告程序) and proceedings for preservation of property.[15]

The following factors explain how the reforms of the civil procedural system in Taiwan became a success:

---

[14] Judicial Weekly (2014).

[15] Xu (2013, pp. 14–15).

(1) the influence of prominent politicians such as Jiang Jing-guo. In his later years, Jiang brought about the separation of trial and prosecution, lifted the martial law and introduced constitutional rules that guaranteed the independence of the Council of Grand Justices from the Judicial Yuan;
(2) an enlargement of judicial power, which allows the judiciary to protect people's rights and restrict the powers of the executive. Such enlargement includes the appointment, transfer and promotion of judicial staff by the judiciary itself, as well as the introduction of the Constitution as the highest law; and
(3) judges and prosecutors being ultimately accountable to the people, thus obtaining their trust and support through judicial independence.[16]

In October 2016, Xu Zong-li, the new President of the Judicial Yuan, proposed six areas of judicial reform: (1) enhancing judicial independence, human rights protection, due process of law and other judicial core values; (2) making court hearings more professional; (3) strengthening the influence of barristers; (4) avoiding contradictory judgments; (5) reducing the workload of judges; and (6) introducing constitutional appeal. Among these areas, improving the efficiency of proceedings and reducing the workload of judges are considered the *conditio sine qua non* for the success of all reforms. Key points include reducing the number of cases, simplifying the procedure, strengthening the parties' obligation to litigate efficiently, making good use of judicial assistants, equipment and other resources, and reducing the workload of judges so that they can concentrate on deciding cases. In addition, judges need to possess the necessary professional knowledge and experience to handle disputes arising from diverse and complex social activities in fields of, for example, medical care, construction, labour, food safety, finance, corporate governance, electronic information and environmental protection.

In Taiwan, case-flow management is mainly adopted in criminal procedure. According to an empirical study on case-flow management in criminal cases conducted by Qiu Zhong-yi, lawyers, public defenders, prosecutors and judges appear to acknowledge that the case-flow management system has reduced the average time for disposing of court cases, improved the quality of judgments and reduced undue delay, which is conducive to a proper and speedy trial and can fulfill the constitutional requirements of a fair, timely and effective hearing.[17] Case-flow management has achieved unexpectedly favourable results in criminal procedure.

6 Conclusion

The mission of justice calls for judicial reforms. Judicial reforms serve the goal of creating a more just legal system. Case-flow management can be regarded as an independent system which can enhance the performance of the judicial system, improve the allocation of resources and reduce the workload of judges. It aims to

---

[16] Liu and Wang (2011, p. 77).

[17] Qiu (2013, p. 218).

draw a distinction between auxiliary matters handled by junior court staff and judicial work handled by judges. This distinction has proved to be successful in Taiwan and has greatly enhanced the performance of the judiciary, resulting in a more efficient judicial system for the citizens and ultimately, a better manifestation of the rule of law.

References

Chiou JY (2013) District court's implementation of the case-flow management system in response to the demand for proper and speedy adjudication—Centered upon Taiwan Hsinchu district court criminal pretrial center. Technol Law Rev 10(1): 213–311 (in Chinese)
Chu JT (2003) Taiwan judicature. Soc Sci Nanjing 2:139–156 (in Chinese)
Gu JC, Zhang YW (2015) Actively promoting Taiwan's ADR mediation education—A sprint to catch up with the United States. The Arbitration Quar 2 (in Chinese)
Judicial Weekly (2007) Case-flow management to enable judges to concentrate on adjudication matters. https://jirs.judicial.gov.tw/GNNWS/NNWSS002.asp?id=8519&flag=1&regi=1&key=&MuchInfo=&courtid=. Accessed July 2020 (in Chinese)
Judicial Weekly (2014) The Judicial Yuan sets out the key points for the implementation of case process management: Formally implemented on 4 September 2014. https://www.judicial.gov.tw/tw/cp-1429-69897-a61e0-1.html. Accessed July 2020 (in Chinese)
Judicial Yuan (2000) Comparative table and general description of specific articles of the civil procedure law. Taipei (in Chinese)
Judicial Yuan (2019a) Central Government General Budget of the Judicial Yuan 2019. https://www.judicial.gov.tw/tw/dl-56431-a9706f2077754bad98cdff37bd177b4f.html. Accessed July 2020 (in Chinese)
Judicial Yuan (2019b) Introduction to the Judicial Yuan. https://www.judicial.gov.tw/tw/cp-209-210-b0504-1.html. Accessed 3 July 2020 (in Chinese)
Li Z (2015) Investigation of the litigation system of the intellectual property court in Taiwan. Intellectual Property 10:64–65 (in Chinese)
Liang Q (2007) On judicial reform in Taiwan. Law Appl 12:31–34 (in Chinese)
Liu KZ, Wang HX (2011) Sixty years of judicial reform in Taiwan: the practice and challenges of judicial independence. Oriental Law 4:69–77 (in Chinese)
Qiu ZY (2013) District court implements case-flow management system (Taiwan Hsinchu district court criminal pretrial center). Technology Law Review 10: 213–311 (in Chinese)
Shen KL (2010) The right to a fair hearing within a reasonable time and case management. Nat Taiwan Univ Law J 39(2):301–349
Xu ZX (2009) Civil law and judicial system. Taipei (in Chinese)
Xu SH (2013) New civil procedure law. Beijing
Xue YH (2016) Taiwan securities group litigation system: Norms and reference. Taiwan Res J 3:9–16 (in Chinese)
Zhang WC (2017) Reform at the commercial and labor courts and tax tribunal. Liberty Times Net. https://news.ltn.com.tw/news/politics/paper/1104533. Accessed July 2020 (in Chinese)

Civil Court Structure in Hong Kong

Ubaid-Ur Rehman

Abstract This contribution examines the introduction of the Hong Kong case management rules in 2009 that resulted from a decade long Civil Justice Reform. An important aspect of the reform was the emphasis on the underlying objectives of the civil procedure rules to enhance cost-effectiveness, promote efficiency and encourage fairness between parties in a dispute. Some of the specific mechanisms designed to achieve these objectives are discussed in this contribution. In addition, there is a brief discussion of the various courts and tribunals that deal with civil cases in Hong Kong and an examination of the means by which the higher courts supervise the case management of the lower courts through appeal procedures. Another important aspect that is examined is the difficulties the judiciary has faced in the recruitment of competent judges and the impact of these complications on case management. Finally, the contribution examines the efficacy of the case management powers granted to judges to rein in parties and shorten trials and delays and the efficacy of ADR processes such as mediation. The contribution concludes that although greater case management powers granted to judges appear to be achieving the desired positive results in terms of proportionality and efficiency, costs remain a concern that need to be the focus of continued reform in the long run.

1 Introduction

From the time it was occupied by the British in 1841 until the resumption of sovereignty by the Chinese government in 1997, Hong Kong was a British colony. During this more than 150 year period, the colonial masters of Hong Kong implemented the common law adversarial system into Hong Kong.[1] The Chinese laws and custom that had been in operation before the cession of Hong Kong were gradually

[1] Wesley-Smith (1994, pp. 87–89).

U.-U. Rehman (✉)
City University Hong Kong, Hong Kong, The People's Republic of China
e-mail: uurehman@cityu.edu.hk

P. C. H. Chan and C. H. van Rhee (eds.), *Civil Case Management in the Twenty-First Century: Court Structures Still Matter*, Ius Gentium: Comparative Perspectives on Law and Justice 85, https://doi.org/10.1007/978-981-33-4512-6_6

supplanted by English law.[2] The consequential effects of the British occupation on the territory's legal traditions were a rapid decline in Chinese law and custom as a source of law.[3] The only exceptions and instances when Chinese law and custom were retained were the circumstances of Hong Kong or its inhabitants where English law was inapplicable.[4] Over time, even this category of laws became increasingly narrow and was mostly confined to traditional Chinese customs such as concubinage (before its abolition in 1971) and the rights and interests of the indigenous inhabitants of the New Territories.[5] Given this backdrop, it is not surprising that Chinese culture had minimal or almost no influence on the shaping of the court structure in Hong Kong. From the time of its establishment as a British colony, expatriate judges were tasked with founding and developing the common law tradition in Hong Kong.[6] The early English judges, who would have had limited knowledge of the local legal customs and traditions, were effectively transplanting a legal system that was foreign to the Chinese natives of Hong Kong. This already difficult task would have been made even more demanding if there had been an effort by the British to supplement the English common law with Chinese law on any significant scale.[7]

The adoption of English law occurred in Hong Kong in incremental stages through the twentieth and twenty-first centuries[8] and by the time of the handover to the Chinese government in 1997, the traditions and the civil procedure rules were almost identical to the rules in England and Wales. Even after China assumed sovereignty over Hong Kong in 1997, in accordance with the 'one country-two systems' principle reached between the UK and the Chinese governments, it was guaranteed that Hong Kong's previous capitalist system and its laws would remain unchanged for 50 years.[9]

From a case management perspective, the adoption of an adversarial system of European origin in the early history of Hong Kong provided certainty and stability in a turbulent area of the world. Although there are many factors that contributed to the rapid rise of Hong Kong as a global force in trade and finance, it is undeniable that the legal system and the assurances it provided played an important part in the success of Hong Kong. However, Hong Kong's civil litigation system was not immune from the inherent deficiencies (especially in relation to case management issues) that can result from an adversarial system in which too much of the discretion and initiative is left in the hands of the litigants. By the turn of the century, the judiciary and the other stakeholders in the civil litigation system were acutely aware of the inefficiency, delay and the spiralling costs associated with conducting civil litigation in Hong Kong.[10]

---

[2] *Ibidem*, p. 205.

[3] *Ibidem*.

[4] *Ibidem*, p. 209.

[5] *Ibidem*, p. 206.

[6] Lin (2016, p. 6).

[7] *Ibidem*.

[8] Wesley-Smith (1994, pp. 88–96).

[9] Article 8 of the Basic Law of the Hong Kong Special Administrative Region.

[10] Wilkinson et al. (2017, p. 7).

2 Case Management and Reforms in the Litigation System

Whilst there is no definition of 'case management' in the Rules of the High Court (RHC), active case management is commonly understood to be the means by which the courts have been directed to achieve the objectives of increasing cost effectiveness and warranting that cases are dealt with in an expeditious and feasible manner.

Prior to 2009, the excessively adversarial nature of civil litigation in Hong Kong had led to immoderations such as delay and complexity.[11] In response to the increasingly apparent need for an overhaul of the system, the Hong Kong judiciary implemented the most radical and sweeping reform in the history of the jurisdiction. The Civil Justice Reform (CJR) was the culmination of almost a decade of consultation and discussions between the stakeholders of the legal system. In 2000, the Chief Justice set up the Working Party on Reform of the Civil Rules and Procedures of the High Court ('the Working Party'). The mandate given to the Working Party was to consider and make recommendations on the workings of the civil litigation system to make it more efficient and less expensive. The Working Party found that apart from the high cost of litigation, the system was slow; it imposed procedural obligations that were disproportionate to the needs of the case; it was susceptible to tactical manipulation of the rules by the parties; it was overly adversarial; it was incomprehensible to many users of the system and it did not address the inequality between wealthy and poor litigants.[12]

The recommendations of the Working Party were accepted by the Chief Justice and new rules were implemented to give effect to the recommendations of the Working Party by the HK Civil Justice (Miscellaneous Amendments) Ordinance 2008 and subsequently reflected in the changes to the RHC and the Rules of the District Court (RDC).[13]

One of the most momentous changes brought upon by the CJR was the introduction of the underlying objectives outlined in the amended RHC.[14] Similar in intention to the overriding objectives in the Civil Procedure Rules in England, the underlying objectives in RHC O.1A, r.1 set out: (a) to increase the cost-effectiveness of any practice and procedure to be followed in relation to proceedings before the Court; (b) to ensure that a case is dealt with as expeditiously as is reasonably practicable; (c) to promote a sense of reasonable proportion and procedural economy in the conduct of proceedings; (d) to promote greater equality between the parties; (e) to facilitate the settlement of disputes; and (f) to ensure that the resources of the Court are distributed fairly.

The underlying objectives were introduced to not only increase cost-effectiveness and procedural expediency but also to ensure fairness between parties and facilitate settlement of disputes.[15] The grant of control to the judges to exercise their case

[11] Final Report (2004, p. 10, para. 31).

[12] Interim Report (2001, p. 6, para. 24).

[13] Zuckerman (2009, p. 49).

[14] RHC O. 1A, r. 1.

[15] RHC and RDC O. 1A, r. 1.

management powers either on application or of their own motion[16] was an aspirational undertaking to achieve the imperatives of effectiveness, efficiency and fairness in the civil litigation system.

In practical terms, the case management rules after the CJR demand firm actions from the litigants. In a typical case, within 28 days after the close of pleadings, the parties to the litigation are required to complete a timetabling questionnaire to enable the Court to give directions relating to management of the case and to fix a timetable for the steps to be taken.[17] In addition to other matters, the questionnaire requires the parties to deal with issues such as joinder of parties, evidence, interlocutory applications, experts, ADR, amendment of pleadings, whether a case management conference and pre-trial review are going to be requested and an estimate of the length of the trial. The filling out of the questionnaire assists in the determination of the directions that are needed in the case.

If the parties are able to reach agreement, within a further 14 days, the plaintiff must file a consent summons containing the agreed directions or timetable for the Court's consideration and approval.[18] If the parties cannot come to an agreement on the case management directions or the defendant fails to file his timetabling questionnaire, the plaintiff must file a case management summons. Upon receipt of the case management summons, the defendant must serve on the plaintiff a notice specifying the orders that can be agreed and his proposal in terms of orders that cannot be agreed. The court can then make case management directions either in the presence of the parties or without a hearing. In cases requiring it, a case management conference (CMC) may also be held. The purpose of a CMC is to increase the efficiency of the interlocutory stage of the proceedings by allowing a judge to acquire the necessary information to give further directions.[19] A CMC can also be used for fixing a timetable for further progress of a case and to even fix the dates for the pre-trial review and the trial. Any outstanding interlocutory applications can also be dealt with at the CMC. If the court had earlier set down a date for a pre-trial review, at the actual pre-trial review, the court will fix the starting date for the trial and confirm or vary the length of the trial in light of the steps taken by the parties during the interlocutory stage. If any further directions are necessary (provided they do not affect the trial date), these will also be given at the pre-trial review.[20]

The implementation of this system that empowers the courts to give clear directions to the litigants in regard to the progress of a case clearly has many advantages. Unlike in the past when litigation was a financial and emotional commitment fraught with uncertainty and doubt, the post-CJR case management regime endeavours to allow the parties and more importantly, the court to dictate the pace of the proceedings from the outset of the case.[21] If a case is to progress through the civil procedure

[16] RHC O. 1B, r. 2.

[17] PD 5.2, B.

[18] *Ibidem*, D.

[19] *Ibidem*, G.

[20] *Ibidem*, H.

[21] Wilkinson et al. (2017, p. 447).

machinery in an efficient and cost effective manner, clear case directions are of paramount importance. The distinct advantage they provide include the ability of the court to control the pace of the case from the start of the proceedings, the focusing of the minds of the parties on the real issues between them and a better understanding of the costs that are likely to be incurred at each separate stage of the proceedings. These factors not only encourage the parties to consider settlement in a more constructive manner but also result in fewer delays and enable a more efficient deployment of judicial resources. The court can use its active case management powers to prevent delays and if necessary impose sanctions on litigants who are deliberately trying to prolong a case. In this respect, the court can order a party to pay a sum of money into court and to specify the consequences of a failure to comply with an order of the court.[22]

The changes brought about by the CJR are not limited to the interlocutory stage of civil proceedings. In order to enhance procedural efficiency and economy during the trial, a number of case management powers have been granted to the courts. At any time before or during a trial, the Court may by direction (a) limit the time to be taken in examining, cross-examining or re-examining a witness; (b) limit the number of witnesses (including expert witnesses) that a party may call on a particular issue; (c) limit the time to be taken in making any oral submission; (d) limit the time to be taken by a party in presenting its case; (e) limit the time to be taken by the trial; and (f) vary a direction made under this rule.[23] In deciding whether to make any such direction, the Court shall have regard to the following matters in addition to any other matters that may be relevant: (a) the time limit for a trial must be reasonable; (b) any such direction must not detract from the principle that each party is entitled to a fair trial; (c) any such direction must not detract from the principle that each party must be given a reasonable opportunity to lead evidence and cross-examine witnesses; (d) the complexity or simplicity of the case; (e) the number of witnesses to be called by the parties; (f) the volume and character of the evidence to be led; (g) the state of the Court lists; (h) the time expected to be taken for the trial; and (i) the importance of the issues and the case as a whole.[24]

3 Horizontal Arrangement

In Hong Kong, there are a number of courts and tribunals that deal with specific types of civil cases. These courts and tribunals include:

(a) The Court of Final Appeal (CFA): Prior to the resumption of sovereignty over Hong Kong by the Chinese government in 1997, the highest appellate court of Hong Kong was the Judicial Committee of the Privy Council in England.[25] Since

[22]RHC O. 1B, r. 1(3).

[23]RHC and RDC O. 35, r. 3A(1).

[24]RHC and RDC O. 35, r. 3A(2).

[25]Wesley-Smith (1994, p. 65).

its inception in 1833, the Judicial Committee of the Privy Council has been the highest court of appeal for British overseas territories and dependencies. With the enactment and commencement of the Hong Kong Court of the Final Appeal Ordinance on 1 July 1997, the CFA replaced the Privy Council and now serves as the highest appellate court in Hong Kong. When it is in session, appeals in front of the court are heard by five judges, comprising of the Chief Justice, three permanent judges and one non-permanent judge (who are either from Hong Kong or from other common law jurisdictions such as the UK, Australia or New Zealand). Most of the appeals to the CFA are from the Court of Appeal although a small number of appeals lie directly from the Court of First Instance.

(b) The Court of Appeal of the High Court (CA): The CA has the jurisdiction to hear appeals on civil and criminal matters. The majority of the cases are from the Court of First Instance and the District Court but the court also hears appeals from the Lands Tribunal.

(c) The Court of First Instance of the High Court (CFI): The CFI has unlimited jurisdiction in all civil matters and it also has jurisdiction in Admiralty matters.[26] In addition, the CFI has an appellate jurisdiction which includes appeals from the decisions of Masters, the Labour Tribunal[27] and the Small Claims Tribunal.[28]

d) The District Court (DC): The DC has jurisdiction to hear and determine any action founded on contract, quasi-contract or tort where the amount of the plaintiff's claim does not exceed Hong Kong $3,000,000.[29] The Court has jurisdiction to hear and determine any action for the recovery of land, where the annual rent or the rateable value of the land, determined in accordance with the Rating Ordinance (Cap. 116), or the annual value of the land, whichever is the least, does not exceed Hong Kong $320,000.[30]

(e) Family Court: Matrimonial cases including divorce, maintenance and custody of children come under the jurisdiction of the DC under its capacity as the Family Court.

(f) The Competition Tribunal: This tribunal was established in 2013 under the Competition Ordinance and has the jurisdiction to hear and decide a variety of applications made by the Competition Commission regarding alleged contraventions of the competition rules. The tribunal has the power to grant the same reliefs and remedies as the CFI.

(g) The Lands Tribunal: The Lands Tribunal was established in 1974 and has jurisdiction to hear and adjudicate cases involving possession of premises by landlords, building management disputes (which may involve interpretation of the Building Management Ordinance and the affairs of the management committees

---

[26]Section 3(2) of HCO.

[27]Section 32 of Labour Tribunal Ordinance, Cap. 25.

[28]Section 28 of Small Claims Tribunal Ordinance, Cap. 338.

[29]Section 32(1) of the District Court Ordinance, Cap. 336.

[30]Section 35 of the District Court Ordinance, Cap. 336.

of a building), compensation cases involving the government and persons whose land may have been resumed or suffered a fall in value due to governmental policies, compulsory sale cases and appeal cases.[31]

(h) The Labour Tribunal: The Labour Tribunal was established in 1973 and enjoys exclusive jurisdiction over disputes between employers and employees.[32] The common types of claims heard in this tribunal include claims by employees for wages (for work done and for termination in lieu of notice), disputes in relation to statutory holidays and rest days, claims for severance and bonus pay and claims by employers for wages (in lieu of notice or termination of contract). The amount of the claim has to exceed Hong Kong $8000 and there is no upper limit on the amount of claim.

(i) The Small Claims Tribunal (SCT): This tribunal was established in 1976 and has exclusive jurisdiction over monetary claims that fall below Hong Kong $75,000.[33] The typical claims handled by the SCT are for debt, service charges, damage to property, goods sold and consumer claims.

From a case management perspective, these courts and tribunals are effective in their operations because, except for the SCT, the differentiation or channelling of cases according to the nature of the claim in the tribunals and courts allows the judges with specialist knowledge in that particular area to preside over the cases. The constant contact with one particular area of the law allows judges to accumulate jurisdictive experience in that distinct area of the law and not only enhances their judicial skills in that area but also allows them to become intimately familiar with the case management issues that may arise in those types of cases.

In relation to the SCT, parties appearing in the SCT cannot be represented by lawyers. However, if they can provide valid reasons, they may be allowed to have a representative appear for them. The litigants or their representatives have to prepare all the witness statements and other documents that are to be used during the trial and they also have to conduct the examination of witnesses during the trial. The filing of a claim in the SCT is relatively straightforward in that a claimant must fill in one form[34] in which he states his particulars and the particulars of the person against whom he is making a claim and another form[35] in which he has to state the amount of the claim (and the breakdown of the calculation) and the reasons of the claim. Once the forms have been filled and a prescribed filing fee has been paid, the tribunal registry will issue the claimant another form[36] with the details of the place, time and date of the call-over hearing. The court bailiff will then send copies of all the forms to the defendant by ordinary post.

---

[31] Sections 6 and 8 and Schedule of Lands Tribunal Ordinance, Cap. 17.

[32] Section 7 of Labour Tribunal Ordinance, Cap. 25.

[33] Section 5(2) of Small Claims Ordinance, Cap. 338.

[34] Form 1.

[35] Form 2.

[36] Form 3.

Any party that is aggrieved by the decision of the adjudicator in the SCT has the option to either apply to the tribunal for review or apply to the CFI for leave to appeal. A review entails the filling of a form and the hearing of the application by the same adjudicator who presided over the original hearing.

A party that opts to apply to the CFI must first apply for leave to appeal within the prescribed time period. If leave is granted, the appeal is then heard by a judge in the CFI. However, the CFI has no jurisdiction to vary the SCT's determinations on questions of fact. If the appellant's appeal is refused, he can further appeal to the CA.

In regard to the CFI, unlike the English civil court system in which the High Court is divided into three divisions, the CFI consists of original jurisdiction and authority of a like nature and extent as that held and exercised by the Chancery, Family and Queen's Bench Divisions of the High Court in England and any other jurisdiction, whether original or appellate jurisdiction, conferred on it by any law.[37] Given its wide jurisdiction, the opportunity for a CFI judge to specialize in a particular area of law may appear to be more restrictive when compared to adjudicators in the various tribunals. However, taking a cue from England, Hong Kong has adopted the system of lists for particular proceedings.[38] This channelling of cases not only allows specialist judges to manage cases but also allows structural differentiation in the handling of the so-called 'hard cases' as opposed to the disposal of the more routine cases. Currently, the lists include the personal injuries list, the commercial list, the construction and arbitration list, the constitutional and administrative law list, the admiralty list and the employees' compensation list. Each list is supervised by a judge who specializes in that particular area of the law and during the interlocutory stages, chambers applications are almost exclusively dealt with by the judge in charge of a particular list.[39]

For each list, the Practice Direction sanctions the judge in charge of the list certain active case management powers and allows the judge latitude in regulating the degree to which these provisions ought to apply to the cases in that particular list.[40] For example, the Practice Direction of the Personal Injuries List[41] contains many provisions which are meant to improve procedural efficiency. The aim of the Practice Direction is to encourage the parties to explore alternative means such as mediation and negotiation to reach consensus and to regard the trial as a last resort.[42] The provisions in relation to a pre-action protocol, the case management questionnaire, the encouragement towards the use of alternative dispute resolution, the preference of a joint approach to the admission of expert evidence on quantum are all examples of efforts by the court to use its case management powers to expedite the resolution of the cases. The lawyers acting for the parties are expected to have

[37] Section 12(2) of HCO.

[38] Wilkinson et al. (2017, p. 839).

[39] *Ibidem*, p. 840. Also see *Broad Mark Ltd v Lin Zhen Zhong* [2012] 5 HKLRD 359.

[40] *Ibidem*, p. 840.

[41] PD 18.1.

[42] Para. 4, PD 18.1.

a firm grasp of the details of their cases, to have an early identification and framing of the issues, and to map out a realistic timetable for the expeditious resolution of the case.[43] Even when it becomes apparent that a trial is going to be inevitable, the parties should consider and take all necessary steps in preparation for the trial, making only such interlocutory applications as are necessarily required for the expeditious resolution of the ultimate dispute and the saving of costs.[44]

4 Current Vertical Arrangements and Their Effectiveness from a Case Management Perspective

The most visible and effective means for the higher courts to supervise the case management of the lower courts is thorough appeal procedures. Any litigant from the SCT to the CFI who feels aggrieved by a decision of the judge or adjudicator can appeal to a higher court to have the matter heard again. These appeal mechanisms afford a losing party the opportunity to present its case to a different tribunal for reconsideration. The right to appeal to a higher court is a welcome feature of the civil litigation system as it prevents injustice and ensures the proper administration of justice by clarifying and developing the law.[45] However, appellate cases can lead to significant additional work for an already strained judicial system and the resultant additional costs and delay can be undesirable. To attain a balance between these opposing interests, the civil litigation system has in place certain procedural devices that essentially limit the cases that may reach the appellate courts.

In respect of appeals to the CA from the CFI judge's decisions, one of these devices is the requirement to obtain leave before lodging an appeal to the CA. Prior to the CJR, in most cases, any final or interlocutory judgment of the CFI in a civil cause could be appealed to the CA as of right.[46] However, after the implementation of the CJR, the new O.59, rr. 2A, 2B and 2C, has set out the procedure for applications to the Court of Appeal for leave to appeal. Whilst a CFI judge's decision at trial and any final decisions still do not require any leave, a CFI judge's decisions in most interlocutory decisions (which are not determinative of a party's substantive rights) require an application for leave to appeal.[47] Leave to appeal from an interlocutory judgment or order of the Court of First Instance in any civil cause or matter should not be granted unless the court hearing the application for leave is satisfied that the appeal has a reasonable prospect of success.[48] In *SMSE v KL*,[49] Le Pichon JA observed that:

[43] Para. 3, PD 18.1.

[44] Para. 5, PD 18.1.

[45] Bowman (1997, Sect. 14.2).

[46] Section 14(1) of HCO.

[47] Section 14AA(1) of HCO.

[48] Section 14AA(4)(a) of HCO.

[49] [2009] 4 HKLRD, para. 17.

> Leave to appeal under Order 59 rule 2B is not lightly granted. The relevant test appears in section 14AA(4) of the High Court Ordinance. In granting leave, the judge must have considered that the test set out in section 14AA(4) had been met. The section requires that the court be satisfied that the appeal has a reasonable prospect of success or there is some other reason in the interests of justice why the appeal should be heard before granting leave. Reasonable prospects of success involves the notion that the prospects of succeeding must be 'reasonable' and therefore more than 'fanciful', without having to be 'probable'.

In an instance when a litigant is required to obtain leave before lodging an appeal, a failure to do so would prevent that party from being able to serve a valid notice of appeal.[50]

Another mechanism for ensuring procedural efficiency and expediting finality in litigation is the use of short time limits to institute appeals. The time limits for appealing CFI decisions to the CA are 14 days[51] from the decision of a CFI judge in most interlocutory applications (for which the leave to appeal must be lodged first) and 28 days[52] for a CFI judge's decision at trial and in a final application. In the post CJR era, although the CA is bound to give effect to the underlying objectives, it nevertheless has to be conscious of the need to reach a just resolution of the issues whilst balancing the rights of the parties. In this regard, the CA has the power to extend these periods. However, the power to grant or refuse the extension is entirely at the discretion of the CA. The factors that will be considered when exercising the discretion include (1) the length of the delay; (2) the reasons for the delay; (3) the chances of the appeal succeeding if time for appealing is extended; and (4) the degree of prejudice to the potential respondent if the application is granted.[53] In the past, the courts have held that this is an unfettered dicretion and an overly rigid or mechanistic approach which focuses solely on the reasons and the length of delay is undesirable. Instead, the courts have encouraged a holistic approach in which all the circumstances of the case are considered and a decision is only reached after considering whether the overall justice of the case requires an exercise of the discretion.[54]

Before the Administration of Justice (Miscellaneous Provisions) Ordinance 2014 came into effect in December 2014, the appeal mechanism for cases to be heard in the Court of Final Appeal (CFA) was considered highly unsatisfactory.[55] Previously, an appeal lay to the CFA 'as of right' from a final judgement of the CA where the matter

---

[50] *Cumbes v Robinson* [1951] 2 K.B. 83.

[51] RHC O. 59, r. 2B(1).

[52] RHC O. 59, r. 4(1)(c).

[53] See *Norwich & Peterborough Building Society v Steed* [1991] 1 W.L.R. 449; *Chiu Sin Chung v Yu Yan Yan, Angela* [1993] 1 H.K.L.R. 225; *Secretary for Justice v Hong Kong and Yaumati Ferry Co. Ltd* [2001] 1 H.K.C. 125. See also *Mak Hau Shing v Oriental Press Group Ltd & Others* [1996] 1 H.K.L.R. 245; *Birkenhead Properties and Investments Ltd v Leung Yiu* [1998] 1 H.K.L.R.D. 527; *Chiu Butt York v Chiu Kwok Lim* [1980] H.K.L.R. 459, CA.

[54] See *Jerry Chen v Whirlpool (Hong Kong) Ltd* [2005] H.K.E.C. 1602 and *Nantong Angang Garments Co. Ltd v Hellman International Forwards Ltd* [2005] H.K.E.C. 1482.

[55] *China Field Ltd v Appeal Tribunal (Buildings)* (2009) 12 HKCFAR 68, para. 16, as *per* Ribeiro PJ.

in dispute amounted to HK$1 million or more[56] or the appeal involved a question which, by reason of its great general or public importance, or otherwise, ought to be submitted to the CFA for decision.[57] The main point of objection was in relation to the former provision as it was argued that the adoption of an arbitrary financial limit to determine the right of appeal enabled any claimant whose claim was above the financial threshold to obtain leave, regardless of the merits of the claim. This situation led to the court having to hear appeals that were unmeritorious.

The new provisions state that all civil appeals to the CFA are subject to discretionary leave from either the CA or the CFA, regardless of the amount involved. This change will theoretically allow the CFA to hear genuine and more meritorious appeals. It has also brought Hong Kong in line with other common law jurisdictions.

5 Court Funding, Court Composition and Case Management

The courts in Hong Kong are financed by the government as the annual budget of the judiciary is part of the overall budget of the government of Hong Kong.[58] The yearly budget of the government is approved on an annual basis by the Legislative Council through appropriation legislation. Over the last decade or so, the Hong Kong government has been able to accumulate significant fiscal reserves through land sales and through the adoption of a conservative monetary policy.[59] Thus, the judiciary has not faced any significant difficulties in securing the necessary financing for the administration of the judiciary.

Therefore, unlike some other jurisdictions,[60] the Hong Kong judiciary's resource deficiencies are not of a financial nature. Instead, the limiting factor is the lack of human capital. A combination of factors including the increasing number of experienced judges reaching retirement age and the reluctance of the more senior and well qualified lawyers to joining the judiciary have resulted in difficulties in judicial recruitment.[61] This problem is especially acute in the higher courts. This has in turn had a knock-on effect on the management of cases because the shortage of experienced judges has inevitably increased delay in the adjudication of cases. The government has recognized this phenomenon and has provided the necessary financial support for the recruitment and appointment of judges. Since 2012, 16 judicial appointments have been made in the CFI and 22 judicial appointments have been

---

[56] Section 22(1)(a) of the Hong Kong Court of Final Appeal Ordinance (Cap. 484).

[57] Section 22(1)(b) of the Hong Kong Court of Final Appeal Ordinance (Cap. 484).

[58] Hong Kong Budget 2017–2018.

[59] South China Morning Post (2017).

[60] Schauffler and Kleiman (2010).

[61] South China Morning Post (2018).

made in the DC.[62] However, despite these efforts, persistent recruitment difficulties continue to be a problem for the judiciary.

Coupled with the difficulties in the recruitment of judges, the judiciary in Hong Kong has also seen a significant rise in the number of unrepresented litigants in civil proceedings and the introduction of the CJR has not had a significant impact on lessening the number of such cases.[63] In 2011, 36% of litigants in the CFI and 51% of litigants in the DC were not legally represented.[64] The figures for 2017 were 32% and 61%, respectively.[65] Whilst it is overly simplistic to attribute the rise in average waiting times for cases in the High Court to merely one or two causes such as the lack of judges or unrepresented litigants, the statistics are nevertheless illuminating. From 2015 to 2017, the average waiting times for cases in the civil fixture list in the High Court have increased from 140 to 163 days.[66]

Currently, civil proceedings in the CFI are heard before single judges and only cases in the Court of Appeal and the Court of Final Appeal are heard by a panel of judges. The adjudication of most cases by a single judge is preferable, effective and constructive from a case management perspective. The increasing number of cases being brought before the courts and the surge in the claims being initiated by litigants in person have not only caused a serious strain on judicial resources but also placed time constraints on the judges who must preside over these cases. Unlike civil law countries where judges are often recruited at a relatively young age and go through extensive on the job training, judges in Hong Kong who are appointed to the High Court are often very experienced and distinguished practitioners who may already be in their late 40s or early 50s when they are appointed. This tradition coupled with the disinclination of some qualified and successful practitioners to accept appointments to the bench have led to a shortage of judges in the upper levels of the judiciary. Faced with an already limited number of judges, it is prudent from a case management standpoint to continue to have cases in the DC and CFI be adjudicated by single judges.

6 Academic Views and ADR

Although the radical reform of the civil procedure rules has been in place for slightly more than 11 years, there have been few comprehensive and structured studies about the effectiveness of the CJR. However, the limited information available does suggest that there is a variance of views on the success of the reform. In regards to case

[62] Hong Kong Judiciary (2016).

[63] Cameron and Kelly (2002, p. 313).

[64] Leung (2015, p. 34).

[65] Hong Kong Judiciary (2017).

[66] *Ibidem.*

management, some judges have expressed confidence in the efficacy of the management powers of the judges to rein in parties and shorten trials and delays.[67] Other commentators have been more skeptical and questioned whether the courts' willingness to tolerate parties' breaches of procedural timetables reflect a lax enforcement attitude.[68] Similar divergence of views have been expressed by judges, practitioners and the users of the court services in relation to the effectiveness of the reform in areas such as discovery and milestone dates.[69]

Statistics from the judiciary suggest that mediation has been one of the more successful aspects of the reform package. As early as the mid 1980s, mediation had been utilized to encourage settlement between parties in Hong Kong.[70] However, the various mediation schemes introduced throughout the last two decades of the twentieth century and the first decade of the twenty-first century were largely confined to specialist areas such as construction and insurance.[71] It was not until the implementation of the CJR that there was a concerted effort to encourage parties to engage in ADR processes to settle their disputes. The biggest impetus for the widespread adoption of mediation for the resolution of civil disputes has been Practice Direction 31 (PD31), which supplements the provisions in the RHC and RDC. The aim of PD31 is to assist the court to discharge its duty to encourage parties to use ADR if it considers it appropriate and to facilitate its use.[72] PD31 further states that 'the parties and their legal representatives have the duty of assisting the court' to discharge this duty[73] and that in 'exercising its discretion on costs, the court takes into account all relevant circumstances. These would include unreasonable failure of a party to engage in mediation where this can be established by admissible materials.'[74] Whilst a party that refuses to participate in mediation may be in danger of being slapped with an adverse order, the sanction is only applicable if a party refuses to mediate.[75]

Whilst most practitioners were guarded about the benefits of mediation at the start of the reform, the practice has increased in popularity as the quality of the mediators in Hong Kong has risen and the public has become more educated about the value of mediation. In 2011, 421 cases with mediation in the CFI were reported to the judiciary. In 159 of those cases, there was either a full or partial agreement between the parties (representing 38% of the total cases). In 2017, 780 cases with mediation in the CFI were reported to the judiciary. In 369 of those cases, there was either a full or partial agreement between the parties (representing 47% of the total cases).[76]

---

[67] Meggitt (2010, p. 169).

[68] *Ibidem.*

[69] *Ibidem.*

[70] Leung (2009, p. 39).

[71] *Ibidem*, p. 40.

[72] Paras. 1 and 2, PD 31.

[73] Para. 1 of PD 31.

[74] Para. 4 of PD 31.

[75] *Golden Eagle International (Group) Ltd v GR Investment Holdings Ltd* [2010] 3 HKLRD 273, as *per* Lam J.

[76] Hong Kong Judiciary Mediation Statistics (2017).

Whilst the above statistics and the growth of mediation is encouraging and indicates that litigants and their legal representatives may be becoming more aware of mediation, there is also consensus in the academic and professional realms that although the reforms have addressed a number of important issues in relation to case management and the efficiency of the civil litigation processes, there are still areas that were not covered by the reform but should be addressed in the future. These include the suitability of discovery of electronic documents and particular issues related to enforcement of judgements.[77]

7 Conclusion

One of the most essential tenets of the Hong Kong Basic Law[78] is the independence of the judiciary.[79] The fundamental concept of separation of powers between the Executive, Legislature and the Judiciary is predicated on the independence of the judicial branch. As such, the judiciary enjoys total independence to adjudicate according to the law without any interference from the other branches of the government. In the period before the implementation of the CJR, the judiciary received recommendations from the Working Party to improve efficiency and reduce delay and all subsequent decisions it made to apply the recommendations were made independently and without any interference from the other branches of the government.

Since the implementation of the CJR, although the management of the litigation process has undergone great changes, the overall framework of civil litigation has remained similar to its structure before the reforms.[80] Also, unlike the English approach that was adopted in the Woolf Reforms, the Working Party adopted a more cautious approach by selectively amending the existing civil procedural code rather than introducing a whole new code. The aim of introducing changes such as the underlying objectives, active case management, timetabling and the use of milestone dates, the new system of sanctioned offers and payments and provisional assessment of costs in the amended code was to enhance the cost-effectiveness of the system, reduce its complexity and reduce delays in litigation.[81] By streamlining the litigation process and encouraging judges to take a more proactive approach in dealing with litigants and their legal representatives, the goals of achieving greater proportionality and greater efficiency are being realized.

One of the biggest practical concerns of the users of a civil litigation system is costs. In effect, all the measures introduced by the CJR were meant to have a

---

[77] Meggitt (2010, p. 172).

[78] The mini constitution of the Hong Kong Special Administrative Region.

[79] Article 85 of the Basic Law of the Hong Kong Special Administrative Region.

[80] Zuckerman (2009, p. 49).

[81] Wilkinson et al. (2017, p. 8).

meaningful impact on the costs borne by the litigants. If courts continue to exercise their active case management powers and enforce the rules and litigants embrace their obligations in an earnest manner, there is no reason to doubt that the reforms will be effective in the long run.

References

Bowman G (1997) Review of the court of appeal (Civil Division)—Report to the Lord Chancellor (Bowman Report), London

Cameron C, Kelly E (2002) Litigants in person in civil proceedings. Hong Kong Law J 32(2):313–342

Final Report (2004) The final report of the Chief Justice's Working Party on Civil Justice Reform, 3 March 2004. https://www.civiljustice.hk/fr/documents/cjr_final_report.pdf. Accessed July 2020

Hong Kong Budget (2017) The Annual Controlling Officer's Report. https://www.budget.gov.hk/2017/eng/pdf/head080.pdf. Accessed June 2020

Hong Kong Judiciary (2016) The Judiciary Administrator's Speaking Notes at the Special Finance Committee Meeting on 1 April 2016. https://www.judiciary.hk/en/other_info/fc_questions/fc_quest1617a.htm. Accessed June 2020

Hong Kong Judiciary (2017) Annual Report Hong Kong Judiciary. https://www.judiciary.hk/en/publications/annu_rept_2017/eng/caseload_hc.html. Accessed June 2020

Hong Kong Mediation Statistics (2017) Hong Kong Mediation statistics for civil justice reform related cases. https://mediation.judiciary.hk/en/figures_and_statistics.html. Accessed June 2020

Interim Report (2001) Civil justice reform: Interim report and consultative paper. 21 November 2001. https://www.civiljustice.hk/ir/documents/FullReport.pdf. Accessed July 2020

Leung R (2009) Hong Kong mediation handbook. Hong Kong

Leung JHC (2015) Lay litigation behaviour in post colonial Hong Kong courtrooms. Language and Law/Linguagem E Direito 2(1):32–52

Lin F (2016) The expatriate judges and rule of law in Hong Kong: Its past, present and future. In: Shetreet S, McCormack W (eds) The culture of judicial independence in a globalised world. Leiden, pp 279–312

Meggitt G (ed) (2010) Civil justice reform—What has it achieved? Hong Kong.

Schauffler RY, Kleiman M (2010) State courts and the budget crisis: Rethinking court services. The Book of the States 42:289–294. https://knowledgecenter.csg.org/kc/content/state-courts-and-budget-crisis-rethinking-court-services. Accessed June 2020

South China Morning Post (2017) Hong Kong's nearly HK$2 tr fiscal reserves should be spent to benefit the people who own them. https://www.scmp.com/business/global-economy/article/2085785/hong-kongs-nearly-hk2tr-fiscal-reserves-should-be-spent. Accessed June 2020

South China Morning Post (2018) Hong Kong's shortage of judges means justice is often delayed. https://www.scmp.com/comment/insight-opinion/article/1888948/hong-kongs-shortage-judges-means-justice-often-delayed. Accessed June 2020

Wesley-Smith P (1994) The sources of Hong Kong law. Hong Kong

Wilkinson M, Cheung ETM, Meggitt G (2017) A guide to civil procedure in Hong Kong, 6th edn. Hong Kong

Zuckerman AAS (2009) The challenge of civil justice reform: Effective court management of litigation. City University Hong Kong Law Review 1(1):49–71

The Formal Adequacy Principle from the Perspective of Judicial Case Management: Macau

Wei Wang

Abstract When Macau's civil procedural rules were codified at the end of 1999, the lawmakers did not make a radical change to the then-existing structure inherited from Portugal. An important guiding principle of 'formal adequacy' was introduced. This contribution explains how the introduction of the formal adequacy principle transformed the case management landscape in Macau. The formal adequacy principle alleviates the procedural rigidity of the past and provides that when a procedure established by law does not fit the specific details of an individual case, the judge should, either at the request of the parties or *sua sponte*, determine the best procedural arrangements for the case.

1 Introduction

In 1999, Macau conducted a thorough review of its civil justice system. Two main goals were formulated: first, adapt the procedural law to the local reality,[1] and second, modernize the civil justice system pursuant to Opinion No. 3/99 concerning the Civil Procedure Code of Macau (CPCM) issued by the *ad hoc* Commission to Monitor and

[1]Prior to the 'handover', the main legal source of the rules governing the adjudication of civil and commercial matters was the Civil Procedure Code of Portugal (CPCP) enacted in 1961, which was applied in Macau pursuant to Government Order No. 19305 issued on 30 July 1962.

[2]Parecer no. 3/99 da Comissão Eventual Destinada a Acompanhar e Participar na Elaboração dos Projectos Relativos aos Códigos Civil, Processual Civil e Comercial sobre Apreciação do Projecto relativo ao Novo Código de Processo Civil de Macau, Legislative Assembly of Macau SAR 2020. The Opinion comprises *Apreciação Técnico-Jurídica do Projecto relativo ao novo Código de Processo Civil de Macau* (drafted by Armando Isaac as Adviser of the Macau Legislative Assembly) and *As Linhas Mestras do Novo Código de Processo Civil de Macau* (drafted by José Manuel Cardoso Borges Soeiro as Coordinator for drafting the CPCM).

W. Wang (✉)
University of Macau, Macau SAR, The People's Republic of China
e-mail: weiwang@um.edu.mo

P. C. H. Chan and C. H. van Rhee (eds.), *Civil Case Management in the Twenty-First Century: Court Structures Still Matter*, Ius Gentium: Comparative Perspectives on Law and Justice 85, https://doi.org/10.1007/978-981-33-4512-6_7

Participate in the Preparation of the Civil Code, Civil Procedure Code and Commercial Code (Opinion).[2] One of the key aspects that required profound reform was the rigid civil procedural rules, which were primarily responsible for the undue delays in civil litigation.

At the international level, both common law and civil law countries are focused on simplifying the procedures for handling cases to enhance the efficiency of civil litigation.[3] Some have even argued for a more radical approach in favour of deformalizing civil litigation altogether.[4]

The question faced by Macau at the turn of the century was whether it should radically overhaul the traditional system of litigation or try to keep a reasonable balance among relevant objectives including efficiency, legal certainty, transparency, *audi alteram partem*, economy of procedure and due process. There was a lively discussion in the Legislative Assembly of Macau about which of the two alternatives should be selected.[5] The result of this debate is reflected in the Preamble of Decree-Law No. 55/99/M approving the CPCM.

The solution the lawmakers arrived at was widely seen as prudent. They were 'aware of the risks arising from the creation of the CPCM in [the] stage of transition.' Of special concern was the danger of giving too much power and discretion to the courts.[6] However, they also kept the enormous backlog of cases in mind and knew that the widespread dissatisfaction with the efficiency of the courts had to be addressed. As a result, the first local code of civil procedure preserved the structure of the CPCP. The procedural framework remained practically intact, but there were significant *qualitative* changes as compared to the CPCP.

Professor Teixeira de Sousa explained that the extent of law reform should not be confused with its depth. The fact that many institutions are modified and many articles are amended does not necessarily mean a profound change in civil procedure. A small number of changes can transform the character of a system by embedding fundamental principles in the law that affect many other parts. The draftsmen of the CPCM chose to reform the litigation system by incorporating principles that have the potential to dramatically change the previously inefficient judicial system.[7] The 'revolutionary' principle of formal adequacy (*princípio da adequação formal*)

---

[3]For example, the famous Woolf Reforms resulted in the enactment of the Civil Procedure Rules 1998 in England and Wales. The Civil Procedure Code of Portugal (CPCP) enacted in 1961 was revised in 1995 and 1996 approved by Decree-Laws No. 329-A/95 and 180/96 respectively, which brought about a profound change to the civil justice system in Portugal, but its application was not extended to Macau as Macau was going through the sovereignty transition process around that time. On the subject of Portuguese civil procedure reform in the mid-twentieth century, see, e.g., De Sousa (1997, pp. 27–28).

[4]See, *inter alia*, Pellegrini Grinover (1991, pp. 25–52).

[5]See note 2 above.

[6]See Decree-Law No. 3/99 of 8 October 1999.

[7]Similar to what Professor Loïc Cadiet mentioned in his article (Cadiet 2011) on the role of the guiding principles embodied in the French Civil Procedure Code, the overall idea of civil litigation is explicitly shown in the first core articles of the CPCM under Title I (Fundamental Provisions) of Book I (Actions).

was highlighted in the Preamble of Decree-Law No. 55/99/M. It is a unique and powerful device of judicial case management vested in the courts 'for the purpose of simplifying the procedure'.[8]

2 Development of Judicial Case Management: The Formal Adequacy Principle

Judicial case management in the 'inquisitorial' sense was introduced into the Macau legal system in the first half of the twentieth century with the promulgation of the Civil Procedure Code of Portugal (CPCP) of 1876,[9] which was structured around the principle of party disposition (*princípio dispositivo*) under a passive court model. This model was replaced by the CPCP of 1939,[10] influenced by the *Zivilprozessordnung* of Franz Klein,[11] which conferred upon the judges the power to ensure the proper conduct of a procedure with a special focus on evidentiary examination and resolution of disputes on the merits.

The idea of effective case management by the judge was further strengthened when the CPCP of 1939 was replaced by the CPCP of 1961, which allowed the court to intervene in any phase of the proceedings in order to promote the efficient resolution of disputes. Meanwhile, the basic idea of trying to strike a balance between party autonomy and the active role of the judge remained unchanged.[12] Nevertheless, none of these reforms worked effectively. Even though provisions on judicial case management were enacted, the court continued with its traditional reactive approach

---

[8]Professor Miguel Teixeira de Sousa considers that judicial case management involves the substantive aspect of directing the proceedings and the instrumental aspect of formal adequacy. To comply with the duty of conducting effective proceedings, the judges resort to the principle of formal adequacy as a key instrument for simplifying and expediting the proceedings. See De Sousa (1997).

[9]CPCP of 1876 was the first Portuguese Code of Civil Procedure which was applicable to Macau soon after its promulgation. The code adopted a liberal approach influenced by Napoleon's *Code de procédure civile* (1806). See, e.g., Van Rhee (2006, p. 129). Together with other codes including the Penal Code of 1852, the Civil Code of 1867 and the Commercial Code of 1888, the Portuguese legal system was adopted in Macau and transformed the Chinese legal landscape under centralized monarchical hegemony, which was rooted in Confucianism, into one based on the rule of law. On the subject of Macau legal history, see e.g., Tong and Wu (2011).

[10]The code was approved by Decree-Law No. 29637 which authorized 'the Government to extend the Code to the colonial empire' including Macau (source: Portuguese Government Gazette No. 123/1939, Series I of 28 May 1939). It took 6 years to achieve the reform initiated by Decree-Law No. 12353 of 26 September 1926. The draftsman of the accompanying report, Professor José Alberto dos Reis, stated that the powers conferred upon the judges included removing all obstacles that hinder the resolution of civil disputes on the merits at an early stage of the proceedings, stopping all kinds of chicanery or abuse, directing the procedure efficiently and making conscientious judgments. See Soares (1985, p. 60).

[11]Professor C.H. van Rhee pointed out that the conception of judicial case management originated from the reform of the 1895 Austrian Civil Procedure Code. See Van Rhee (2008, pp. 11ff).

[12]This was emphasized in the Preamble of the CPCP of 1961 approved by Decree-Law No. 44129 of 28 December 1961. It came into force in Macau on 1 January 1963. See note 3 above.

instead of adopting the new proactive approach. As a matter of fact, while the court is permitted to intervene in the proceedings so as to remove any obstacles hindering the efficient disposition of civil cases, it is not entitled to change any procedural arrangements established by law.

The predominance of the rigid legal principles governing litigation procedure impeded the successful implementation of judicial case management. It was not until the enactment of the CPCM when Macau finally made a substantial change to its civil justice system by establishing a new guiding principle of civil procedure called the 'formal adequacy principle'. Different from other time-limiting procedural principles that have been discussed at great length for a couple of decades, the principle of formal adequacy in the context of judicial case management remains a relatively underdeveloped area in civil law jurisdictions.[13] It first appeared, as a result of civil procedure reform,[14] in Article 265-A of the CPCP:

(1) Where the procedural track established by law does not fit the specific circumstances of the individual case, the judge should, on its own initiative, adapt the proceedings with the agreement of the parties (Quando a tramitação processual prevista na lei não se adequar às especificidades da causa, deve o juiz, oficiosamente e com o acordo das partes, adaptar o processado).

(2) When performing the assigned function referred to in the previous paragraph, the judge should determine the procedural steps most suitable for finding the truth and making the correct judgment, and exclude those which are manifestly improper for the purpose of the process (Na execução da atribuição referida no número anterior, determina o juiz a realização dos actos que melhor se adequem ao apuramento da verdade e acerto da decisão, prescindindo dos que se revelem manifestamente inidóneos para o fim do processo).

In addition to the general provision, some specific rules further defining the formal adequacy principle were incorporated in Article 31 of the CPCP. Paragraphs 2 and 3 of this article provide that different procedural tracks can be combined if the judge authorizes the parties to do so.

The aforementioned Article 265-A has been criticized for two reasons. First, the requirement for an agreement between the parties would obviously complicate the application of the provision, considering the difficulty for the contending litigants to reach a consensus on this matter. Second, such requirement would also be inconsistent with Article 31.[15] As such, the initial version of Article 265-A was revised as follows:

> Where the procedural track established by law does not fit the specific circumstances of the individual case, the judge should, after hearing the parties, determine *sua sponte* the procedural steps which best suit the purpose of handling the case and make adaptations accordingly (*Quando a tramitação processual prevista na lei não se adequar às especificidades da causa, deve o juiz oficiosamente, ouvidas as partes, determinar a prática dos actos que melhor se ajustem ao fim do processo, bem como as necessárias adaptações*).

Macau lawmakers have incorporated the principle of formal adequacy into the CPCM. Although the development of such principle in Macau is far behind that in

[13] See, e.g., Costa e Silva (2011, p. 138).

[14] See note 3 above.

[15] See, e.g., Brito (1997, pp. 31–69).

Portugal, Macau lawmakers have critically reflected on the Portuguese experience to find a solution for Macau. Thus, the provision on formal adequacy embedded in Article 7 of the CPCM is partially derived from Article 265-A of the CPCP introduced by Decree-Law No. 180/96 of 25 September. Article 7 of the CPCM states that:

> Where the procedural track established by law does not fit into the specific circumstances of the individual case, the judge should, after hearing the parties, determine *sua sponte* the procedural steps which best suit the purposes of handling the case (*Quando a tramitação processual prevista na lei não se adeque às especificidades da causa, deve o juiz oficiosamente, ouvidas as partes, determinar a prática dos actos que melhor se ajustem aos fins do processo*).

By omitting the final part of Article 265-A of the CPCP, the Macau lawmakers intended to leave 'a broader practical scope' for the principle of formal adequacy.[16]

Article 7 of the CPCM is different from the CPCP in two major respects:[17] First, the idea underlying Article 7 is not simply to give the judge a choice among the various procedural options set out in the law. Instead, the judge is empowered to adopt a procedure not expressly provided by law. Second, as regards the procedural tracks, Article 7 does not restrict the option to one within the existing law. Instead, it enables the judge to create *ex novo* a procedure for handling the case,[18] which is not provided by the law.[19]

The justification for the court to deviate from the existing legal provisions governing the rules of procedure is the instrumental function of civil procedure as emphasized in Decree-Law No. 55/99/M approving CPCM.[20] In other words, civil procedure is not only used to achieve its own objective, but it also serves as a tool for the court to achieve the overriding objectives set out in Article 6 of the CPCM, namely the seeking of truth and the fair resolution of the dispute, which are the core

---

[16] As regards the conceptional scope of Art. 265-A CPCP, see, *inter alia*, De Sousa (1995, p. 364). Note, however, that since 2006, Portuguese lawmakers have revised twice the general clause of formal adequacy which is now embodied in Art. 547 CPCP enacted in 2013: 'The judge should adopt the procedural track suitable for the specific circumstances of the case, and adapt the content and the form of the procedural acts to the purpose intended to be achieved in order to ensure a due process' (*O juiz deve adotar a tramitação processual adequada às especificidades da causa e adaptar o conteúdo e a forma dos atos processuais ao fim que visam atingir, assegurando um processo equitativo*).

[17] See note 3 above.

[18] See Pellegrini Grinover (1991). The author correctly pointed out that the judge may adopt a 'substitute sequence' and 'fix a new order of acts not provided for by the law, which may be the mere combination of different procedural patterns or the imposition or omission of certain acts.'

[19] In some jurisdictions, the judge is given a choice out of different courses of action. For instance, under English civil procedure, the judge, according to the value of the claim and other factors, may decide to proceed in one of the three different ways prescribed in the Civil Procedure Rules 1998, namely the small claims proceedings (Rule 26), the fast track (Rule 27) or the multi-track (Rule 28). Also, in France, the court may choose, as an alternative to the long track (*circuit long*: Arts. 763-787 NCPC), the fast track (*circuit court*: Art. 760 NCPC) or the medium track (*circuit moyen*: Art. 761 NCPC). *Cf.* note 14 above.

[20] For an analysis of the instrumental nature of civil procedure, see also: e.g., De Sousa (1993, pp. 35–36 and 42ff).

principles for access to justice. Ultimately, as emphasized by the Hon. Mr. Justice Borges Soeiro (the coordinator for drafting the CPCM), the essential role of the formal adequacy principle is enshrined in Article 1 of the CPCM. It guarantees there is legal recourse to enforce every right.[21]

3 Legal Regime of the Formal Adequacy Principle

3.1 General Provision

The principle of formal adequacy is set out in Article 7 of the CPCM in the form of a standard clause (*cláusula geral*) with a regulative nature,[22] providing direction and guidelines to apply the principle in Macau. This principle does not specify all the particular decisions that need to be made on a case-by-case basis. As stated in the Opinion, the *raison d'être* for the consolidation of the normative framework is to 're-regulate civil proceedings'.[23] It is different from the tradition overemphasizing formal rules which 'attempt to foresee and regulate in detail each step of the procedure, transforming the CPC into a primer without freedom of action'.[24] This is due to a shift in the approach taken by the lawmakers, who adopted a general instead of a closed-ended provision with more flexibility in the procedure to contribute to the protection of substantive rights. Therefore, such a provision does not contain any internal restrictions on the application of the principle or the original purpose it was designed for.[25]

However, the formal adequacy principle is rarely applied. As pointed out by Armando Isaac, formal adequacy is an inadequate tool to rearrange the legal procedure in order to achieve the objectives of civil procedure, namely the seeking of truth and a fair resolution of the dispute. As such, it is supplementary, and its application is only justified when the directly applicable rules of procedure do not provide for the special circumstances of specific cases, such as the nature of the claim, the cause of action, the evidence provided, the perspective of final resolution or settlement of the dispute and the practical effects of the legal action. Therefore, the principle of formal adequacy should not be considered as part of the regular civil procedure, but a 'divergence' to promote procedural efficiency or a more effective action through an approximation of the material truth.[26]

---

[21] See note 2 above.

[22] *Cf.* Cordeiro (1984, p. 1184).

[23] See note 2 above.

[24] See Freitas (1995, p. 10).

[25] See note 2 above.

[26] See Isaac (2000, pp. 59–85).

Within this context, the consolidation and interpretation of Article 7 of the CPCM requires careful scrutiny.[27] The judge plays a key role in developing a reasonable outcome in alignment with various interrelated interests in the process.[28] The final decision will be made only after considering all relevant interests and the corresponding rights so as not to violate the fundamental rights under judicial protection. The recognition of these interests constitutes the general requirements for and the conceptual scope of the formal adequacy principle.[29]

3.2 General Requirements

3.2.1 Audi Alteram Partem

According to Article 7 of the CPCM, the powers given to the judge under the principle of formal adequacy should be exercised only after hearing the petition of the parties. In other words, respecting the principle of *audi alteram partem* (*princípio do contraditório*) is the first *sine qua non* to trigger the formal adequacy principle. Under Article 3(3) of the CPCM, the judge should not rule on the facts of a case or on points of law without hearing the parties, even if the court itself initiates the ruling.

Traditionally, the principle of *audi alteram partem* focused solely on allowing the parties to defend against the claims brought by the counterparties,[30] and this approach is still valid today. As pointed out by Enrico Tullio Liebman, '[i]t is an elementary requirement of justice to give all parties the opportunity and possibility to defend themselves before the judge issues any judgment'.[31] However, it is no longer considered the complete definition of *audi alteram partem*. The idea of avoiding 'surprise decisions' has been added to the principle in order to ensure that the parties are not taken by surprise by any court decisions based on issues that have not been litigated.[32]

Case law has further expanded the principle of *audi alteram partem* with two elements—participation and influence.[33] In other words, *audi alteram partem* is feasible only if the parties have the opportunity to participate in the hearing and such participation should be capable of exerting influence on the court decision. Evidently, no one can influence a decision without participating in the proceedings, nor is any

---

[27] *Cf.* Robert (1997, p. 235), Isaac (2000, pp. 59–85).

[28] Geraldes (1997, p. 70).

[29] *Cf.* Isaac (2000).

[30] *Cf. inter alia*, Manuel (1993, pp. 379–380).

[31] Liebman (1992, p. 93).

[32] The reshaped conception of *audi alteram partem* originated from the constitutional guarantee of the right to be heard (*rechtliches Gehör*) set out in Art. 103(1) of the German Constitution (*Grundgesetz*). See Freitas (1996, p. 96).

[33] *Ibidem.*

participation considered authentic without the possibility of influencing the decision of the court. Otherwise, hearing the parties will merely be symbolic. Therefore, as far as the application of the formal adequacy principle is concerned, an effective hearing of the parties is indispensable. Omission of an *effective hearing* would render the hearing null under Article 147(1) of the CPCM if such omission affects the decision of the case. Moreover, according to Article 653(f) of the CPCM, the final decision of a case may be subject to review for its failure to observe the principle of *audi alteram partem* due to any omission or invalidity of the service of process on the defendant (*citação do réu*).[34]

3.2.2 Equality of the Parties

Apart from the principle of *audi alteram partem*, the principle of equality of the parties before the court provides that a decision will be considered as impartial, fair or duly reasoned only if equal treatment (i.e. equality of arms) has been given to both parties.[35] Furthermore, Article 4 of the CPCM requires the court to ensure that the parties have a *de facto* equal status in exercising their rights. Therefore, when, while applying the formal adequate principle, it is considered appropriate to reverse the legally prescribed order or to insert, exclude or create procedural steps, the court should guarantee that the parties can participate equally in the process.

3.2.3 Respect for the Principle of Cooperation

The principle of *audi alteram partem* now includes the idea of court participation through dialogue with the parties. In order to allow the parties to participate and exert influence on the court decision, they need to be informed and clear about the relevant factual and legal questions. Therefore, the principle of cooperation provides an important means for realizing *audi alteram partem* in practice.

According to Article 8 of the CPCM, when the court intervenes in the proceedings, the parties should cooperate with the court in a timely and effective manner in order to obtain a just solution to the dispute. For this purpose, the judge may at any time during the proceedings hear the parties or their representatives, invite them to clarify the facts or law that may be relevant to the case and make the counterparties aware of the necessary diligence. The invited persons, whenever notified, are obliged to appear and provide clarifications as requested, without prejudice to the requirements listed in Article 442(3) of the CPCM.[36] When a party alleges any serious difficulty

---

[34] See, e.g., Da Silva and De Lima (2006, pp. 36–37).

[35] Alfredo Soveral Martins compared the principle of equality of the parties to the scales of justice: Martins (1995, p. 170).

[36] Art. 442(3) provides that the duty of collaboration ceases when it involves (a) infringement of the physical or moral integrity of a person, (b) intrusion into his private life, home, or correspondence,

in obtaining the document or information which may prejudice any right or the compliance with any procedural duty, if justified, the judge shall remove the relevant obstacles.

As noted by Professor Teixeira de Sousa, the principle of cooperation concerns various duties that the court should comply with, including (i) the duty of exerting inquisitorial powers, that is, the court should conduct its own investigation on the cases (Art. 6(3) CPCM); (ii) the duty of prevention or warning, where the court is obliged to prevent irregularities resulting from remediable omissions or deficiencies (Art. 6(2) CPCM); (iii) the duty of clarification, when the parties have doubts about the claims or the relevant procedural acts (Art. 8(2) CPCM); (iv) the duty of collaboration, that is, the court should assist the parties in removing the obstacle that may prejudice their right or compliance with the procedural duty (Art. 8(3) CPCM); and (v) the duty to consult the parties, namely to alert the parties to matters that the court may raise on its own motion and to enable the parties to influence the judge's decision, thus avoiding any surprise decision.[37]

3.2.4 Predictability/Legal Certainty

Legal certainty, which is closely related to the very notion of the rule of law, is an important guarantee to the parties. There is no doubt that the traditional civil justice system has provided predictability and legal certainty to the parties who at the outset acknowledge the total procedural *iter*, enabling the court to control the proceedings. In other words, formal rules are considered a safeguard against arbitrary action of the court which is the holder of judicial power. Additionally, formal rules of procedure provide choice and freedom. Nevertheless, on the assumption that legal certainty comes from predictability, what matters the most is to guarantee the parties that they will have previous knowledge of the proceedings besides the knowledge provided by statute. As long as the system ensures predictability, legal certainty will also be guaranteed, even if such predictability derives from a source other than the law.

In cases where the formal adequacy principle applies, *audi alteram partem* is a mandatary prerequisite. As shown above, according to the modern interpretation of *audi alteram partem*, the judge is required to participate in the process and exercise, *inter alia*, the duty of consultation in light of the principle of cooperation, thereby bringing to the parties' knowledge the information regarding alternative proceedings in order to ensure predictability and thus legal certainty.

(c) infringement of professional, official or state secrecy, without prejudice to paragraph 4 of this article relating to the exemption of such secrecy according to the law.

[37] See De Sousa (2017).

4 Effectiveness of Judicial Case Management by Implementation of the Formal Adequacy Principle

4.1 Adequacy by Way of Derogation from the Rule

As seen above, the principle of formal adequacy replaces the procedural track laid down in the law so long as the provisions of the law do not fit the circumstances of the individual case.

4.2 Aggregation of Parties and Claims

4.2.1 Aggregation of Parties (*Coligação*)

Under the heading of 'Aggregation of plaintiffs and defendants' (*coligação de autores e de réus*), Article 64 of the CPCM provides that two or more plaintiffs may jointly take an action against one or more defendants based on different claims if the cause of action is the same or the claims are interrelated. Prior to the revision of the civil procedural law, the parties were strictly required to litigate their claims within the same procedure. However, under the current provision in Article 65 of the CPCM, when the claims are litigated through different procedures but are not manifestly incompatible, the court may authorize an aggregation of procedures if there is relevant interest between the parties or if it is indispensable for a fair resolution of the dispute (para. 3). The court will then rearrange the procedures to fit them into the authorized joinder litigation (para. 4). Thus, the principle of formal adequacy has made aggregation of claims corresponding to different procedural tracks possible.

4.2.2 Aggregation of Claims (Cumulação de Pedidos)

The principle of formal adequacy is applicable to both initial and successive aggregation of claims. The initial aggregation of claims refers to various claims entailing different legal consequences submitted at the outset of the judicial action by the plaintiff against the same defendant. The aggregation of claims can be divided into aggregation of parallel claims and aggregation of alternative or subsidiary claims, among other categories provided for by the CPCM (Art. 390 *et seq.*).

Aggregated parallel claims are litigated simultaneously.[38] Therefore, substantive compatibility between the claims is required. As to the aggregation of parties, Article

[38]This should be distinguished from an apparent aggregation of claims. For example, in an action for recovery of property (*acção de reivindicação*), Art. 1236 of the Civil Code of Macau (CCM) provides that the owner may claim simultaneously recognition of his right to the property and its recovery. This is considered a typical situation of the apparent aggregation of claims. *Cf.* Brito (1997).

65 of the CPCM is also applicable to the aggregation of parallel claims. Moreover, the principle of formal adequacy is applicable to the aggregation of alternative claims,[39] and subsidiary claims,[40] if the law provides different procedural rules for these claims, unless the obstacles as specified in Article 65 of the CPCM exist.

Apart from aggregating various claims at the outset of the proceedings, the plaintiff may further formulate additional claims during the proceedings or by way of amendment of the claims or the cause of action under Articles 216 and 217 of the CPCM.

4.2.3 Counterclaims (*Reconvenção*)

Article 218 of the CPCM provides that the defendant may bring counterclaims against the plaintiff in accordance with the requirements as stated in this article. Prior to the enactment of the CPCM, an identical procedure was required, which made it more difficult for the defendant to file counterclaims. Now, the counterclaims submitted by the defendant do not need to be of the same type of procedure as the plaintiff's claims. The judge may grant the relevant authorization in accordance with Article 65(3)(4) by virtue of Article 218(3) of the CPCM.

4.2.4 Interim Relief (*Procedimentos Cautelares*)

The CPCM provides for common interim relief (Arts. 326-337 of the CPCM) and specified interim relief (Art. 338 *et seq.*), which are measures intending to guarantee effective judicial protection.[41] If the claims for relief are litigated through different proceedings, the court may authorize an aggregation provided that such aggregation does not lead to apparent incompatibility (Art. 326(4)).

Although the law does not expressly require compatibility of jurisdiction as in Article 65(1) or substantive compatibility of claims as in Article 391(1) of the CPCM, the common understanding is that these requirements are also applicable to the aggregation of interim relief.

---

[39] Alternative claims are based on alternative liabilities established in substantive law (Art. 536 of CCM).

[40] Subsidiary claims are formulated together with the main claim to eventually replace the latter in case it fails.

[41] The following are considered examples of specific interim relief: provisional recovery of possession (*restituição provisória de posse*), suspension of corporate resolutions (*suspensão de deliberações sociais*), provisional maintenance (*alimentos provisários*), arbitration of provisional remedies (*arbitramento de reparação provisória*), seizure (*arresto*), and a ban on the execution of new work (*embargo de obra nova*). These types of relief are available if there is a risk of irreparable damage.

4.3 *Judicial Management*

It is incumbent on the judge to refer cases to the procedural track that can best address the specifics of the case. In practice, this does not cause any problems when complex litigation requires additional procedural steps which are not prescribed by law. However, when it comes to the exclusion of procedural steps established by law, the application of the formal adequacy principle may become more difficult.[42] Professor Teixeira Sousa proposed that minimum standards should be followed in applying the principle of formal adequacy, namely the parties must be given the opportunity to submit facts and law as well as to provide evidence on disputed matters.[43]

4.4 *Consequences of the Infringement of Procedures Ordered by the Court*

What is the consequence of the parties failing to comply with the procedural requirements laid down by the court? On the one hand, the letter of law only renders the procedural acts that the law does not admit or the omission of acts or formalities prescribed by law as grounds for nullity (Art. 147 of the CPCM). However, on the other hand, the choice of procedure made by the court has binding force in light of the formal adequacy principle enshrined in Article 7 of the CPCM. Infringement of such choice will lead to procedural nullity as stipulated in Article 147 of the CPCM.[44]

What if the judge himself does not comply with the decision he has made? The answer is the same as above, that is, the procedure chosen by the court is in principle as binding on the court as on the parties.[45]

5 Conclusion

When Macau civil procedural rules were codified at the end of 1999, the lawmakers did not make a radical change to the then-existing structure inherited from Portugal. An important guiding principle of 'formal adequacy' was introduced. The formal adequacy principle, as an integral part of judicial case management, provides that when a procedure established by law does not fit the specific details of an individual case, the judge should, either at the request of the parties or *sua sponte*, determine the best procedural arrangements for the case *sub judice*.

---

[42]De Sousa (2017).

[43]*Ibidem*.

[44]Cf. De Sousa (1997, p. 38).

[45]Cf. Freitas (1996, p. 17).

References

Brito PMD (1997) O novo princípio da adequação formal. In: Teixeira Souza M (ed) Aspectos do novo processo civil. Lisboa, pp 31–69

Cadiet L (2011) Introduction to French civil justice system and civil procedural law. Ritsumeikan Law Rev 28:331–393

Cordeiro AM (1984) Da Boa Fé no Direito Civil II. Coimbra

Costa e Silva P (2011) Legalidade das formas de processo e gestão processual ou as duas faces de Janus. Revista de Legislação Legislativa Brasilia A 48:137–149

Da Silva APC, De Lima VMP (2006) Código de processo civil de Macau: Anotado e comentado. Macau

De Sousa MT (1993) Introdução ao processo civil. Lisboa

De Sousa MT (1995) Apreciação de alguns aspectos da 'Revisão do processo civil projecto'. Revista da Ordem dos Advogados 55(II): 353–416

De Sousa MT (1997) Estudos sobre o novo processo civil. Lisboa

De Sousa MT (2017) Novas orientações da reforma do código de processo civil. In: International conference on civil procedure reform—Civil procedure reform and future orientation (Conference proceedings) (Macau) (unpublished)

Freitas JLD (1995) Em torno da revisão do direito processual civil. Revista da Ordem dos Advogados 55(I): 5–18

Freitas JLD (1996) Introdução ao processo civil—Conceito e princípios gerais à luz do código revisto. Coimbra

Geraldes ASA (1997) Temas da reforma do processo civil. 1—Princípios fundamentais. 2—Fase inicial do processo dec larativo. Coimbra

Isaac AL (2000) O Princípio da adequação formal—Ensaio de algumas nótulas e dúvidas. Univ Macau Boletim da Faculdade de Direito 10:59–85

Liebman ET (1992) Manuale di diritto processuale civile: Principi I. Milano

Manuel A (1993) Domingues de Andrade. Noções elementares de processo civil, Coimbra

Martins AS (1995) Direito processual civil. Coimbra

Pellegrini Grinover A (1991) Deformalização do processo e deformalização das controvérsias. Revista de Informação Legislativa 3(1):25–52

Robert A (1997) Theorie der juristischen Argumentation: Die Theorie des rationalen Diskurses als Theorie der juristischen Begründung (trad. Castelhana: Theoría de la argumentación jurídica: La teoría del discurso racional como teoría de la fundamentación Jurídica) Madrid

Soares FL (1985) Processo civil de declaração. Coimbra

Tong IC, Wu YN (2011) Legal transplants and the ongoing formation of Macau legal culture. Isaidat Law Rev 1(1):619–645

Van Rhee CH (2006) The influence of the French Code de procédure civile (1806) in 19th century Europe. In: Cadiet L, Canivet G (eds) De la commémoration d'un code à l'autre: 200 ans de procedure civile en France. Paris, pp 129–165

Van Rhee CH (2008) The development of civil procedural law in twentieth century Europe: From party autonomy to judicial case management and efficiency. In: van Rhee CH (ed) Judicial case management and efficiency in civil litigation. Antwerp, Oxford, Portland, pp 11–26

The Litigation Superpower's Case Management Cure for Adversarial Ills

Richard Marcus

Abstract This contribution examines how adversarial excesses in the American system are contained through judicial case management. It begins with an introduction to the US court system and an explanation of American exceptionalism in procedure. America's unique procedural attributes, while linked by many to a 'litigation explosion', also created the need for managerial judging. The contribution then examines the role of judicial settlement promotion in American courts. In some state courts, 'settlement weeks' became prominent; rather than hold one or two trials to resolve cases, judges would instead convene numerous settlement conferences to hammer out agreed resolutions. Indeed, judges command a special authority that, if used properly, could set parties on the right course in settlement negotiations. The contribution highlights both the innovations in judicial management and the results of judicial settlement promotion during the last half century. It concludes that the overall experience of judicial case management has been positive.

1 Introduction

Twenty years ago, it seemed that the US was the unquestioned litigation superpower in the world.[1] It was surely the prime example of the adversarial style of civil litigation. The combination of relaxed pleading standards, a broad right to amend pleadings, even broader discovery, class actions, emotional damage recoveries and possible punitive damage recoveries, and the right to jury trial meant that the stakes of this litigation could be very high. And beginning in the 1960s, legislatures in the US created more and more rights to sue that seemed to fuel a litigation 'boom'.

[1] Marcus (1999, pp. 71–118).

R. Marcus (✉)
The University of California, Hastings College of the Law, CA, USA
e-mail: marcusr@uchastings.edu

P. C. H. Chan and C. H. van Rhee (eds.), *Civil Case Management in the Twenty-First Century: Court Structures Still Matter*, Ius Gentium: Comparative Perspectives on Law and Justice 85, https://doi.org/10.1007/978-981-33-4512-6_8

Altogether, these developments fueled a reaction, and even access to court could be regarded as a zero-sum game.[2]

One response to these developments began in the 1960s—increased judicial management of civil litigation. In a significant sense, this response authorized American judges to constrain the broad powers enjoyed by American lawyers.[3] This movement has gained force during the last half-century, particularly in the US federal courts. It has also served as a model for similar efforts in other countries, even countries with significantly different legal cultures. This paper introduces the American movement.

2 The General Structure of American Court Systems

Any consideration of the case management approach of a nation's judicial system must begin with an appreciation of the architecture of the court system. In the US, that is particularly important because the court systems are numerous and complex.

2.1 *State v Federal Court*

This paper will focus mainly on the American federal court system, though with occasional references to the state courts in California. Nonetheless, it is important to appreciate at the outset that there is a wide diversity of judicial systems in the US. Each state (all 50) has its own, and so do the District of Columbia and Puerto Rico. As a consequence, at any location in the US there are two parallel court systems—the federal court and the local court system. And the very great majority of civil cases are heard in the state court systems, not the federal one.

As one might imagine, several of these state court systems are quite large. For example, Los Angeles Superior Court alone has nearly 500 Superior Court judges. That is more than half the number of US District Judges in the entire federal court system. The point to be kept in mind is that this variety means that practices—such as managerial judging—vary a great deal from place to place. These state courts have jurisdiction over some specialized matters, such as family law matters, but for the most part they are courts of 'general jurisdiction' handling all sorts of cases.[4]

Nevertheless, the federal court system has been the leader in innovation at least since the Federal Rules of Civil Procedure were adopted in 1938. Roughly half the

[2] Marcus (2017, pp. 53–75).

[3] Marcus (2003b, pp. 3–28).

[4] Another set of 'courts' is not addressed here—adjudication before administrative tribunals before 'administrative law judges'. Many of these are specialized courts, dealing exclusively with labor or securities or social benefits matters. In much of the world, these institutions would likely be regarded as courts alongside others, but in the American scheme they are not and they are not addressed in this paper.

states (though not most of the larger ones) have adopted procedure rules that copy the federal rules. More important for this paper, the federal courts have been leaders in the development of case management.

2.2 *American Exceptionalism in Procedure*

It need hardly be emphasized that US procedure is exceptional, but the features that make it exceptional also explain its early embrace of managerial judging.

Since the adoption of the Federal Rules in 1938, American civil procedure has been distinctly receptive to plaintiffs.[5] Those distinctive features bear directly on judicial control over lawyers. Because pleading requirements are quite relaxed, judges cannot often dismiss cases of dubious validity. Because there is a right to jury trial, American judges are rarely in a position to decide who should win the case. Unless there is no rational basis in the evidence for a jury decision in favor of one side, the court may not award judgment to either party.[6]

At the same time, American lawyers were, by the mid-20th century, uniquely empowered to employ the court system's authority to their advantage. A prime example of that was the power to initiate discovery, including the right to serve subpoenas[7] on nonparties as well as to demand that other parties provide access to documents and respond to pretrial questioning under oath. Particularly due to technological change (first the photocopier, and more recently the development of email and other digital methods for communicating and for storing data) the power to demand discovery could appear to impose very substantial costs and burdens on parties and nonparties. The increasing prominence of the 'Internet of Things' (IoT; devices that record and communicate data about everyday behavior of people) will only increase these costs and challenges; some time ago it was estimated that some 20 billion IoT devices would be in use worldwide by the year 2021.

[5]The English court in *Smith Kline & French Laboratories Ltd. v Bloch* [1983] 1 W.L.R. 730 (C.A. 1982) recognized these distinctive features: 'As a moth is drawn to the light, so is a litigant drawn to the United States. If he can only get his case into their courts, he stands to win a fortune. At no cost to himself, and at no risk of having to pay anything to the other side. The lawyers will conduct the case 'on spec' as we say, or on a 'contingency fee' as they say ... There is also in the United States a right to trial by jury. These are prone to award fabulous damages. They are notoriously sympathetic and know that the lawyers will take their 40%. All this means that the defendant can be readily forced into a settlement. The plaintiff holds all the cards.' While recognizing that this portrait of American litigation is overdrawn, one must also recognize that it captures some essential differences between American litigation and litigation in most of the rest of the world.

[6]This reality is reflected in the American rules on summary judgment and directed verdict, which provide that the court may award judgment only in cases in which the evidence will not rationally support the party against whom judgment is entered. See, e.g., Fed. R. Civ. P. 50(a) (judgment as a matter of law); 56(a) (summary judgment).

[7]See Fed. R. Civ. P. 45 (authorizing a lawyer to issue a subpoena to a nonparty—without any advance review or authorization by a judge—requiring either appearing at a deposition to testify under oath or production of documents, or both).

By the 1970s, the procedural opportunities in American-style litigation had generated a backlash against what some described as a 'litigation explosion'. One must approach this label with caution. There surely was a significant increase in the frequency of litigation in the US during the mid-20th century. To some extent, it was a result of legislation creating new rights to sue. To some extent it was a result of expanded rights to sue for constitutional violations. To some extent it was encouraged by legislation that offered successful plaintiffs the opportunity to recover their attorney fees from losing defendants, which created a new 'public interest bar'. In a very real sense, it resulted from a distinctive American enthusiasm for private enforcement rather than public enforcement of public law.[8]

These developments contributed to the emergence of managerial judging, described below.

2.3 *The Broad Authority of American First Instance—'Trial'—Courts*

In much of the world, it seems that first instance courts are not regularly the last stop for civil litigation.[9] Instead, they are merely a prelude to the real resolution in a higher court. That is not the American way. To the contrary, appellate review is ordinarily allowed in the US only after entry of a 'final judgment'. That final judgment, in turn, can occur only after all claims involving all parties are fully resolved by the trial court. Of all cases filed, only a small proportion ever reach that point.

At the same time, the standard of review for many decisions that American judges make on critically important matters like the scope of discovery or leave to amend a pleading or join an additional party to the case are subject to review only for an 'abuse of discretion'. It is said that this phrase sounds worse than it is, but it is surely true that persuading an appellate court that the judge has abused discretion is a considerable challenge even when the case has finally reached the point when appellate review is possible.

Owing to the limits on their authority to decide the merits of cases, these 'trial' courts have authority at trial only to rule on the admissibility of evidence and to instruct the jury (which will decide which party wins) on the legal rules that apply to the case. Those sorts of decisions involve weighing multiple factors in the context of the specific case, rather than application of some transcendental legal 'rules,' a circumstance that explains the 'abuse of discretion' standard for reviewing their rulings.

---

[8]For a review of the issues that result from this American orientation, see Burbank et al. (2013, pp. 637–722).

[9]For more extensive discussion, see Marcus (2012, pp. 105–26).

2.4 Complex v Simple Cases

Because American courts ordinarily entertain all sorts of cases, there is no single formula for all of them. Some are very 'simple'. To take one example, a significant proportion of civil matters pending in our federal courts consists of requests by claimants of social benefits for judicial review of denial of those benefits in the administrative law court system of our Social Security Administration.[10] The issue raised in each of those cases is whether there was 'substantial evidence' in the administrative record to support denial of benefits.

In 1938, when the Federal Rules were introduced, it is likely that the great majority of civil cases were of some 'simple' variety. By the end of the Second World War, concerns had arisen about more complex litigation, called 'protracted litigation' at the time. The advent of this challenging litigation initially produced an effort to design streamlined methods of trial. An abiding debate, therefore, is whether the 'learning' gained through management of complex litigation should inform the handling of all litigation.

Meanwhile other forces prompted the federal courts to devise new methods of dealing with repetitive litigation. In the late 1950s, the government obtained convictions for price fixing against a number of high officials of companies that made heavy electrical equipment. Those convictions led to an outburst of suits brought against these companies by the purchasers of this heavy equipment, which came to be known as the Electrical Equipment Cases. This outburst of litigation (around 2,000 separate cases) threatened to overwhelm the federal courts.

The Chief Justice responded by appointing an ad hoc committee of judges to foster uniform treatment of these cases in federal courts across the country.[11] The ad hoc committee persuaded the judges handling the actual cases to collaborate on how to manage them. The experiment was proclaimed a success, and the federal court system was not overwhelmed.

That success produced proposals that Congress make this technique permanent and, in 1968, it created the Judicial Panel on Multidistrict Litigation, with authority to transfer cases from around the country to a single judge it selected for all pre-trial proceedings.[12] This authority has recently proved very important. Indeed, of all civil cases pending in the US federal court system now, more than one third are subject to a combination order from this Judicial Panel.

Some state court systems also responded to the challenge of complex and dispersed litigation. For example, California created an authority like the federal Judicial Panel to combine cases from throughout the state's court system before a single judge. In addition, most metropolitan California superior courts created 'complex litigation departments,' which afforded tailored judicial handling to a select few cases felt to

---

[10] See 42 U.S.C. § 405(g) for the provision for such judicial review, which states that the claimant does so by filing 'a civil action'.

[11] For a review of these developments, see Marcus (2008, pp. 2245–2296).

[12] 28 U.S.C. § 1407.

justify that treatment. In a real sense, then, complex litigation was the stimulus for developing case management techniques.

3 The Emergence of Widespread Case Management in US Courts

The American case management movement was largely a result of various factors just described. Actually, as Professor Kessler has recently written, it may be that the current movement involves a return to early 19th century characteristics of American litigation in some state courts, particularly those of New York.[13] Unlike what seems to have been the case on the European continent under the influence of the French code of 1806,[14] the judges in the New York courts kept control of fact-gathering and development of the cases before them. Lawyers chafed at limitations on their ability to control their own cases.

By the mid-19th century, that judicial control was receding under the pressure of growing judicial business and also lawyer pressure for control of their cases. At that time, however, the distinctive American practices regarding pleading and discovery had not been introduced, so litigation was in that sense a much more constrained activity.

The advent of the Federal Rules in 1938, with 'notice pleading' and broad discovery, removed many of those constraints. The advent of the photocopier, and later email and other digital methods of communication and record-storing, magnified the importance of constraint.

One approach might be to introduce rigid constraints on discovery. From time to time, such proposals have been made, and sometimes acted upon.[15] But even when such limits have been imposed, they have always been subject to a court order altering the limits. And the great range of kinds of cases before the court has meant that tailoring would often support exceeding the general limits, while in many cases the actual discovery would not approach those limits. Limits appropriate for the simplest cases could not conceivably be appropriate for massive complex litigation, and the range of cases in between was very large.

Instead of rigid limits, then, the move was toward tailored judicial direction designed for the individual case. That move began in various federal district courts—principally in New York and San Francisco—during the 1960s. A critical first ingredient was the 'single assignment' system, under which civil cases are assigned to a single judge for their entire duration, from filing to final judgment.

---

[13] Kessler (2017).

[14] van Rhee reports that the French code of 1806 relied on a laissez faire attitude toward civil litigation that left the control of litigation to the lawyers. See van Rhee (2005, pp. 3–24).

[15] See, e.g., Fed. R. Civ. P. 30(a)(2)(i) (limiting parties to 10 depositions); 30(d)(1) (deposition must not be longer than one day of seven hours); 33(a)(1) (no more than 25 interrogatories may be served).

The single assignment system empowered courts to supervise pretrial litigation more closely. In some places, the judges made vigorous use of this opportunity. For example, Chief Judge Robert Peckham of the federal court in San Francisco described a typical judicial management conference with the attorneys in the 1970s, a meeting held at the beginning of the case that 'warns the attorneys that they have a vigilant judge ... The conference can also give the judge a 'feel' for the case and the attorneys; he may pick up early signals that an attorney tends to be careless or to procrastinate, perhaps warranting a fairly rigid timetable and a warning that it will be strictly enforced.'[16]

Not all federal judges did this sort of thing in the 1970s; indeed, most did not. But starting in 1983, the national rules required all federal judges to take some such steps in almost all their cases.[17] Beginning in 1983, the Federal Judicial Center included more and more coverage of such techniques in 'baby judges' school,' introductory training offerings for recently-appointed federal district judges. More and more of those appointed to be federal district judges had experience with judicial case management from their practice careers. What began as the exception gradually became the norm in federal court.

The result is that, though it is not universal, case management is increasingly the customary method of the American federal judicial system. And it has increasingly been adopted in American state courts. The Complex Litigation departments of California Superior Courts, for example, employ techniques very much like those in the federal courts. Several California Superior Courts have also adopted a single assignment system for all civil cases, enabling their judges to exercise similar control over those cases.

Perhaps the most aggressive versions of this judicial control occur in federal-court cases centralized by the Judicial Panel on Multidistrict litigation. The Manual for Complex Litigation, which went into its 4th edition in 2004, provides an extensive menu of suggested techniques for judges to manage what may sometimes be thousands of combined individual cases. Besides adopting schedules like those developed for ordinary individual cases, this judicial power extends to appointing 'lead' and 'liaison' counsel for both sides, directing that all other lawyers cede authority to those the court has designated, requiring all parties to contribute to a fund used to pay for the work done by those lawyers and, on occasion, even abrogating the right of other lawyers to collect the 'contingent' fee provided by their contracts with their clients.[18]

---

[16]Peckham (1981, pp. 781–82).

[17]See Fed. R. Civ. P. 16(b)(3) (requiring that judge enter a scheduling order in every case that limits the time to join other parties, amend the pleadings, complete discovery and file motions, and also authorizes provisions in the scheduling order about a wide variety of other pretrial concerns).

[18]For an example, see In *re Vioxx Products Liability Litigation* 574 F.Supp.2d 606 (E.D. La. 2008), in which the judge capped contingent percentage fees for all lawyers involved in the 'consolidated' litigation of claims from use of a pharmaceutical product at 32% of any settlement amounts, and directed also that any funds for 'common benefit' work done by lead or liaison counsel should be deducted from that figure. In the judge's view, this case was a 'quasi class action' even though it was not conducted pursuant to Fed. R. Civ. P. 23, the federal class-action rule. The judge explained that

This pattern of judicial activity was not borrowed from any other judicial system. To the contrary, it has sometimes served as a model for development of similar case management techniques in those countries. A prime example is the work of Lord Woolf in England & Wales in the 1990s. Called upon to design new procedures for the English courts' handling of civil cases, Lord Woolf carefully studied the US experience with case management.[19]

Based on his study of American practices, Lord Woolf proposed what Professor Zuckerman described as 'a radical departure from past practice' by emphasizing case management.[20] Due to the configuration of the English judicial system, Lord Woolf could not recommend a single assignment system. But he did provide for teams of 'procedural judges' to set and enforce schedules, a feature that Professor Andrews described as 'the cornerstone' of the new procedure.[21]

In sum, as with other procedural initiatives, one could say that American case management is another part of American exceptionalism. But in some ways it resembles the judge-centered mode of conducting litigation that exists in many countries, particularly those following the civil law tradition.

4 American Resistance to Case Management

As noted above, not all American federal judges wholeheartedly embraced the case management movement. Indeed, as one might gather from the absence of rigid directives on such matters as the amount of discovery allowed in individual cases, the American judiciary enjoys singular independence in handling civil litigation. This independence is a feature of a more general judicial independence in the US. As a consequence, long after judicial management was enshrined in the national procedure rules, it remained dead letter in some district courts, or at least some federal courtrooms.

---

such measures would meet 'a growing need to protect the public's trust in the judicial process'. In part, the judge relied on provisions of the collective settlement agreement in the case, and asserted that 'this Court is uniquely situated to examine the reasonableness of attorneys' fees for claimants enrolled in the global settlement.' In *re Zyprexa Products Liability Litigation* 424 F.Supp.2d 488 (E.D.N.Y. 2006), is another example. This is not to say that such rulings are common, but as the judge in the *Vioxx* case said, 'settlement agreements such as the one currently before the Court will likely become more common.'

[19]Lord Woolf recognized the American influence when he said in his preliminary report regarding how to respond to the problems he had diagnosed in English civil litigation: 'It includes increased activity on the party of the judiciary. This is well understood in the United States where case management has been employed for some time.' Woolf (1995, p. 31). As I wrote at that time: 'It is obvious that American input influenced the Woolf Report. Indeed, it should be apparent to readers of the Report that its central recommendation—inaugurating a system of case management—is essentially based on the experience of the American federal courts' Marcus (1995a, p. 231).

[20]Zuckerman (2003, p. 1).

[21]Andrews (2003, p. 1).

4.1 Academic Resistance

Besides lawyers and judges unmoved by urgings toward 'efficiency,' case management prompted resistance in a significant sector of the legal academy. Professor Resnik's 1982 article *Managerial Judges*[22] objected that 'Judicial management has its own techniques, goals, and values, which appear to elevate speed over deliberation, impartiality, and fairness.'[23]

There were salient points to be made against case management of the modern sort. One was that it actually increased the cost of litigation in many smaller cases because it required lawyers to perform unnecessary tasks. This argument focused on the original emergence of case management in complex litigation, and emphasized that what was good for complex litigation was not good for normal litigation.

A second strand of argument was that case management cut against the first principle of 'transsubstantivity,' the notion that the same set of procedure rules govern all cases. Although the Federal Rules have always had some exceptions to that idea,[24] in general they set a framework for all litigation and supplanted old common law procedures that were specifically designed for each type of case.

The objection was that the modern approach to case management gave judges too much discretion.[25] Coupled with the possibility that judges would indulge their own predispositions about various sorts of claims, it added the risk that the judge would also indulge antagonisms against lawyers or parties that resulted from the ongoing intimacy of the case management process itself.

Chief Judge Peckham of the San Francisco federal court was the chief architect of the national rules enshrining case management in the federal system. He responded to Professor Resnik's criticisms, saying that Professor Resnik 'wishes to preserve the laissez-faire character of the adversarial system. I contend, however, that our adversarial system has run amok and that the movement toward judicial oversight represents an effort to preserve the best qualities of the system.'[26]

As noted above, the gradual evolution of the federal judiciary has made case management more pervasive. The most recent edition of the *Manual for Complex Litigation* thus advises that '[f]air and efficient resolution of complex litigation requires at least that … the court exercise early and effective supervision (and, where necessary control).'[27]

---

[22] Resnik (1982, pp. 374–448).

[23] *Ibidem*, p. 380.

[24] See, e.g., Fed. R. Civ. P. 9(b) (imposing special pleading requirements on fraud cases).

[25] For discussion of this trend, see Marcus (2003a, pp. 1561–1616).

[26] Peckham (1985, p. 265).

[27] Federal Judicial Center (2004, § 10.1).

4.2 Resistance to the Multidistrict Litigation Process

More recently, intense criticism has been directed at the multidistrict litigation process that results from the centralizing efforts of the Judicial Panel on Multidistrict Litigation. For decades lawyers not selected as 'lead' or 'liaison' counsel have objected that judges wield too much authority in such cases and interfere with the attorney-client relationship.

In the last decade, however, the volume of cases subject to centralization has grown considerably, and a significant number of academic critics have charged that judges managing such cases run roughshod over the rights of lawyers and litigants in their efforts to resolve these gargantuan collections of litigation.[28] In significant ways, these criticisms echo the early criticisms of case management more generally.

These objections have produced proposals that special procedure rules be adopted to manage multidistrict litigation[29] and also has prompted legislation that has passed one house of Congress.[30]

---

[28] A recurrent critic is Professor Burch. See, e.g., Burch and Williams (2017, pp. 1445–1537), Burch (2015, pp. 71–142, 2017, pp. 67–166). See also Burch (2019).

[29] Formal proposals for rule changes addressed to reported problems with multidistrict litigation have been presented to the US Judicial Conference's Advisory Committee on Civil Rules, the body responsible for considering and drafting changes to the Federal Rules of Civil Procedure. Those proposals are presented and discussed in the agenda book for the 7 November 2017 meeting of the Committee, pp. 469–544, available at www.uscourts.gov. Accessed 10 June 2020.

[30] The Fairness in Class Action Litigation Act of 2017, H.R. 985, passed the House of Representatives on March 9, 2017. § 5 of the bill would add provisions to 28 U.S.C. § 1407, which governs multidistrict litigation, for any consolidated cases involving claims for personal injury. Among other things, it would require every such plaintiff to submit 'a submission sufficient to demonstrate that there is evidentiary support (including but not limited to medical records) for the factual contentions in plaintiff's complaint regarding the alleged injury, the exposure to the risk that allegedly caused the injury, and the alleged cause of the injury.' Such a requirement may resemble pleading requirements in many other countries, but is quite different from the customary pleading burden in the US. The bill would also require that the plaintiff 'receive not less than 80% of any monetary recovery obtained in that action by settlement, judgment or otherwise.' As noted above in footnote 18, in such proceedings judges have sometimes relied on a 'quasi class action' concept to support limitations of attorney fee payments. Thus, in the *Vioxx* litigation the judge limited attorney fees to 32% (plus costs). Very often 'contingent fees' in the US are for a larger proportion of any settlement or judgment. Limiting fees and costs to 20% of any recovery would be a very substantial change. H.R. 985 did not pass the US Senate, however, and it lapsed when a new Congress was seated in January 2019. No such bill has been introduced in the current Congress, which sits through January 2021. Further Congressional elections are to occur in November 2020.

5 Link to Settlement Promotion

At more or less the same time that judicial management became prominent in American federal courts, another judicial initiative was coming to the fore—judicial settlement promotion. That initiative combined with judicial management was to foster a fairly broad transformation of judicial behavior in civil cases.

The classic image of American civil litigation was that the judge was not involved until trial unless the parties had a motion, and that motion practice was limited. Under the 'master calendar' system that persisted into the 1980s, a given case might be the responsibility of a number of judges before it reached judgment.

With divided judicial responsibility for civil litigation, the lawyers were in control. From many perspectives, this was a good thing; the lawyers were more likely than the judge to understand the nuances of given cases.[31] The American judge, on the other hand, might seem a 'blind and blundering intruder' when intervening in the matter.[32]

With active judicial management, the judge would be more familiar with the case and feel more responsibility for its resolution. One thing that judges perceived was that often the parties would 'leave it to the lawyers' and avoid making hard decisions about the resolution of the case until the last moment. The image of 'settlement on the courthouse steps' represented what judges increasingly regarded as a judicial failure; if the case could be settled, it would save a lot of money (and judicial time) if that could be done early in the litigation rather than at the last minute.

Meanwhile, litigants and lawyers were waking up to a similar reality. Particularly in commercial litigation pitting commercial entities against one another, corporate management increasingly recoiled at the cost and drain of full-scale litigation followed by a settlement that could have been obtained years sooner at lower cost and with less effort. Moreover, creative parties were recognizing that settlement resolutions offered more flexibility than the prospect of 'winner take all' results in court.[33]

Putting judicial management together with settlement promotion and the idea that agreed outcomes might be preferable to litigated decisions could seem to invite untrammelled judicial control of the actual result of litigation. In some state courts, 'settlement weeks' became prominent; rather than hold one or two trials to resolve cases, judges would instead convene numerous settlement conferences to hammer out agreed resolutions.

There was much to be said in favor of this judicial activity. Many lawyers favored settlement promotion, perhaps in part because trials held risks for them but mainly because experience taught them that settlement on the courthouse steps subjected their clients to unnecessary expense and turmoil. It was said that the only ones who like trials were clients, but also that clients tended too often to be unrealistic about

---

[31] For a classic statement of this perspective, see Fuller (1949, pp. 706–707).

[32] For the classic statement of this view, see Frankel (1975, pp. 1031–1059).

[33] For a classic statement of these views, see Lieberman and Henry (1986, pp. 424–439).

their chances at trial. Bringing clients to their senses was one of the things judges could do when lawyers could not accomplish it.[34]

In at least some situations, however, this 'litigation in the shadows' seemed to supplant the existing body of legal rules with a negotiated set of substitute rules effected through settlement of litigation. Probably the most prominent version of that sort of thing in the 1990s was the settlement class action.[35] In 1997, the Supreme Court overturned a huge class action settlement of thousands of asbestos personal injury claims. This settlement substituted for the tort system of individual litigation in court what the Court called 'a nationwide administrative claims processing regime'.[36] The Court held that this sort of arrangement was more appropriate to legislation, and beyond the authority of judges acting as judges.

Despite this 1997 decision, the practice known as 'settlement class certification' continued to operate on a reduced scale. The growing importance of multidistrict centralization of litigation offered a substitute route to a similar goal when combined with active case management and judicial settlement promotion.[37] Some judges came to regard such multidistrict proceedings as 'quasi class actions' subject to judicial control in a manner similar to the control of class actions that rules give to the judge.[38] A striking example came in litigation involving a pharmaceutical product called Vioxx. Under the leadership of a federal district court judge in New Orleans, Louisiana, and with support from state courts judges from California and New Jersey, a nationwide settlement of thousands of claims for a total fund of $4.85 billion was reached.[39]

There seems little doubt that the judicial press toward settlement, particularly in multidistrict litigation, is quite strong. There is fierce debate about whether this is a good thing or a bad thing. But it does serve to illustrate what some would say is the dystopia that can result when too much judicial power is combined with too much judicial discretion and a pervasive push toward a non-litigation result.

6 Conclusion

This contribution should end on an optimistic rather than a pessimistic note. It has highlighted both the innovations in judicial management and the results of judicial

---

[34]See Brazil (1984, pp. 15–19), reporting survey results showing that lawyers want judges to participate actively in settlement discussions and offer candid assessments of case strengths and weaknesses.

[35]For discussion, see Marcus (1995b, pp. 858–908).

[36]*Amchem Products, Inc. v Windsor* 521 U.S. 591 (1997).

[37]For discussion, see Sherman (2008, pp. 2205–2224).

[38]In particular, Fed. R. Civ. P. 23(e) provides that only the judge can approve a settlement of a class action, and that approval depends on whether the judge finds the settlement 'fair, reasonable and adequate'.

[39]For a discussion of this settlement, see In *re Vioxx Products Liability Litigation* 874 F.Supp.2d 606 (E.D. La. 2008).

settlement promotion during the last half century in the US. Lest the reader leave with the impression that these movements have created a dystopia, it is important to emphasize that the overall experience of judicial case management has been positive.

Many American lawyers recognize that judicial management holds a key to more expeditious and less expensive litigation. They realize that lawyerly game-playing, particularly in regard to discovery, is wasteful and distracting. To some extent, even the national rules have moved away from a wholehearted embrace of adversarial excesses. Thus, Rule 1 was amended in 2015 to say that the parties bear a responsibility to 'secure the just, speedy, and inexpensive determination of every action' and the accompanying Committee Note recognized that '[e]ffective advocacy is consistent with—and indeed depends upon—cooperative and proportional use of procedure.'[40]

But Nirvana has not arrived in American litigation despite this effort to shift somewhat away from the most vigorous form of adversarial behavior. Instead, American lawyers will increasingly find that American judges provide what some call 'adult supervision' as an antidote and constraint to the unique latitude granted lawyers in this system.

For other judicial systems in which the lawyers have never had such latitude, it may be that developing a judicial management 'cure' is less urgent. Indeed, it may be that the innovations introduced in the US in the last half century resemble longstanding practices in many other judicial systems in which the court has long had a more prominent role. But for any who want to explore ways to enhance judicial supervision of litigation, studying the American experience would be a good idea.

References

Andrews N (2003) English civil procedure. Oxford

Brazil W (1984) Settling civil cases: What lawyers want from judges. Judges' J 23:15–19

Burbank S, Farhang S, Kritzer H (2013) Private enforcement. Lewis Clark Law Rev 17:637–722

Burch EC (2015) Judging multidistrict litigation. New York Univ Law Rev 90:71–142

Burch EC (2017) Monopolies in multidistrict litigation. Vanderbilt Law Rev 70:67–166

Burch EC (2019) Mass tort deals: Backroom bargaining in mass tort litigation. Cambridge

Burch EC, Williams M (2017) Repeat players in multidistrict litigation: A social network analysis. Cornell Law Rev 102:1445–1537

Federal Judicial Center (2004) Manual for complex litigation, 4th edn

Frankel M (1975) The search for truth: An umpireal view. Univ Pennsylvania Law Rev 123:1031–1059

Fuller L (1949) The problems of jurisprudence. New York

Kessler A (2017) Inventing American exceptionalism. New Haven, London

Lieberman J, Henry J (1986) Lessons from the alternative dispute resolution movement. Univ Chicago Law Rev 53:424–39

Marcus R (1995a) Deja vu all over again? An American reaction to the Woolf Report. In: Zuckerman AAS, Cranston R (eds) The reform of civil procedure: Essays on 'access to justice'. Oxford

[40] See Fed. R. Civ. P. 1.

Marcus R (1995b) They can't do that, can they? Tort reform via Rule 23. Cornell Law Rev 80:858–908
Marcus R (1999) Malaise of the litigation superpower. In: Zuckerman AAS (ed) Civil justice in crisis. Oxford
Marcus R (2003a) Slouching toward discretion. Notre Dame Law Rev 78:1561–1616
Marcus R (2003b) The new role of American judges: Reining in the American litigator. Hastings Int Comparative Law Rev 27:3–28
Marcus R (2008) Cure-all for an era of dispersed litigation? Tulane Law Rev 82:2245–2296
Marcus R (2012) Appellate review in the reactive model: The example of the American federal courts. In: Uzelac A, Van Rhee CH (eds) Nobody's perfect: Comparative essays on appeals and other means of recourse. Cambridge, pp 105–126
Marcus R (2017) Misgivings about American exceptionalism: Court access as a Zero-Sum game. In: Uzelac A, Van Rhee CH (eds) Revisiting procedural human rights: Fundamentals of civil procedure and the changing face of civil justice. Cambridge, pp 53–75
Peckham R (1981) The federal judge as case manager: The new role in guiding a case from filing to disposition. California Law Rev 69:770–805
Peckham R (1985) A judicial response to the cost of litigation: Case management, two-stage discovery planning and alternative dispute resolution. Rutgers Law Rev 37:253–278
Resnik J (1982) Managerial judges. Harvard Law Rev 96:374–448
Sherman E (2008) The MDL model for resolving complex litigation if a class action is not possible. Tulane Law Rev 82:2205–2224
Van Rhee CH (2005) Introduction. In: van Rhee CH (ed) European traditions in civil procedure. Cambridge, pp 3–23
Woolf Lord (1995) Access to justice: Interim report to the Lord Chancellor on the civil justice system. London
Zuckerman AAS (2003) Civil procedure. London

Framing the Structure of the Court System from a Case Management Perspective: New Trends in Brazilian Law

Antonio Cabral

Abstract Just as elsewhere, in Brazil case management has always been met with enormous enthusiasm. However, its widespread application as a tool for enhancing efficiency should be approached with caution. Hasty solutions might cause more harm than good in terms of effective results. Moreover, the conjunction of less tangible institutional factors, contrary trends, and specificities of different legal systems may indicate that the world is far more complex than appears at first sight. New tools for managing conflicts and procedures are not immune to criticism and limitations. However, the tools should be seen as a starting point for the further development of case management.

1 Introduction: What Is Case Management?

Case management is the control over a judicial proceeding. From pretrial to post-trial, efficiency, speed, and quality, are pivotal factors of effective case management. Successful case management ensures proper resource operation and less expense for the parties. Additionally, there should be indicators available that enable a predetermination of the results of the proceeding. Constant monitoring of what occurs within proceedings is crucial to allow adjournments and adjustments.

This article partially corresponds to an Introductory Report that the author presented at the IAPL Conference in Tianjing (China) in 2017.

A. Cabral (✉)
University of Rio de Janeiro, Rio de Janeiro, Brazil
e-mail: antoniocabral@uerj.br

P. C. H. Chan and C. H. van Rhee (eds.), *Civil Case Management in the Twenty-First Century: Court Structures Still Matter*, Ius Gentium: Comparative Perspectives on Law and Justice 85, https://doi.org/10.1007/978-981-33-4512-6_9

2 Who Manages?

The study of the management of tasks in a judicial proceeding frequently focuses on the judiciary. The emphasis of the jurisdictional role of the judges, in any case, is not unusual, as well as the prominence of the instruments at their disposal to ensure the procedure is efficient. Moreover, the administrative side of the management role should also be highlighted, either performed by the judge or the judiciary. These management activities, although performed by judges, are described as administrative rather than jurisdictional. Case management, therefore, is a task that sits between adjudication and judicial administration.[1]

The judge is a key figure within the management of cases.[2] On the administrative side, in some parts of the common law world, court administration has been delegated to court staff. In the Roman-Germanic tradition, this task has been predominantly performed by judges, with the assistance of the judiciary's personnel (civil servants or others).[3] In recent years, alternatives to the management of courts by judges have been developed. These initiatives aim to put other government bodies, such as the executive branch, in charge of case management. In the jurisdictions where this has occurred, controversies have arisen. These controversies have demonstrated the idea that when judicial case management is not performed by judges, it could lead to a violation of the trias politica by allowing forms of constraint, pressure, or external influence to be imposed on judicial decisions.[4]

Subsequently, with regard to adjudication in common law legal systems, judges were granted powers to decide which legal procedures are to be applied. This flexibility allows more suitable adaptation to the circumstances of the particular case and increases efficiency.[5] There is the belief that in order to achieve greater efficiency, case management had to be implemented by the managing judge (the so-called 'court control of litigation').[6] It is deemed that, if judges are to exercise their jurisdictional powers efficiently, they must hold powers that allow them to adapt the manner in which procedures are performed in order to attain optimal results.

---

[1] See Jeuland (2017).

[2] Many authors still depict the judge as a passive umpire or a detached decision maker, but the increasing discretion related to case management powers shows that the judge becomes more and more a 'strategic player in the litigation game', as Bone highlights: Bone (2007, pp. 1996–1997).

[3] Jeuland (2017), Röhl (1998, pp. 242ff).

[4] Ferejohn (1999, pp. 353–384).

[5] Mainly in the USA, but also in England since the reforms resulting from the Woolf Report: Flood et al. (2007, pp. 133–188), Clarke (2009, pp. 33–49). In the United States of America, there was no provision in statutory law, but the constant concerns of legal scholars and the judiciary led to a progressive acceptance of judges' procedural management powers, always with regard to greater efficiency of the results. See Resnik (1982, pp. 374ff and 419–431), Marcus (2008, pp. 2274–2275). For Brazil, see Gajardoni (2008, pp. 162ff), Tiemi Ono (2016, p. 3).

[6] Van Rhee (2008, pp. 3–4). About the subject, Andrews (2003, p. 333), Resnik (1986, pp. 524 and 534–535), Dodge (2014, p. 333), Turner (2009, p. 79), Almeida (2011, p. 289), Moreira and Novidade (2001, pp. 185–186). See also Sorabji in this volume.

The Brazilian Code of Civil Procedure (hereinafter, CPC) incorporated judicial case management in Article 139(vi), which allows the judge more flexibility in the setting of deadlines and allowing of evidence. Also, Articles 69 and 55 § 3 enable the aggregation of claims on the grounds of efficiency.[7] In some proceedings, the judge can decide to stay proceedings or to continue litigation on the merits of a case, under Article 685. Article 357 of the CPC also establishes a 'procedural phase' for the organization of the procedure, especially regarding pretrial activity, under Article 373 § 1. In complex cases, it provides that the court should set a date for a hearing that allows the parties to discuss organizational issues with the judge (Article 357 § 3). The statutes intend to grant the judge powers to manage the proceedings, thus, assuring greater adaptability and flexibility of the formalities. This allows a more suitable and efficient judicial process, resulting in a more effective system of accessing justice.[8]

While many legal scholars are in favour of a management role of judges,[9] judicial case management has attracted a lot of criticism.[10] This criticism is seen in countries where the role of the judge is more restricted and passive; the transformation of the judge to the contrary[11] has increased the risk of compromising impartiality. Such risks can be mitigated as management functions can be exercised through moderate restraint. Within the principle of cooperation, the dichotomy between the prevalence of public and private interests can be resolved if all the relevant players seek the same objectives regarding the proceeding. This entails all parties want the proceeding conducted in a correct, efficient and just manner. The management of proceedings by the judges would not represent a risk to their impartiality or independence, but rather a natural and necessary activity for the administration of justice in the contemporary world, aiming to provide greater efficiency and effectiveness to the results of the procedure.[12]

In either adjudication or performance of judicial administration, there is a widespread view that the management task is predominantly a state activity. Whether case management is conducted by the executive branch or by the judiciary itself, the parties to court proceedings are beneficiaries, not active players.

[7]If no other evidence is needed, the Code of Civil Procedure grants the judge the power to decide the case on the merits (whether totally or partially) by summary judgment, i.e. without a trial hearing or taking of testimonial or expert evidence (Arts. 354 and 356). In Brazilian legal literature, see Marinoni, Arenhart and Mitidiero (2016, p. 47), Gajardoni et al. (2015, p. 72), Didier (2001). Didier (2016, p. 119), speaks of a 'jurisdictional adaptation of the procedure', giving other examples of normative provisions that reinforce the normative basis of this adaptability. In the same sense, Dos Santos Bedaque (2006, pp. 63ff and 109–112), Cabral (2010, p. 63).

[8]Oliveira and Mitidiero (2012, pp. 74ff), Garcia Medina (2015, p. 115).

[9]Peckham (1981, pp. 770–773).

[10]Molot (2003, pp. 29ff).

[11]McGovern (1997, p. 1869).

[12]Fix-Fierro (2003).

3 What to Manage? Aggregation of Cases, Conflict Management, and Court Management

In the judicial sphere, existing court proceedings need to be handled judicially or extrajudicially. This practice could be described as 'one-case management' or conflict management. The former seeks to resolve a dispute already brought before the courts and the latter provides a suitable solution. It also acknowledges the importance of arbitration for certain disputes and instruments of alternative dispute resolution.[13]

There are increasing numbers of studies on the management of judicial structures (i.e. court management). Court management is understood as the management of the staff and budget of the court, infrastructure, IT, and so on.[14] Court management has become an important topic in recent years. This aspect of management activity focuses on the possibility of the courts expanding their structures, sectors and benches, promoting the qualification and training of judges, clerks, and other court officials.

Thus, court management aids in the development of management practices and improving court organization. The legal system must be equipped with suitable organizational conditions in order for judges to perform their duties. Therefore, efficiency is crucial in achieving successful court management and organization.

4 How to Manage? Objectives and Benefits of Case Management

Case management encompasses both the initial stages and the fact-finding phase. However, there are also case management activities in the enforcement stage, known as post-trial case management.[15] Legal literature focuses on the objectives of case management and court management. The issues discussed include efficiency, cost-benefit analysis, and the time frame of proceedings. Case-flow management is also highlighted. All of this depends on when the management activity is implemented. For example, pre-trial case management is concerned with cost and time reduction; whereas post-trial case management is predominantly concerned with effectiveness and efficiency.[16]

In order to achieve these objectives, the legal system would have to adopt modern techniques,[17] and various methods to implement case management. To guarantee efficiency, it would be necessary to allow greater adaptability to the specificities of each dispute within the procedure. Ordinary proceedings can no longer satisfy the

[13]Cabral (2017a, pp. 342–359), Cabral and Da Cunha (2016, pp. 471ff).

[14]Jeuland (2017).

[15]Resnik (1982, pp. 391 and 413–414).

[16]*Ibidem*.

[17]Didier (2008, p. 41).

peculiarities of each conflict, which, in the late 20th century, led to the proliferation of special proceedings. The parties may opt for special proceedings which provide more specific procedural handling of cases in which substantive law does not fit the generalized format of the ordinary proceeding. Besides the varied and diversified proceedings, depending on the substantive law litigated in each case, many legal systems, especially in the civil law tradition, experienced the establishment in statutory law of several types of summary and fast-track proceedings, among which the small claims model is widely disseminated. To reduce costs, management activity is commonly associated with the formal loosening of procedures. Reducing formalities and adding flexibility to the proceedings would enable the prevention of nullities of procedural legal acts, thus making it feasible for the judicial procedure to better serve the purposes of effective dispute resolution, solving the litigated substantive legal issues. A more flexible procedure would contribute to adaptability and would be more suitable to provide effective relief.

Subsequently, to guarantee adequate case-flow management, the judge should be able to schedule proceedings.[18] In Brazil, the new CPC provides the possibility of the judge and the parties to agree upon the schedule for the performance of procedural acts (Article 191), including the taking of forensic evidence (Article 357 § 8). As regards the reduction of costs, many studies have been conducted on cost management, in other words, the management of procedural costs.[19] This management is now operated by cost allocation orders and decisions to distribute cost burdens among parties and third-parties.[20] In the past decades, cost allocation has been strongly influenced also by 'litigation agreements' (or 'negotiated procedure') such as legal expenses insurance and third-party funding.

5 New Perspectives on Case Management

Traditionally, the problem of an excessive caseload before the courts was solved by establishing court practices for the whole tribunal: the management of civil servants, structure, budget, etc. However, in the judicial sphere, management was dealt with from the perspective of each lawsuit. The increase in efficiency of various proceedings was in reality the effect of the management of individual court actions rather than general management activity. If judges could implement a suitable pace and timeframe for each case, while accounting for costs and the fulfilment of all fundamental guarantees, the optimal resolution of each case would have a large-scale impact on many other lawsuits, since they would also be conducted accordingly. Therefore, the repercussion of case management on court management was not the goal of the case management activity in itself, as it was monitored on a case-by-case basis.

---

[18] Resnik (1986, p. 523).

[19] Davis and Garrett (2014, pp. 483, 488–489).

[20] Hurst (2009, pp. 171–181), Machado Alves (2016, p. 194).

In recent times, adjudication mechanisms of a jurisdictional nature, applied by a judge within judicial proceedings, are beginning to flourish. They enable the management of many procedures at once. Examples are standard-solution procedures, and proceedings for the resolution en bloc of multiple claims on the same issue of fact or law, such as test claims, model proceedings, and pilot-judgments.[21]

Through the use of these techniques, case management is targeted from a macro-procedural perspective, in what could be called multiple-cases management. The biggest difference is that these techniques promote large-scale solutions.

6 New Developments in Case Management: Nature of the Parties, Litigation Agreements and Lack of Case Management

The changes within the objectives as well as the techniques and methods of case management have modified the role of the person in charge of case management. This shift is natural in regard to the principle of cooperation in contemporary civil procedure that concerns the key stakeholders. Moreover, there is a collective ideology that relevant players should partake in case management.[22]

Subsequently, there has been a global trend in the increased study and the significance of litigation agreements. These agreements provide proof that procedural management often assigns a leading role to the parties. Through the negotiation of the rules of procedure, parties outline a format of proceeding that suits their interests and adapts the judicial process to their needs, thus, ensuring a more efficient judicial system. Litigation agreements are akin to an arbitration proceeding. The nature of these agreements allows for greater predictability of the outcome of the proceedings. For example, the legal rules applicable to the litigation proceeding may have been agreed in the initial stages of the legal relationship, in other words, when the party signed a contract including the agreement.

The new Brazilian CPC is possibly the most modern piece of legislation on this subject. Article 190 states:

> When the action deals with rights that permit the resolution of the dispute by the parties themselves, the parties can stipulate changes in the procedure to adapt it to the specific requirements of the case and can agree upon their powers and procedural legal rights and obligations, before or during the proceedings.
>
> Either upon request or on its own motion, the judge shall control the validity of the agreements set forth in this article, denying their application only in the case of nullity or abusive inclusion of such terms in adhesion contracts or in cases where any of the parties is in a manifestly weaker position.

Additionally, Article 200 states:

[21] See Cabral (2016a, pp. 263–281).

[22] Tatiana Machado Alves remarks that a case management approach exclusively focused on the judge's activity is only part of the story. Machado Alves (2016, p. 84).

> The legal acts of the parties consisting of unilateral or bilateral declarations of will shall immediately produce the constitution, modification or extinction of procedural legal rights.

Article 190 in conjunction with Article 200 provides for general clauses of litigation agreements. These enable the parties to create a legally valid litigation agreement, specifically regarding procedural aspects.[23] The ability of parties to negotiate the procedure is a very powerful management tool. Albeit, it has not yet been thoroughly discussed in studies on case management.[24] The Brazilian CPC shows how litigation agreements can be used as case management instruments. For example, in the organizational phase, Article 357 § 2 provides that the parties can agree on the issues of fact that will be litigated or submit to the court a choice of law agreement.

Consequently, litigation agreements have generated a major shift in the activity of procedural management. Case management always concerns a pending case whereas litigation agreements deal with cases that are yet to come before the courts and before the dispute even occurs. The goals differ: one manages pending disputes whereas the other aims at avoiding litigation. Preventing litigation has arguably created a 'no-case management system'. Additionally, litigation agreements also change special proceedings. In the past, the adaptation of judicial proceedings was a legislative task, as a result of the creation of special statutory proceedings. Nowadays, these special proceedings have become increasingly unnecessary, due to ordinary proceedings becoming more adaptable.[25]

---

[23] Cabral (2016b).

[24] Among all general reporters at the (2017) IAPL Conference in Tianjin, only Sorabji mentioned the subject. Sorabji (2017, pp. 62–63). In China, Wang reports that there is little space for the parties to agree on proceedings, for the judges tend to play a leading role in the definition of procedural rules. Wang (2017, pp. 20ff).

[25] Another aspect of the topic which has been little explored concerns the fact that these procedural agreements represent a rearrangement of the relationship between substantive law and procedural law. Litigation agreements can, indirectly, increase or reduce the costs of the implementation of rights, by rendering their enforcement more or less difficult; and they can establish a new evidentiary logic (burden of proof, evaluation of evidence, etc), causing an impact on substantive law because they change the prognosis of spontaneous compliance with the rules. As is the case with any contract, an improvement in the procedural legal position of one party could represent an advantage gained by the opposing party, e.g. in substantive law, such as a price reduction. A consumer may negotiate a lower price by agreeing to clauses that allow greater 'seizability' of her assets or easier attachment in execution proceedings. Therefore, the contract may not deal merely with the choice of more efficient procedures: the parties frequently agree on procedure against the backdrop of the expectation of the impact of those provisions on substantive law. And, mainly in contracts signed prior to the emergence of the dispute, contractually designing future in-court proceedings may generate incentives for individual behaviour. By undertaking obligations and regulating procedure, the parties are indirectly delineating incentives that favour compliance with their legal obligations. This aspect of litigation agreements has been little studied but indicates that these agreements are not only a form of conventional case management, but also a means of reshaping or remodelling the interactions between procedure and substantive law.

7 The New Structure of Court Management: A Global Trend in New Public Judicial Management, Outsourcing Justice and Privatization

The search for a more efficient judicial procedure is omnipresent in today's world. The traditional, stricter approach does not meet the demands of modern society. The need for 'new judicial public policies' has been expressed for a significant period of time. Without fail, there is currently a strong tendency for the application of new public management to court management.[26]

This new public management movement requires efficiency indicators for state performance, which involves effective management, transparency, and accountability.[27] Public management requires that the judiciary, firstly, defines relevant objectives and then, plans and targets that seek to achieve the standards of quality defined on the basis of developed indicators.[28] In addition, there must be a strict control of results in order to review the judicial policies previously adopted.[29]

New public judicial management underlines the need for greater flexibility and adaptability, but the movement also aims at heightening the qualifications of the staff responsible for court administration. In recent years, hiring professionals for specific sectors has been increased and functions have been transferred to private persons, which is qualified as justice outsourcing.[30] Moreover, bodies are also created outside the judiciary for administrative and budgetary management.[31] Court managers are appointed as well.[32] In rare instances, this means the revaluation of the qualification of

[26]The call for new public judicial management was observed in Australia, New Zealand and England, and spread throughout several European countries such as the Netherlands, Belgium, France and Germany. In the majority of countries that implemented the guidelines of new public judicial management, there have been reports of positive experiences with this type of court administration, and the fear that there could be some type of undue interference in the judicial activity or judges' independence has proven to be purely speculative. Loth and De Werd (2003, p. 319), Scott and Sturm (2006, p. 566). In Germany, Röhl (1998, p. 241), Hoffmann-Riem (1997, pp. 4ff).

[27]Hess (2006, pp. 143ff), Hoffmann-Riem (1997, p. 5), Eifert (1997, pp. 75ff), Contini and Carnevali (2010, pp. 1–2, 6, 12).

[28]Contini (2010, p. 111ff), Fabri et al. (2005), Ng et al. (2008, pp. 58–64), Porcelli (2009), Sodan (2005, pp. 766–767), Pauliat (2008, p. 108), Röhl (1998, p. 241), Loth and De Werd (2003, pp. 318–319).

[29]Langbroek (2007, pp. 112–113), Contini and Carnevali (2010, pp. 7–8).

[30]See Uzelac (2010, pp. 86–87), Yarkov and Abolonin (2010, p. 225).

[31]Mäurer (2000, p. 68), Langbroek (2007, pp. 112–113). It is important to highlight that court management does not need to be carried out necessarily by the judiciary itself (judge-only). One could imagine comissions or commitees formed by members of both the judiciary and parliament. In the traditional debate, judicial independence and judges' accountability are values considered to be clashing values. Trying to tackle this issue, see Contini and Mohr (2007, pp. 28, 39ff). About the relationship between the judicial budget and judges' independence: Douglas and Hartley (2003, pp. 441–453), Baar (1999, pp. 399–351), Wheeler (1979, pp. 134–149).

[32]Karpen (1999, pp. 993ff), Papier (2002, pp. 2587–2590), Pauliat (2008, pp. 96, 99, 101 and 108), Contini and Carnevali (2010, pp. 7–9), Jeuland (2017, pp. 21ff).

judges for a particular administrative task.[33] The transfer of management activities to a technical, professional body has a correlation with increasing efficiency. This occurs because judges do not normally have the required expertise for certain tasks and further proper training is costly and time-consuming. Changes can occur more easily with staff other than judges; when judges are responsible for court management, they cannot be removed for a lack of managerial achievements.[34]

8 Specialization of Courts

With regard to the structure of court management, many legal systems around the world are promoting the establishment of specialized units. The most common form of specialization is attributing exclusive subject-matter jurisdiction to certain courts.[35] This specialization sometimes assigns cases to independent branches of the judiciary like labour courts but is much more frequent at first instance and appellate courts, such as a chamber or panel, that is specialized in certain subject-matter.[36]

9 Proposals for the Development of Case Management: Case Assignment Management, Functionality, and Management of the Rules Governing the Allocation of Competences

Case assignment management is the development of systems that distribute cases among judges and courts in order to achieve an optimal result regarding both quantity and quality of cases litigated. Functionality is an intrinsic characteristic of case management.[37] Moreover, the fundamental objective is a structured system, based on creating a suitable division of tasks among the various decision-making

[33] Kramer (2001, p. 3449), Loth and De Werd (2003, p. 318).

[34] In Latin America, however, this is rare: in most courts, judges or judicial civil servants remain as those responsible for court administration. There is a strong lobby, especially from judges' associations, against any kind of justice outsourcing or privatization.

[35] Uzelac (2014, p. 148), Mak (2008, p. 2).

[36] In Brazil, at the State level, the division of competences between the Tax, Civil, Family and Commercial Courts is well known. Within the Federal jurisdiction, in the various circuits, there are specific courts for social security, environmental, agrarian, tax and tax foreclosure, intellectual property, trademark and home loan matters, or matters regarding the Hague Convention on the Civil Aspects of International Child Abduction (among others).

[37] McGovern (1986, pp. 440ff).

centres.[38] Additionally, efficiency parameters allow for an optimal organization and distribution of work.[39]

The most suitable tool to manage mass litigation has been debated. Some advocates argue that the best solution is to focus on class arbitration as a model; the solution for mass litigation would be to take proceedings out of the judiciary.[40] The costs of those arbitration proceedings, however, demonstrate this might not be a viable alternative for poor and developing countries.

Another method that has been developed to manage the court system concerns the aggregation of cases in which the same issues of law or fact are litigated.[41] The rise of mechanisms for the consolidation and centralization of individual proceedings has been recognized, regardless of the *perpetuatio iurisdictionis*. This method is displayed across several jurisdictions: multidistrict litigation orders in the USA, centralization of multiple actions in Brazil, or consolidation in Portugal, the latter being when several actions that are pending before different trial and appellate courts are joined for fact-finding and taking of evidence or for a joint trial.[42]

Various types of aggregation of claims[43] are used to manage large numbers of cases on similar subject-matters. This aggregation can assure uniformity of final results and reducing cost and time.[44]

These tools are different from the class or collective actions models. In fact, during the 20th century, the emergence of the previous models for redress was seen as an empowerment mechanism for associations and institutions to seek judicial protection for collective rights. However, the more recent forms of aggregation of claims are clearly seen as a management instrument and often have the goal of expediting the litigation process.[45]

---

[38] Mitidiero (2013, p. 13).

[39] Definition by Elaine Mak: Mak (2008, p. 2), along with Hol and Loth (2004, pp. 67–89).

[40] Strong (2016), Roque (2014).

[41] The idea is to provide relief for a larger number of people at once. McGovern (1983, pp. 5–9).

[42] Cabral (2017b).

[43] Aggregation in a broad sense occurs in any case in which more than one person or entity is a plaintiff or a defendant. Resnik (1991, p. 23). Yeazell (1989, p. 44), rejects such a wide approach because it would mask 'an important distinction between voluntary joinder and involuntary participation, which causes questions regarding 'free riders' and 'kidnapped' participants.

[44] Resnik (1991, p. 37).

[45] And more and more, class actions that in their origin were seen as empowerment tools, are starting to be looked at as management tools as well. See Resnik (1991, pp. 47–48).

10 Court Management, Specialization Focused on Judges, and Specialized Itinerant Judges

As seen previously, specialization normally consists of attributing exclusive competences to chambers, units, and, occasionally, to an entire court. Specialization also contributes towards efficient case assignment management and the specialization of judges.[46]

Some jurisdictions have adopted mechanisms of this nature that could also be successful in many other jurisdictions. In the future, groups of itinerant judges could be sent out to address the caseload of courts. These itinerant judges would be appointed to cover the annual court holidays and other absences as substitutes, and, also, to provide additional help to counter excessive caseloads. The idea is to ensure functional mobility with greater flexibility in the management of court structures.[47] In this way, without excluding the judge to whom the case was originally assigned, a more efficient performance is enabled in terms of quality.[48]

11 Concluding Remarks

Case management has always been met with enormous enthusiasm. However, its widespread application as a tool for enhancing efficiency should be approached with caution. Hasty solutions might cause more harm than good in terms of effective results. It is important to recognize what has actually happened and what is the future of case management. Moreover, the conjunction of less tangible institutional factors, contrary trends, and specificities of different legal systems may indicate that the world is far more complex than this short contribution suggests. The new tools for managing conflicts and procedures are not immune to criticism and limitations. However, the tools should be seen as a starting point for the further development of case management.

References

Almeida D (2011) O case management inglês: Um sistema maduro? Revista Eletrônica de Direito Processual 7:283–335

Andrews N (2003) English civil procedure: Fundamentals of the new civil justice system. Oxford

[46]Uzelac (2014, p. 149). Commenting the South African experience, Van Loggerenberg says that we must not only think of the variety of services (in the multidoor or multi-access logic), but also of the variety of tasks attributed to judges and the variety of their capabilities and expertises (multitasked and multi-skilled). Van Loggerenberg (2014, pp. 187–188).

[47]This characteristic is seen as fundamental to assure efficiency in court management. Langbroek and Fabri (2007a, p. 17).

[48]Langbroek and Fabri (2007b, p. 296).

Baar C (1999) The development and reform of court organization and administration. Public Administration and Development 19(4):339–351
Bone RG (2007) Who decides—A critical look at procedural discretion. Cardozo Law Rev 28:1996–1997
Cabral A (2010) Nulidades no processo moderno: Contraditório, proteção da confiança e validade prima facie dos atos processuais, 2nd edn. Rio de Janeiro
Cabral A (2016a) Standard-solution procedures and mass litigation. Int J Procedural Law 6:263–281
Cabral A (2016b) Les conventions sur la procédure en droit processuel brésilien. Revue internationale de droit comparé 3:629–648
Cabral A (2017a) Mediation und Schlichtung nach brasilianischem Recht. Zeitschrift für Vergleichende Rechtswissenschaft 3:342–360
Cabral A (2017b) Juiz natural e flexibilização de competência. Rio de Janeiro
Cabral A, Da Cunha L (2016) Negociação direta ou resolução colaborativa de disputas. Revista de Processo 259:471–489
Clarke A (2009) The Woolf reforms: A singular event or an ongoing process? In: Dwyer D (ed) The civil procedure rules ten years on. Oxford, pp 33–49
Contini F (2010) The reflective court: Dialogue as key for 'quality work' in the Swedish judiciary. In: Langbroek P (ed) Quality management in courts. Strasbourg, pp 1–27
Contini F, Carnevali D (2010) The quality of justice in Europe: Conflicts, dialogue, and politics. Italian National Research Council: Research Institute on Judicial Systems
Contini F, Mohr R (2007) Reconciling independence and accountability in judicial systems. Utrecht Law Rev 3(2):26–43
Davis LA, Garrett PA (2014) Case time and cost management for plaintiffs in multidistrict litigation. Louisiana Law Review 74:483–506
Didier Jr F (2001) Sobre dois importantes, e esquecidos, princípios do processo: Adequação e adaptabilidade do procedimento. Revista dos Mestrandos em Direito da UFBA: 224–238
Didier Jr F (2008) Apontamentos para a concretização do princípio da eficiência do processo. Revista Magister de Direito Civil e Processual Civil 52. Available at: http://www.lex.com.br/doutrina_24598622_APONTAMENTOS_PARA_A_CONCRETIZACAO_DO_PRINCIPIO_DA_EFICIENCIA_DO_PROCESSO.aspx. Accessed June 2020
Didier Jr F (2016) Curso de direito processual civil, vol 1, 18th edn. Salvador
Dodge J (2014) Facilitative judging: Organizational design in mass-multidistrict litigation. Emory Law J 64:329–382
Dos Santos Bedaque JR (2006) Efetividade do processo e técnica processual. São Paulo
Douglas J, Hartley R (2003) The politics of court budgeting in the states: Is judicial independence threatened by the budgetary process? Public Adm Rev 63:440–454
Eifert M (1997) Das neue Steuerungsmodell—Modell für die Modernisierung der Gerichtsverwaltung? Die Verwaltung: 75–96
Fabri M, Jean JP, Langbroek P, Pauliat H (eds) (2005) L'administration de la justice en Europe et l'évaluation de sa qualité. Montchrestien
Ferejohn J (1999) Independent judges, dependent judiciary: Explaining judicial independence. Southern California Law Rev 72:353–384
Fix-Fierro H (2003) Courts, justice, and efficiency: A socio-legal study of economic rationality in adjudication. Oregon
Flood J, Whyte A, Banakar R, Webb J (2007) Case assignment in English courts. In: Langbroek P, Fabri M (eds) The right judge for each case: A study of case assignment and impartiality in six European judiciaries. Antwerp, pp 133–188
Gajardoni F (2008) A flexibilização do procedimento processual no âmbito da common law. Revista de Processo 163:161–178
Gajardoni F, Dellore L, Roque A, Oliveira Jr Z (2015) Comentários ao CPC de 2015: Parte geral. São Paulo
Garcia Medina JM (2015) Direito processual civil moderno. São Paulo

Hess B (2006) Effektiver Rechtsschutz vor staatlichen Gerichten aus deutscher und vergleichender Sicht. In: Gottwald P (ed) Effektivität des Rechtsschutzes vor staatlichen und privaten Gerichten. Bielefeld, pp 121–170

Hoffmann-Riem W (1997) Wahrheit, Gerechtigkeit, Unabhängigkeit und Effizienz—Das Magische Viereck der Dritten Gewalt? Juristen Zeitung: 1–8

Hol A, Loth M (2004) Reshaping justice: Judicial reform and adjudication in the Netherlands. Maastricht

Hurst P (2009) Costs orders as a case management tool. In: Dwyer D (ed) The civil procedure rules ten years on. Oxford, pp 171–181

Jeuland E (2017) Toward a new court management and the rise of the court manager. General report, IAPL Conference 2017 (unpublished)

Karpen U (1999) Brauchen wir einen Gerichtsmanager? In: Isensee J, Lecheler H (eds) Freiheit und Eigentum: Festschrift für Walter Leisner zum 70. Geburtstag, Berlin, pp 989–1001

Kramer B (2001) Modernisierung der Justiz: Das Neue Steuerungsmodell. Neue Juristische Wochenschrift 47:3449–3453

Langbroek PM (2007) Case assignment in Dutch courts. In: Langbroek PM, Fabri M (eds) The right judge for each case: A study of case assignment and impartiality in six European judiciaries. Antwerp, pp 105–131

Langbroek PM, Fabri M (2007a) Internal case assignment and judicial impartiality: Comparative analysis. In: Langbroek PM, Fabri M (eds) The right judge for each case: A study of case assignment and impartiality in six European judiciaries. Antwerp, pp 17–22

Langbroek PM, Fabri M (2007b) Is there a right judge for each case? A comparative study of case assignment in six European countries. European J Legal Stud 1(2):292–315

Loth MA, De Werd MFJ (2003) Teilaspekte der Gerichtsorganisation in den Niederlanden im Überblick. Deutsche Richterzeitung

Machado Alves T (2016) O gerenciamento processual no Código de Processo Civil de 2015: Mecanismos para a gestão cooperativa da instrução probatória e integração da atuação dos sujeitos processuais. PhD thesis, Universidade do Estado do Rio de Janeiro

Mak E (2008) Balancing territoriality and functionality: Specialisation as a tool for reforming jurisdiction in the Netherlands, France, and Germany. International Journal for Court Administration: 1–8

Marcus RL (2008) Cure-all for an era of dispersed litigation? Toward a maximalist use of the multidistrict litigation panel's transfer power. Tulane Law Review 82:2245–2296

Marinoni LG, Arenhart S, Mitidiero D (2016) Curso de processo civil, vol 2. São Paulo

Mäurer U (2000) Justiz—Aufbruch oder Abbruch? Ressourceneinsatz und Arbeitsleistung der Justiz, Deutsche Richterzeitung: 65ff

McGovern FE (1983) Management of multiparty toxic tort litigation: Case law and trends affecting case management. The Forum 19:1–23

McGovern FE (1986) Toward a functional approach for managing complex litigation. University of Chicago Law Rev 53:440–493

McGovern FE (1997) Rethinking cooperation among judges in mass tort litigation. UCLA Law Review 44:1851–1870

Mitidiero D (2013) Cortes superiores e cortes supremas: Do controle à interpretação, da jurisprudência ao precedente. São Paulo

Molot JT (2003) An old judicial role for a new litigation era. Yale Law Journal 113:27–118

Moreira JCB, Novidade U (2001) O código de processo civil inglês. In: Temas de direito processual—sétima série. São Paulo, pp 185–186

Ng GY, Velicogna M, Dallara C (2008) Monitoring and evaluation of courts activities and performance. Int J Court Administration 1(1):58–64

Oliveira CA, Mitidiero D (2012) Curso de processo civil, 2nd edn. São Paulo

Papier HJ (2002) Zur Selbsverwaltung der Dritten Gewalt. Neue Juristische Wochenschrift: 2585ff

Pauliat H (2008) Le modèle français d'administration de la justice: Distinctions et convergences entre justice judiciaire et justice administrative. Revue française d'administration publique 125(1):93–110
Peckham RF (1981) The federal judge as a case manager: The new role in guiding a case from filing to disposition. California Law Review 69:770–805
Porcelli F (2009) Measurement of technical efficiency: A brief survey of parametric and non-parametric techniques. Paper, University of Warwick. Available at: http://www2.warwick.ac.uk/fac/soc/economics/staff/fporcelli/porcelli_dea_sfm.pdf. Accessed June 2020
Resnik J (1982) Managerial judges. Harvard Law Rev 96(2):374–448
Resnik J (1986) Failing faith: Adjucatory procedure in decline. University of Chicago Law Review 53:494–560
Resnik J (1991) From cases to litigation. Law and Contemporary Problems 54(3):5–68
Röhl KF (1998) Vom Gerichtsmanagement zur Selbstverwaltung der Justiz. Deutsche Richterzeitung: 241–250
Roque A (2014) Arbitragem de direitos coletivos no Brasil: Admissibilidade, finalidade e estrutura. PhD thesis, Universidade do Estado do Rio de Janeiro
Scott J, Sturm SP (2006) Courts as catalysts: Rethinking the judicial role in new governance. Columbia Journal of European Law 13(3):565–594
Sodan H (2005) Das Spannungsverhältnis von Qualität und Quantität in der Justiz. Die Öffentliche Verwaltung: 764–771
Sorabji J (2017) Managing claims. General report. IAPL Conference 2017 (unpublished)
Strong SI (2016) Class, mass, and collective arbitration in national and international law. J Int Econ Law 19(3):749–754
Tiemi Ono T (2016) A flexibilização procedimental: Uma comparação entre os sistemas jurídicos brasileiro, inglês e português. Revista de Processo 254:407–427
Turner R (2009) 'Actively': The word that changed the civil courts. In: Dwyer D (ed) The civil procedure rules ten years on. Oxford, pp 77–88
Uzelac A (2010) Privatization of enforcement services: A step forward for countries in transition? In: Van Rhee CH, Uzelac A (eds) Enforcement and enforceability: Tradition and reform. Antwerp, pp 83–101
Uzelac A (2014) Mixed blessing of judicial specialisation: The devil is in the details. Russian Law J 2(4):1–17
Van Loggerenberg D (2014) Specialization of South African judges and courts: Multi-skilled, multi-tasked, multi-access. Russian Law J 2(4):187–203
Van Rhee CH (2008) Introduction. In: Van Rhee CH (ed) Judicial case mangement and efficiency in civil litigation. Antwerp, pp 1–9
Wang F (2017) The history and future of civil judicial management in China. IAPL Conference 2017 (unpublished)
Wheeler R (1979) Judicial reform: Basic issues and references. Policy Studies Journal 8(1):134–149
Yarkov V, Abolonin V (2010) Enforcement in Russia: A short outline. In: Van Rhee CH, Uzelac A (eds) Enforcement and enforceability: Tradition and reform. Antwerp, pp 217–232
Yeazell S (1989) Collective litigation as collective action. Unive Illinois Law Rev 1989(1):43–68

Structure of the Court System and Case Management: Lessons from England & Wales

John Sorabji

Abstract This paper discusses the approach to case management taken in English and Welsh civil procedure. It examines the nature of case- and costs management of proceedings, while looking at the purpose for which cases are to be managed. In respect of the latter, it outlines how English and Welsh case management is to be carried out to secure proportionality through 'dealing with cases justly' rather than securing 'justice on the merits'. Additionally, it considers how this aim is achieved through structural features of case management i.e., through procedural case tracks which give expression to a form of structural proportionality within the Civil Procedure Rules. Finally, it examines recent innovations in case management through looking at both the move from case management to dispute management and then developments that provide for greater party control over the scope of procedure.

1 Introduction

Case management has a long, albeit chequered, history in English and Welsh (English) civil procedure. It was first attempted via the summons for directions procedure following significant reforms to English civil justice in the 1870s. Repeated failed attempts to make that process work were made during the 20th century.[1] Discrete developments saw it introduced in Commercial Court and Technology and Construction Court proceedings.[2] General case management applicable to all civil proceedings was then proposed, but not implemented, in the 1980s.[3] Its introduction was, once again, recommended in the 1990s as part of the Woolf Reforms in the light of developments in case management in the United States of America and

[1] Rosenbaum (1917, p. 75ff), Diamond (1959, p. 43).

[2] Reynolds (2010, p. 194).

[3] Hodgson (1988, pp. 154–162).

J. Sorabji (✉)
University College of London, London, UK
e-mail: j.sorabji@ucl.ac.uk

P. C. H. Chan and C. H. van Rhee (eds.), *Civil Case Management in the Twenty-First Century: Court Structures Still Matter*, Ius Gentium: Comparative Perspectives on Law and Justice 85, https://doi.org/10.1007/978-981-33-4512-6_10

Australia.[4] That recommendation finally and formally introduced case management into English civil procedure via the Civil Procedure Rules in 1999.[5] Its introduction was further supplemented, following further reforms in 2013, by costs management i.e., by court management of party costs of proceedings.[6]

In this contribution the following aspects of English case and costs management are considered: first, its purpose; secondly, the nature of case and costs management, including the introduction and operation of procedural case tracks as an aspect of case management; and, finally, developments in case management.

2 Case Management's Purpose

The civil court structure, which is funded by a combination of general taxation and litigant fees,[7] in England is both hierarchical and specialised. Its hierarchy is straightforward.[8] The apex court is the United Kingdom Supreme Court.[9] It has no trial jurisdiction, and only hears appeals which raise points of law of general public importance.[10] Below the UK Supreme Court is the Court of Appeal of England and Wales. It has both civil and criminal appellate jurisdiction. In civil matters, it hears both first appeals, i.e., appeals from trial judgments or interim applications, and second appeals i.e., appeals from decisions made on a first appeal from, for instance the High Court.[11] It too has no trial jurisdiction.

Below the Court of Appeal sits the High Court, which has trial, appellate and supervisory (judicial review) jurisdictions. It is divided into three specialist Divisions: the Queen's Bench Division; the Family Division; and the Chancery Division.

[4]Woolf (1995, pp. 26–56), Woolf (1996, pp. 14–91); see, for instance in respect of the United States, Resnik (1982, p. 374).

[5]CPR 1.4; CPR Part 3; and see PD (Case Management) [1995] 1 WLR 262.

[6]CPR 3.12–3.18.

[7]Brooke (2008). The relationship between the two is predicated on the assumption that the civil courts should be entirely self-funded from fee income, see Ministry of Justice (2013, p. 4 and 9), as *per* Vara S, M.P, 'For many years [now], the civil and family courts have operated under the principle that those who use the courts should pay the full cost of the service they receive'. That objective is, however, yet to be realised. The approach to fee income has no bearing on the court's structure or its approach to case management.

[8]For a detailed outline see, Chase et al. (2017, pp. 167–170).

[9]Strictly speaking it is not a court of England and Wales. The United Kingdom is divided into three wholly separate legal jurisdictions: England and Wales; Scotland; and Northern Ireland. Each jurisdiction has its own judges, court structures and legal professions. The United Kingdom Supreme Court is not a part of any of these jurisdictions. It is separate from them, but hears civil appeals from each of the apex appellate courts within those jurisdictions.

[10]Appeals are not as of right. Either the UK Supreme Court or the Court of Appeal must grant permission to appeal. The UK Supreme Court as a consequence of the permission to appeal requirement and the general public importance threshold test hears between 80–120 appeals per year. See UK Supreme Court (2018) for further details on appeal numbers.

[11]For a detailed account of the nature of the civil appeal process, see Burton (2013).

Within those Divisions further specialisation is achieved through, for instance, the Commercial Court, the Technology and Construction Court and the Patent Court. Further specialisation is then achieved through 'specialist lists' which sit within those courts e.g., the Financial List. Such specialisation is intended to ensure that claims are allocated to judges with appropriate expertise within the court structure.[12] The High Court's trial jurisdiction is generally confined to money claims over a value of £100,000.[13] Finally, below the High Court sits the County Court, which has both trial and appellate jurisdiction; the latter being a form of internal appeal where a decision of a district judge (the junior level of County Court judge) may be appealed in certain instances to a Circuit Judge (the senior level of County Court judge).[14]

Historically, the English courts operated under two distinct civil procedural codes: the Rules of the Supreme Court governed practice and procedure in the High Court and Court of Appeal; and, the County Court Rules did the same in the County Court.[15] The latter differing substantively from the former due to their greater simplicity: a mark of the need for a more proportionate, cost-effective approach to the lower value claims that were to remain the County Court's fundamental focus. Both sets of rules operated according to what might now be described as an implicit overriding objective: that practice and procedure should be applied by the court consistently, as Zuckerman rightly described it with *the principle of doing justice on the merits* i.e., substantive justice.[16] In Bowen LJ's words, the RSC—and equally the CCR—were to be applied by the courts in order to ensure that they were able ... *to decide the rights of parties* ...[17] In 1999 the RSC and CCR and their implicit overriding objective were replaced by a new singular civil procedural code applicable to all civil proceedings in the Court of Appeal, High Court and County Court: the Civil Procedure Rules (CPR),[18] and its explicit overriding objective, which as now formulated states that the court must *deal with cases justly and at proportionate cost*.[19] As the Chief Justice of Hong Kong's Civil Justice Reform Working Party correctly noted this did not mean that the new procedural rules were to be applied so as to secure justice on the merits or substantive justice.[20] On the contrary, it marked a significant shift in procedural philosophy away from that aim.[21] This shift takes as its starting point that the achievement of justice on the merits remains fundamental. It is however no

---

[12]UK Courts and Tribunals Judiciary (2017).

[13]For a full account of its and the County Court's jurisdiction see: High Court and County Courts Jurisdiction Order (1991).

[14]See CPR Part 52.

[15]See the Rules of the Supreme Court (SI 1776/1965) and County Court Rules (SI 1687/1981).

[16]Zuckerman (2006, p. 27).

[17]*Cropper v Smith* (1884) 26 ChD 700, pp. 710–711.

[18]SI 3132/1998.

[19]CPR 1.1.

[20]See Chief Justice's Working Party on Civil Justice Reform (2004, pp. 46 and 48–49), Meggitt and Aslam (2009, p. 111).

[21]*Three Rivers District Council and Others v Governor and Company of the Bank of England (No 3)* [2003] 2 AC 1, p. 153.

longer to be an unalloyed objective of procedure. It is to be treated as equal to, and balanced by, a commitment to achieve procedural justice, a fair process. By this is not however simply meant a fair process for particular litigants in any particular case before the courts. If that were the case, it would be all too easy for fair process to be equated with a process that was sufficient to provide a fair trial and a judgment on the merits. In other words, it would be easy to conflate fair process with securing justice on the merits. On the contrary, fair process was to be judged by whether the court could—while securing a cost-effective, efficient and speedy process for parties to particular claims—ensure that sufficient court resources were available to enable other claims to obtain an equitable, a proportionate, share of the court's overall resources.[22] As Lord Dyson MR described it, the CPR's overriding objective required that no individual claim should receive more than its fair share of the court's time and resources.[23] The reason for this was that

> Doing the proper administration of justice goes beyond the immediate parties to litigation. It requires the court to consider the needs of all litigants, all court-users. This idea finds expression in the overriding objective.[24]

As he went on to say, *Dealing with cases justly does not simply mean ensuring that a decision is reached on the merits. It is a mistake to assume it does.*[25] This reform was then explained in more detail by Lord Dyson MR in the Court of Appeal's judgment in the Mitchell decision, when it endorsed his previous extra-judicial explanation of the new approach under the CPR's overriding objective as follows:

> … the Woolf reforms and now the Jackson reforms were and are not intended to render the overriding objective, or rule 3.9, subject to an overarching consideration of securing justice in the individual case. If that had been the intention, a tough application to compliance would have been difficult to justify and even more problematic to apply in practice. The fact that since 1999 the tough rules to which Lord Justice Brooke referred have not been applied with sufficient rigour is testament to a failure to understand that that was not the intention.
>
> The revisions [in 2013] to the overriding objective and to rule 3.9, and particularly the fact that rule 3.9 now expressly refers back to the revised overriding objective, are intended to make clear that the relationship between justice and procedure has changed. It has changed not by transforming rules and rule compliance into trip wires. Nor has it changed it by turning the rules and rule compliance into the mistress rather than the handmaid of justice. If that were the case then we would have, quite impermissibly, rendered compliance an end in itself and one superior to doing justice in any case. It has changed because doing justice is not something distinct from, and superior to, the overriding objective. Doing justice in each set of proceedings is to ensure that proceedings are dealt with justly and at proportionate cost. Justice in the individual case is now only achievable through the proper application of the CPR consistently with the overriding objective.[26]

---

[22]For a detailed discussion see, Sorabji (2014).

[23]Woolf (1995, p. 26).

[24]Sorabji (2014, p. 128). Also see *Beachley Property Ltd v Edgar* [1997] PNLR 197, p. 6, as *per* Lord Woolf MR.

[25]Sorabji (2014, p. 127).

[26]Sorabji (2014, p. 131), as endorsed in *Mitchell v News Group Newspapers Ltd* [2013] EWCA Civ 1537, [2014] 1 WLR 795, paras. 38 and 39. In this Lord Dyson MR echoed Woolf (1996, p. 24),

The starting point then to understand case management in England is that: first, the same approach applies across all civil courts due to the introduction of a single procedural code, the CPR, in 1999; and secondly, and crucially, that code is not intended to enable or ensure that the civil process is applied by the courts so as to ensure justice on the merits in each individual claim. The civil process is, on the contrary, as focused on securing effective distributive justice for all litigants as it is corrective justice for individual claims. This is to be achieved by ensuring that each claim receives no more than a proportionate share of the court's overall resources, as anything more than that would improperly reduce the share available to other litigants in other proceedings.[27] In certain cases this would mean that the court would have to refuse to permit a claim to proceed to trial and judgment.[28] As the Court of Appeal explained in *Vinos v Marks & Spencer Plc*,

> Justice to the defendant and to the interests of other litigants may require that a claimant who ignores time limits prescribed by the rules forfeits the right to have his claim tried.[29]

In other cases, it would mean refusing the parties to take certain procedural steps, such as submitting evidence, which might reduce the court's ability to secure justice on the merits i.e., it might reduce the quality of justice.[30] While such decisions might appear unjust in the context of individual cases, they were however just when the individual case in which such steps were taken was, and is, viewed in the broader context of securing access to an effective justice system for all litigants.[31] This new approach to litigation saw then the replacement of a commitment to achieve substantive justice to a commitment to achieving proportionate justice.[32]

---

when he stated that 'to … preserve access to justice for all users of the system it is necessary to ensure that individual users do not use more of the system's resources than their case requires. This means that the court must consider the effect of their choice on other users of the system.'

[27] A point also and quite properly emphasised in respect of comparative approaches taken in Australia and Vanuatu: see *Aon Risk Services Australia Ltd v Australian National University* [2009] HCA 27; and, Jensel (2010, p. 28), 'Proportionality principle—This is associated with the philosophical theories of 'distributive justice', … The central theme of the Woolf report [which formed the basis of the CPR] was that a sense of proportionality should guide the management of litigation—to apply the limited resources available within the civil justice system in such a way as to meet the greatest need …'

[28] *Flaxman-Binns v Lincolnshire County Council* [2004] 1 WLR 2232.

[29] *Ibidem*, para. 26.

[30] A point Lord Woolf MR had emphasised in the run-up to the CPR's introduction in *Beachley Property Ltd v Edgar* [1997] PNLR 197.

[31] See both *Mitchell v News Group Newspapers Ltd* [2013] EWCA Civ 1537, [2014] 1 WLR 795 and, in respect of Australia, *Aon Risk Services Australia Ltd v Australian National University* [2009] HCA 27.

[32] Sorabji (2014).

3 The Nature of Case and Costs Management

The CPR's overriding objective specified the aim of procedure and how it was to be carried out. It was thus a purposive provision, which set the direction of travel for the CPR. The CPR did not only effect this principled change to the approach to litigation, it also effected a substantive change to the manner in which cases would be managed. It did so initially in two ways through the introduction of procedural case tracks and the introduction of court-controlled case management. These mechanisms were added to in 2013 when, as a consequence of reform recommendations made by Sir Rupert Jackson, costs management was introduced.[33]

4 Procedural Case Tracks—Structural Proportionality

English civil justice had since the early 19th century worked on the assumption that not all claims required the same level of process. With the introduction of the County Courts in the 1840s,[34] a two-tier civil justice system existed with simpler, lower value claims being dealt with under the simpler, more rudimentary and cheaper procedure in those courts, while the more complex and high value cases were dealt with in the superior common law and chancery courts[35] and then, from the 1870s, the High Court and Court of Appeal.[36] This rudimentary approach to matching claims to process was, however, identified as being deficient in the 1990s. For instance, the simplest, lowest value claim in the County Court would have received the same process as the most complex, highest value claim in that court. Notwithstanding the dual forms of process afforded by the RSC and CCR a 'one-size fits all' approach to process was in fact in place in both the County and High Courts. As the Woolf Report put it critically, *the same procedures to all cases regardless of financial weight, complexity or importance.*[37]

To overcome this, in effect blanket approach, the Woolf reforms introduced a more tailored approach; one which built on the hierarchical approach to proportionality that the existence of the County and High Courts instantiated. This new approach centred on the introduction into English civil procedure of a form of structural proportionality via the creation of three procedural case tracks: the small claims track; a fast track; and a multi-track.[38] While all three tracks are available in the County Court, only the multi-track is available in the High Court. Allocation to track is primarily determined

[33] Jackson (2009). For a clear explanation of the costs management reforms see: Jackson (2016, pp. 127–139).

[34] The County Courts (England) Act 1846.

[35] The Courts of Common Pleas, of King's or Queen's Bench, of Exchequer, and the Court of Chancery.

[36] Following the Judicature Act 1873–1875 reforms; see Sorabji (2014, p. 14).

[37] Woolf (1995, p. 19).

[38] *Ibidem*, p. 28.

by claim value. Value is not, however, determinative.[39] Other factors that go to determine allocation are: the remedy sought; the complexity of the issues; the amount of oral evidence required; the views and circumstances of the parties.[40]

The small claims track applies to claims with a value up to £10,000 (albeit personal injury claims for which the value is up to £1,000 are allocated to the small claims track). It offers a very rudimentary form of process. Disclosure is limited to documents parties intend to rely upon. Expert evidence is not the norm. Case management directions are standardised[41] and case management hearings are rarely necessary and rarely take place. Trials are listed for an hour to three hours and operate an informal process, in which the judge has a generally investigative role i.e., the norms of the adversarial process do not generally apply. Fixed and limited cost recovery applies.[42] The fast track offers a greater but still limited form of process and is for claims with a value above £10,000 and up to £25,000. Disclosure is generally limited to documents parties intend to rely upon and those which are adverse to their case. Expert evidence is limited to a single, joint, expert witness.[43] The pre-trial process is limited in time[44] and trials are limited to a day, with a fixed recoverable cost regime broadly in place.[45] The multi-track is reserved for claims above £25,000.[46] This provides the whole panoply of procedure, with case management directions matching the process to the claim on a case-by-case basis.[47] Given the dissimilarity of claims above £25,000, a fourth track, the intermediate track which would operate on a fixed recoverable cost basis, may be introduced as a result of recent reform recommendations, which accepted that the current three track approach did not provide a sufficient degree of process matching to claim value i.e., it was an approach that did not give effect to structural proportionality effectively.[48] If introduced this new track will apply to claims between the value of £25,000 and £100,000.[49]

---

[39] Woolf (1996, p. 9), CPR 26.6(3); CPR 26.6(4); CPR 26.7(1).

[40] CPR 26.8(1).

[41] These being, that '1 Each party must deliver to every other party and to the court office copies of all documents on which he intends to rely at the hearing no later than ... [14 days before the hearing] (These should include the letter making the claim and the reply); 2 The original documents must be brought to the hearing; 3 [Notice of hearing date and time allowed]; 4 The parties are encouraged to contact each other with a view to trying to settle the case or narrow the issues. However the court must be informed immediately if the case is settled by agreement before the hearing date; 5 No party may rely at the hearing on any report from an expert unless express permission has been granted by the court beforehand. Anyone wishing to rely on an expert must write to the court immediately on receipt of this Order and seek permission, giving an explanation why the assistance of an expert is necessary': see CPR PD27 Annex B; CPR 27.4(1)(b).

[42] See CPR Part 27.

[43] CPR 28.2(1); CPR PD28 Appendix.

[44] CPR PD 28 para. 3.12. Trials are to take place within thirty weeks of allocation to the fast track.

[45] See CPR Part 28.

[46] CPR Part 26.

[47] See CPR Part 29; esp., CPR 29.2.

[48] Jackson (2017).

[49] *Ibidem*, pp. 99–113.

Through providing three, and perhaps soon four, procedural templates the procedural case tracks are the primary means through which the CPR implements a proportionate approach to case management. It embeds at a sub-macro level, the macro level being that created by the County and High Court hierarchy, the CPR's overriding objective within the overall structure of civil process.[50] The case tracks are thus the primary means through which, as May LJ put it, the CPR is able,

> … so far as is practicable, [to] allot to individual cases an appropriate share of the court's resources while taking account of the need to allot resources to other cases.[51]

To achieve this, in a way, promotes proportionality. Through creating three broad forms of process applicable to different categories of claim, the CPR avoids the need of using court time and resources, and party time and resources, devising a *bespoke procedure* for each claim.[52] It thus facilitates a more efficient rationing of procedure, which could not occur if the court had to spend its time devising specific forms of pre-trial case management on a case-to-case basis. Equally, through adopting what can be described as a 'value-plus' approach to track allocation, the CPR's case tracks ensure that different cases—albeit categories of case—are treated differently. A one-size fits all approach is not in place because: first, low value cases are afforded a different level and degree of process than mid- and high value cases; and secondly, where other factors justify it a case may and can be allocated to a track other than that to which their value would otherwise assign it i.e., a low value claim that involves allegations of fraud or dishonesty calling for a greater degree of disclosure and cross-examination than otherwise available on the small claims track could be allocated to the fast or multi-track. In this way, the court can ensure that cases are allocated sufficient process to enable them to be managed justly and proportionately both in terms of what that particular case requires and in terms of the need to ensure that no more than a proportionate share of the court's resources are allocated to each case. At the sub-macro, structural, level the case tracks thus provide procedural, case management templates which promote both proportionate justice for the individual claim but also for the justice system as a whole.[53]

5 Case Management

Within each of the procedural case tracks individual claims will be subject to case management. As noted above, this will be minimal, and generally unnecessary, for small claims. For fast track and multi-track claims there will however be active court-based case management; active on the part of the court because it rather than the parties is in control of the case management process. This is a consequence of

---

[50]That it did so was not without criticism, see Sorabji (2014, p. 191), for a discussion.

[51]*Adoko v Jemal* CA 22 June 1999, para. 7.

[52]Zuckerman (2014, p. 633).

[53]CPR 1.1(2)(e).

the Woolf reforms which eliminated party-control of case management in order to enable the court to give proper effect to it, and through case management, to the CPRs' overriding objective.[54] As Lord Clarke MR explained it,

> Taken together, the overriding objective [in CPR Pt 1] and active judicial case management [notably CPR r.3.1] seek to ensure that each case is afforded no more than a proportionate amount of judicial and party resources, that the real issues in dispute are identified and concentrated upon by the court and the parties, and that the claim is dealt with expeditiously.[55]

This is achieved through procedural judges taking control of the management of claims from the time they are allocated to track; allocation being based on information provided by the court to the parties via the parties' statements of case and then a Directions Questionnaire.[56] While this is not done via docketing of cases to specific procedural judges, that possibility exists albeit it is not used generally,[57] it is done through management, and the tailoring of case management directions within the scope permitted by each track, by specialist procedural judges—district judges in the County Court and Masters in the High Court. Given the differential approach to case management across the three case tracks there is, inevitably, greater hands-on case management in the fast and multi-track than in the small claims track; the greatest degree of case management being in the multi-track. The effective management of claims by the court in furtherance of the overriding objective includes the following actions:

(a) *encouraging the parties to co-operate with each other in the conduct of the proceedings;*
(b) *identifying the issues at an early stage;*
(c) *deciding promptly which issues need full investigation and trial and accordingly disposing summarily of the others;*
(d) *deciding the order in which issues are to be resolved;*
(e) *encouraging the parties to use an alternative dispute resolution procedure if the court considers that appropriate and facilitating the use of such procedure;*
(f) *helping the parties to settle the whole or part of the case;*
(g) *fixing timetables or otherwise controlling the progress of the case;*
(h) *considering whether the likely benefits of taking a particular step justify the cost of taking it;*
(i) *dealing with as many aspects of the case as it can on the same occasion;*
(j) *dealing with the case without the parties needing to attend at court;*
(k) *making use of technology; and*
(l) *giving directions to ensure that the trial of a case proceeds quickly and efficiently.*[58]

---

[54] CPR 1.2; CPR 1.3; CPR 1.4; CPR Part 3; *Kesslar v Moore & Tibbits* [2005] PNLR 17, para. 27.

[55] Clarke (2007).

[56] CPR 26.3(1).

[57] For a discussion of docketing see Jackson (2016, pp. 101–102).

[58] CPR 1.4.

Case management is not, however, simply based on the idea that the court is in charge of the pre-trial process. It is not a straightforward reversal of the pre-CPR position where, as an aspect of the principle of party autonomy, the parties had control over the pre-trial process. The approach to case management is essentially a partnership between court and parties, with the court taking the leading role and the parties being required to co-operate with the court in ensuring that the case management process is carried out effectively. This co-operative approach is given expression through the imposition of an obligation on parties to assist the court in furthering the case management process.[59] It is one thing to create such an obligation, it is however another to ensure that it operates effectively. Here arises a fundamental problem for case management: procedural non-compliance.

Compliance with case management directions i.e., effective co-operation by parties with the court, is essential if the court is to ensure that claims are dealt with justly and at proportionate cost. It is necessary to ensure that claims only utilise their fair share of the court's time and resources and do not, by utilising more than that, adversely affect other litigants and their ability to receive and utilise a fair share of those resources. Historically non-compliance with procedural obligations bedevilled English civil procedure. Non-compliance was generally forgiven in order to enable the court to ensure that claims were determined on their substantive merits i.e., so as to ensure justice on the merits was done.[60] The basis of this approach was articulated most clearly by Bowen LJ in *Cropper v Smith* (1884) 26 Ch D 700, when he explained the approach courts should take to non-compliance and the question whether relief from sanctions for non-compliance should be granted,

> … the object of the Courts is to decide the rights of parties, and not to punish them for mistakes they make in the conduct of their cases by deciding otherwise than in accordance with their rights … I know of no kind of error or mistake which, if not fraudulent or intended to overreach, the Court ought not to correct, if it can be done without injustice to the other party. Courts do not exist for the sake of discipline, but for the sake of deciding matters in controversy, … It seems to me that as soon as it appears that the way in which a party had framed his case will not lead to a decision of the real matter in controversy, it is as much a matter of right on his part to have it corrected, if it can be done without injustice … It could always be done without injustice if a payment of costs could remedy any prejudice, as 'costs were the universal panacea'.[61]

The problem with this approach was, as Zuckerman has rightly pointed out, that it led to a generally complacent approach to the prosecution of claims. Knowing that the court's approach was one which tended towards leniency in the pursuit of justice on the merits, led lawyers to adopt an approach to rule-compliance which treated directions as guidelines to be followed at will rather than as rules to be complied with. A culture of non-compliance in turn led to a culture of satellite litigation as non-defaulting parties sought to persuade the court not to follow its general approach but

---

[59]CPR 1.3.

[60]Sorabji (2014, pp. 67–74), Zuckerman (2015, p. 1).

[61]*Cropper v Smith* (1884) 26 Ch D 700, pp. 710–711. The origin of the approach was, however, *Tildesley v Harper* 10 ChD 393.

to enforce sanctions for non-compliance on the facts of their particular case. Non-compliance, complacency and satellite litigation led to a particularly acute form of adversarial litigation culture, which the Woolf reforms criticised,[62] and which resulted in claims being conducted inefficiently and at excess cost.[63]

To ensure that the culture of complacency was not replicated under the CPR, the courts were to take a stricter approach to non-compliance with case management directions. This did not however take effect from 1999, primarily because the courts continued to approach questions of non-compliance on the basis that the CPR's overriding objective gave precedence to securing justice on the merits.[64] By 2009, ten years after the CPR was introduced, the approach to case management and non-compliance was noted to be as follows,

> … courts at all levels have become too tolerant of delays and non-compliance with orders. In so doing they have lost sight of the damage which the culture of delay and non-compliance is inflicting upon the civil justice system. The balance therefore needs to be redressed.[65]

Following reforms in 2013 the culture of complacency came to an abrupt halt. Following two Court of Appeal judgments which emphasised the importance of rule compliance to render case management effective and the need to do this to secure the effective distribution of court resources across all litigants whilst ensuring that parties litigated at proportionate cost to themselves, the approach from *Cropper v Smith* was consigned to history.[66] The present approach to non-compliance with case management directions is now, as summarised by the High Court in *Su-Ling v Goldman Sachs International* [2015] EWHC 759 (Comm), that

> a much stricter view is taken nowadays of non-compliance with the Civil Procedure Rules and directions of the Court. The achievement of justice means something different now. Parties can no longer expect indulgence if they fail to comply with their procedural obligations because those obligations not only serve the purpose of ensuring that they conduct the litigation proportionately in order to ensure their own costs are kept within proportionate bounds but also the wider public interest of ensuring that other litigants can obtain justice efficiently and proportionately, and that the courts enable them to do so.[67]

The court in carrying out its various case management roles, and parties in assisting or co-operating with the court in the effective management of claims, do so now

---

[62] Woolf (1995, p. 8).

[63] Zuckerman (2003, p. 31), Zuckerman (2004).

[64] Sorabji (2015, p. 81).

[65] Jackson (2009, p. 397).

[66] *Mitchell v News Group Newspapers Ltd* [2013] EWCA Civ 1537; [2014] WLR 795; *Denton v TH White Ltd & Others* [2014] EWCA Civ 906; [2014] 1 WLR 3926 at [81], where it was explained in the context of relief from the consequences of non-compliance, that while some '… judges have adopted what might be said to be the traditional approach of giving pre-eminence to the need to decide the claim on the merits. That approach should have disappeared following the Woolf reforms. There is certainly no room for it in the post-Jackson era'; *Prince Abdulaziz v Apex Global Management Ltd & Anor* (Rev 2 [2014] UKSC 64, [2014] WLR 4495; *The Prudential Assurance Company Ltd v HM Revenue and Customs* [2016] EWCA Civ 376 at [21].

[67] [2015] EWHC 759 (Comm), para. 38.

in the full knowledge that a strict approach to compliance is required and will be enforced. In this way, the English courts are adopting an approach which is eliminating both a culture of complacency over compliance with case management directions, and parties are no longer able to adopt such an approach and equally are being discouraged from engaging in satellite litigation concerning non-compliance. On the contrary, the courts are attempting to introduce a culture of co-operation in procedural matters between the parties and are actively discouraging them from seeking to take advantage of procedural mis-steps by their opponents.[68]

In 2013, as a consequence of the Jackson reforms,[69] case management was bolstered by an additional management obligation: costs management.[70] This was understood to be, as Jackson LJ put it, a 'logical consequence' of the introduction of case management.[71] In essence it requires the parties to consider at the start of a claim what work is going to be needed to be done throughout the course of proceedings, to prepare a budget for that work and then try to agree between each other that budget. As Jackson LJ described it, once that is done,

> The court must be satisfied that it is reasonable and proportionate for the parties to expend that level of costs on procedural steps.[72]

Once the costs budget is approved, unless the court agrees to vary it at a later stage, the parties will know the extent of costs that they may incur which are capable—in principle—of being recovered under the indemnity rule i.e., under the loser pays costs rule. The rationale for this innovation, which in practice was created with hostility by some lawyers,[73] was: first, it provided parties with a clear understanding of their potential cost risk if their claim or defence failed, while also giving them clarity over their own solicitor-client costs; secondly, and this flowed from the first point, it enabled clients to have the knowledge to exert more effective control over their own costs;[74] thirdly, it would help to ensure that the costs of litigation were kept within a defined budget, one which was proportionate to the value, complexity etc., of the claim; fourthly, it ensured that case management conferences were more effective. It had been noted that there was a tendency for such conferences, ones where the court was supposed to get to grips with cases and determine what specific management directions were needed, to become formulaic exercises. The need to engage more closely with the nature of the claim via the costs budget as part of the costs management process (which took place in what was to become a case and costs management hearing before a procedural judge) thus made case management more effective. As Jackson LJ put it, *Price tags attached to the work focus attention on*

---

[68] *Freeborn v Marcal* (t/a Dan Marcal Architects) [2017] EWHC 3046 (TCC).

[69] Jackson (2009).

[70] CPR 3.12–3.18; PD 3E—Costs Management.

[71] Jackson (2016, p. 127).

[72] *Ibidem.*

[73] *Ibidem*, p. 131.

[74] *Ibidem.*

the question of whether certain items of work really need to be done at all.[75] As such it better enabled the court to further the overriding objective. While it may be the case, as was noted in *Sharp v Blank: To adapt Søren Kierkegaard's well-known words: 'Litigation can only be understood backwards; but it can only be litigated forwards'*,[76] effective costs management, both in itself through requiring parties to focus on what needs to be done and at what cost, and by rendering through that case management more effective, is reshaping English procedure so that claims are managed from the start with a greater focus on the aim of ensuring that they are dealt with justly and at proportionate cost.

6 Developments in Case Management

The Woolf and Jackson reforms have embedded case and costs management into English civil procedure. In addition to these developments there have been two further discrete developments; the first concerns the growth of alternative dispute resolution (ADR), the second concerns specialist forms of case management procedure.

First, ADR. The court has no power to mandate the use of ADR as part of the case management process in England.[77] It does however have a duty, in furthering the overriding objective to promote the use of ADR. It has the power to take steps, as part of its case management functions, to encourage parties to engage in ADR.[78] Furthermore, it can require parties to take part in an early neutral evaluation process.[79] The court's approach to ADR is however undergoing development at the present time. This is taking place in two ways. First, there is a developing understanding that ADR is not something which stands outside or in competition to the case management process. On the contrary, the modern view is that ADR stands at the heart of the litigation process. As Lightman J put it in *Hurst v Leeming, ADR* lies *at the heart of today's civil justice system.*[80] It is because of a further consequence of the introduction of the Woolf reforms and the CPR's overriding objective. This is a fundamental shift in the approach taken to case management. Under the pre-Woolf system if case management had been introduced its aim would have been to manage claims to trial and judgment in order to better secure justice on the merits. The CPR and its focus on dealing with cases justly and at proportionate cost has meant a shift in approach. It is one that has only recently been realised and articulated. In an examination of the practice and procedure of the High Court's Chancery Division in the *Chancery Modernisation Review* of 2013, Sir Michael Briggs, concluded that case management under the CPR was not concerned with managing claims to trial and judgment. On the

[75] *Ibidem*, p. 133.

[76] [2017] EWHC 3390 (Ch), para. 25.

[77] *Halsey v Milton Keynes General NHS Trust* [2004] 1 WLR 3002.

[78] CPR 1.4(2)(e).

[79] CPR 3.1(2)(m).

[80] *Hurst v Leeming* [2001] EWHC 1051 (ChD).

contrary case management meant, and means under the CPR, *the management of the dispute resolution process as a whole.*[81] This marks a fundamental shift in approach away from the court and case management process taking the delivery of justice on the merits via a court judgment as the primary aim of the litigation process. Secondly, this is a shift which is currently being further developed through the creation of an online small claims process, which embeds facilitated negotiation, mediation and early neutral evaluation into the case management process; such ADR approaches to be carried out by legally trained court staff or case officers rather than by judges.[82] The intention here is to ensure that parties are not only provided with information about the availability of ADR schemes, but rather that ADR becomes a normal, generally applicable, step in the pre-trial process that the court will facilitate. Again, rather than being an adjunct to the case management and trial process, by developing a new, mainly online, form of case management process for low value claims (at least initially), ADR is being taken into the mainstream process. Case management will not be pre-trial management. It will be dispute resolution management.

Secondly, specialist case management. Two forms of specialist case management procedure are currently being trialled, via pilot schemes within the CPR, in England. Each is available for high value commercial and business disputes i.e., they are aimed at cases that would otherwise be allocated to the multi-track. The two pilot schemes were: the shorter trial procedure,[83] and the flexible trial procedure.[84] These schemes are based on the idea that parties to high value, commercial disputes may—by agreement and with court approval—opt-out of the multi-track process. The two processes operate as follows,

> … The Shorter Trial Procedure provides for a fixed length trial of a maximum of four days, with the trial to be held within ten months of issue of proceedings. Claims are docketed and subject to limits on time to comply with procedural obligations and on disclosure and evidence.
>
> … The Flexible Trial Procedure enables the normal process to be adapted to the parties' needs. It aims at facilitating agreement on modifications, and limits, to disclosure, expert and other evidence and submissions.
>
> Both are intended to provide parties and their lawyers the opportunity to adopt a form of process that best serves their needs in the pursuit of judgment. Looked at in a broader context they are an innovation which seeks to bring the procedural flexibility of various forms of alternative dispute resolution within the formal court setting. As such they are intended to enable parties to ensure that procedural rules that are already well-adapted to their needs, can be individually tailored to an even greater extent.[85]

The pilot schemes are now incorporated formally into the CPR as CPR PD57AB. As yet these new procedures have been little utilised, although they provide the basis for parties and the court to adopt creative approaches to the management of

[81] Briggs (2013, p. 68).

[82] For a discussion see Sorabji (2017), Etherton (2017).

[83] CPR PD 51 N.

[84] CPR PD 51 N. Also see PD 51P—Pilot for Insolvency Express Trials.

[85] CPR PD 51 N; Thomas (2016, para. 35).

claims, albeit such creativity will need to remain consistent with the CPR's overriding objective.

7 Conclusion

Case management has since it was introduced in 1999 become an integral and effective part of English civil procedure. Its effective incorporation has not necessarily been smooth, as the problems concerning non-compliance illustrated. It is however now fully embedded into all areas of litigation and across claims of all values and types, albeit its application is tailored to the nature and requirements of particular cases at macro (Court), sub-macro (procedural case track) and micro (case specific case and costs management) levels. The age of the passive English judge is now long gone. Consistently with the overriding objective, it is applied both to promote access to trial and judgment and consensual dispute resolution via ADR. It is also in a state of development through the introduction of innovative, case management schemes which permit parties to devise their own forms of case management, and trial process, as well as through the development of new online schemes that embed ADR into the case management process itself. It is a feature of English civil procedure which is likely to see further developments in the future.

References

Briggs M (2013) Chancery modernisation review: Final report. https://www.judiciary.uk/wp-content/uploads/JCO/Documents/CMR/cmr-final-report-dec2013.pdf. Accessed July 2020

Brooke H (2008) Should the civil courts be unified? https://www.judiciary.gov.uk/wp-content/uploads/JCO/Documents/Speeches/brooke_report_ucc.pdf. Accessed 20 June 2020

Burton M (2013) Civil appeals, 2nd edn. London

Chase O, Hershkoff H, Silberman L, Sorabji J, Sturner R, Taniguchi M, Varano V (2017) Civil litigation in comparative context, 2nd edn. St. Paul, MN

Chief Justice's Working Party on Civil Justice Reform (2004) The final report of the Chief Justice's Working Party on Civil Justice Reform. 3 March 2004. https://www.civiljustice.hk/fr/documents/cjr_final_report.pdf. Accessed July 2020

Clarke MR (2007) The supercase—Problems and solutions: Reflections on BCCI and equitable life. Annual KPMG Forensic Lecture. 29 March 2007

County Court Rules (Northern Ireland) 1981

Diamond M (1959) The summons for directions. Law Quart Rev 75:43–52

Etherton T (2017) The civil court of the future. https://www.judiciary.gov.uk/wp-content/uploads/2017/06/slynn-lecture-mr-civil-court-of-the-future-20170615.pdf. Accessed 20 June 2020

High Court and County Courts Jurisdiction Order (1991). https://www.legislation.gov.uk/uksi/1991/724/contents/made. Accessed 20 June 2020

Hodgson M (1988) Civil justice review: Report of the review body on civil justice. London

Jackson R (2009) Review of civil litigation costs: Final report. London. https://www.judiciary.uk/wp-content/uploads/JCO/Documents/Reports/jackson-final-report-140110.pdf. Accessed July 2020

Jackson R (2016) The reform of civil litigation. London
Jackson R (2017) Review of civil litigation costs: Supplemental report fixed recoverable costs. Judicial Office. https://www.judiciary.gov.uk/wp-content/uploads/2017/07/fixed-recoverable-costs-supplemental-report-online-2-1.pdf. Accessed 20 June 2020
Jensel A (2010) Jensel's Civil Court's Practice. Canberra
Meggitt G, Aslam F (2009) Civil justice reform in Hong Kong—A critical appraisal. Civil Justice Quarterly 28:111–131
Ministry of Justice (2013) Court fees—Proposals for reform. https://consult.justice.gov.uk/digital-communications/court-fees-proposals-for-reform/supporting_documents/courtfeesconsultation.pdf. Accessed 20 June 2020
Resnik J (1982) Managerial judges. Harvard Law Rev 96:374–448
Reynolds M (2010) Of civil procedure and settlement. Civil Justice Quart 29(2):194–204
Rosenbaum S (1917) The rule-making authority in the English Supreme Court. Boston
Rules of the Supreme Court (1965 Reprint)
Sorabji J (2014) English civil justice after the Woolf and Jackson Reforms—A critical analysis. Cambridge
Sorabji R (2015) English civil justice: Another attempt at a new approach to justice. Revista de Processo 40(243):81–102
Sorabji J (2017) The online solutions court—A multi-door courthouse for the 21st Century. Civil Justice Quart 36(1):86–108
Thomas CJ (2016) Commercial justice in the global village: The role of commercial courts. https://www.judiciary.gov.uk/wp-content/uploads/2016/02/LCJ-commerical-justice-in-the-global-village-DIFC-Academy-of-Law-Lecture-February-2016.pdf. Accessed 20 June 2020
UK Courts and Tribunals Judiciary (2017) Launch of Business and Property Courts. https://www.judiciary.gov.uk/announcements/launch-of-business-and-property-courts/. Accessed 20 June 2020
UK Supreme Court (2018) The Supreme Court annual report and accounts. https://www.supremecourt.uk/news/the-supreme-court-annual-report-and-accounts.html. Accessed 20 June 2020
Woolf L (1995) Access to justice: Interim report. London. https://www.i-law.com/ilaw/doc/view.htm?id=36837. Accessed July 2020
Woolf L (1996) Access to justice: Final report. London. https://webarchive.nationalarchives.gov.uk/20060213223540/, http://www.dca.gov.uk/civil/final/contents.htm. Accessed July 2020
Zuckerman AAS (2003) Civil procedure. London
Zuckerman AAS (2004) Enforcing compliance with deadlines. Civil Justice Quarterly 23:231–243
Zuckerman AAS (2006) Zuckerman on civil procedure: Principles of practice, 2nd edn. London
Zuckerman AAS (2014) No justice without lawyers—The myth of an inquisitorial solution. Civil Justice Quarterly 33:355–375
Zuckerman AAS (2015) The continuing management deficit in the administration of civil justice. Civil Justice Quart 34(1):1–10

Framing the Structure of Court Systems from a Case Management Perspective: Lessons from Hungary

Viktória Harsági

Abstract The old Hungarian Code of Civil Procedure (Act III of 1952), which has been modified significantly since its entry into force, did not follow a uniform concept. After the political transformation of Hungary, the Code of Civil Procedure struggled with the problem of 'belonging' and 'finding its proper place'. The main innovations of the new Code of Civil Procedure passed in 2016 include the systemic realization of the effectiveness of court proceedings, diverting claims away from court proceedings, and establishing procedural rules promoting agreements between the parties. This paper concentrates on the following topics: case allocation, preparatory phase, innovation at the first instance level, incapacity to prove, unlawful evidence, remedies, and collective redress mechanisms.

1 Vertical Arrangements

In Hungary, based on the principle of separation of powers, Act IV of 1869 provided that justice and public administration shall be carried out by separate organs of the state. This Act has laid the foundation for the modern administration of justice in Hungary after the Compromise of 1867,[1] which was followed by legislation regulating the structure and operation of the courts.[2] A four-level regular court system and several special court systems had evolved by the first decade of the 20th century.

According to Kengyel, 'after the Communist takeover, Eastern and Central European countries were forced to change their court systems according to the Soviet pattern … [D]estruction of the old Hungarian court system began at the end of the 1940s.' Institutions such as the two-level appeal system and the administrative courts were abolished under Act XI of 1949 and Act II of 1949 respectively. By abolishing

[1]The Austro-Hungarian Compromise of 1867 established the dual monarchy of Austria-Hungary.
[2]Kengyel (2008, p. 91).

V. Harsági (✉)
Pázmány University, Budapest, Hungary
e-mail: harsagi.viktoria@jak.ppke.hu

P. C. H. Chan and C. H. van Rhee (eds.), *Civil Case Management in the Twenty-First Century: Court Structures Still Matter*, Ius Gentium: Comparative Perspectives on Law and Justice 85, https://doi.org/10.1007/978-981-33-4512-6_11

the courts of appeal, the four-level court system was reduced to a 'three-level system of justice in conformity with the unity of local, territorial and supreme courts in socialist countries.'[3]

After the political transition to democracy in Hungary at the end of the 1980s, no corresponding changes in the structure of the Hungarian court system were made until the 1997 Amendment of the Constitution. This rendered the de facto reorganization of the courts of appeal possible after years of repeated changes in their perceived purpose. The courts of appeal were reincorporated into the system of courts in order to reduce the overburdening caseload of lower-level (i.e. local) courts and the Supreme Court. As a result, the four-level court system in Hungary was re-established as in the era preceding World War II.

Following the judicial reform in 2011 (under Act CLXI of 2011 on the Organization and Administration of Courts), the names and the structure of Hungarian courts have been changed. Starting from 1 January 2012, the court system comprises of four levels with one level of appeal. The lowest-level courts are the local courts (helyi bíróság) renamed as district courts (járásbíróság) with effect from 1 January 2013. The second level is constituted by 19 courts of justice (törvényszék) and the Municipal Court of Justice, the latter being substituted by the county courts and the Municipal Court of Budapest on 1 January 2012. The third level consists of five courts of appeal, which were incorporated into the court system at two stages in 2003 and 2005 respectively. Finally, at the top of the hierarchy is the Curia, which replaced the Supreme Court on 1 January 2012.

The new Act CXXX of 2016 on the Hungarian Code of Civil Procedure (2016 HCCP), coming into force on 1 January 2018, did not change the two-level system of first instance courts in Hungary. Cases are now tried at first instance by the district courts and the courts of justice. In civil cases, only local courts (i.e. district courts) had general first-instance jurisdiction before the 2016 HCCP. Starting from 2018, the courts of justice are granted general jurisdiction at first instance under the 2016 HCCP, which also stipulates mandatory legal representation before the courts. By doing so, the 2016 HCCP basically restores the traditions of 1911—it introduces a uniform set of procedural rules,[4] and abolishes the rules of the former HCCP pertaining to small claims and rules relating to matters of special importance that classified cases based on the value of the claim. The uniform system of procedural rules under the 2016 HCCP is designed for the courts of justice. For cases before the district courts, deviation from these rules is permitted only if the parties involved are not legally represented.

Cases falling within the first-instance jurisdiction of the courts of justice can be appealed to the courts of appeal. Review petitions are heard by the Curia, which is also responsible for ensuring the uniformity of judicial practice.

Effective case management is to be achieved by the distribution of cases between the two courts of first instance (i.e. the courts of justice and the district courts), such that cases of more special character or of greater complexity and cases involving

[3] *Ibidem*, p. 93.

[4] Varga (2014, pp. 139–140); Varga (2013, pp. 492, 496–498).

substantial claims will be commenced at higher-level courts of justice. The jurisdiction of district courts extends to: (a) property disputes where the value of the claim does not exceed thirty million forints (ca. 87,000€) or cannot be determined (except for actions related to copyright, neighbouring rights and industrial property rights, actions for general damages or compensation for pain and suffering related to the exercise of official authority, actions launched in the public interest, actions concerning the formation and lawful operation of a legal person, disputes between legal persons and their current or former members, and disputes between current or former members arising from their membership relations); (b) actions related to personal status; and (c) enforcement actions (Section 20 of 2016 HCCP).

2 Horizontal Arrangements

The labour courts functioned as first instance courts from 1973 until 2020. They exclusively tried cases at first instance. Labour courts dealt with employment relations and employment contracts, as well as other cases falling within their subject-matter jurisdiction. Appeals against the decision of the labour courts were heard by the courts of justice. Administrative courts also functioned as specialised courts—in the same structural unit as labour courts—from 2013 until 2020. The jurisdiction of the administrative courts included judicial review of administrative decisions. Appeals against the decisions of administrative courts were heard by the courts of justice as well.[5] As of 1 January 2018, a separate code of administrative procedure came into force, and this area of law is no longer governed by the HCCP. The labour and administrative courts have been abolished, and from 1 April 2020, the general first instance court is competent in matters that were formerly subject to the jurisdiction of the labour and administrative courts.

The 2016 HCCP has not essentially changed the rules on jurisdiction, but it contains some novelties with regard to consumers through introducing rules of exclusive jurisdiction that cater to the interests of the weaker party. Based on the principle of *actor sequitur forum rei*, territorial jurisdiction is determined by the defendant's domicile. The 2016 HCCP allows the parties—unless provided otherwise in the Act—to make a choice of court agreement and establish the territorial jurisdiction of a court in relation to their property rights or any future dispute that may potentially arise regarding their specific legal relation. The parties may conclude such an agreement orally (with written confirmation) or in writing, in a form which is consistent with the established business practices of the parties, or if in the course of international trade, in a form which is consistent with the commercial customs with which the parties are or should have been familiar and which are commonly known and adopted in the given business sector.

[5]Kengyel and Harsági (2013, pp. 324–325), cf. Varga (2014).

In the absence of exclusive territorial jurisdiction, instead of choosing the court with general territorial jurisdiction over the defendant, the plaintiff may at his own discretion bring the action before the court of:

1. the place where the person entitled to enforce the claim is domiciled, if the action is for imposing a maintenance obligation;
2. the place where the immovable property is situated, if the action is related to the ownership or possession of an immovable property or a right *in rem* encumbering the immovable property;
3. the place where the contract is concluded or where it is to be performed, if the action is for enforcing a contractual claim;
4. the domicile in Hungary or, in the absence thereof, the Hungarian place of residence of the plaintiff, if the action is for enforcing a contractual claim of a consumer against an undertaking; and
5. the geographical location where the damage was caused, if the action is for claiming compensation in tort (Sections 27–28 of 2016 HCCP).

3 Complexity Arrangements

The Fundamental Law of Hungary provides that court cases shall be adjudicated by a panel of judges or by a single professional judge (Article 27). Only professional judges may act as single judge or the panel chair. Civil cases at first instance are usually heard by one professional judge. In cases relating to the protection of industrial property rights (which require more specialized expertise), the panel shall consist of three professional judges, two of whom shall have a higher level of education.

In the era preceding the political transition in Hungary, it was common for trials to be conducted by lay assessors in the spirit of 'involvement of the people'. Nowadays, lay assessors merely appear in labour disputes. The courts hear labour cases at first instance in panels of three, including one professional judge as the presiding judge and two lay assessors.[6] During the proceedings, professional judges and lay assessors share the same rights and obligations.

The panel at second instance consists of three professional judges. The Curia shall also hear cases in panels of three professional judges, but if the case is of extreme complexity or of special social significance, the Curia may order a panel of five professional judges (Section 9 of 2016 HCCP).

Violation of the rules relating to the composition of courts may result in the annulment of the judgment.

[6] Lay assessors are nominated by Unions to represent the interests of employees and employers.

4 Legal Historical Perspectives

Hungarian civil procedure is based on German-Austrian civil procedural law. However, some characteristics of socialism can still be detected. Since the political transition to democracy in Hungary, the country has adopted the Western approach, and the Hungarian legal system began to lean towards Western systems (often under the influence of European Union law) in the 1990s.[7] Therefore, on one hand, Hungarian civil procedural law is not a pure national creation. It was developed under the influence of Western (or European) institutions, which is a natural consequence of the fact that Hungary has attached itself to Western culture right from its conception. On the other hand, Hungarian civil procedure is not a pure piece of Western law. Hungary did not simply adopt foreign civil procedural institutions, but made substantial modifications to Western law which suited the country's situation.[8]

For 150 years, Hungarian civil procedure has followed German-Austrian law. Influence by the French legal system can also be observed to a certain extent. This may, amongst others, be traced back to German and French scholarship from the 19th and the beginning of the 20th century respectively, which had a strong impact on Hungarian law. Other influences also came with varying degrees of intensity in different historical periods. For example, the influence of Soviet law, and to a small degree, the influence of the common law system could also be noticed. However, their impact on the Hungarian civil procedure was very limited.[9]

The beginning of the 20th century was a turning point in the history of the Hungarian Code of Civil Procedure. The outdated and anachronistic Code of Civil Judicial Procedure of 1868, which was still based on written proceedings, mediacy and a rigid system of proof, was replaced by the Code of Civil Procedure of 1911 (1911 HCCP). The preparatory work for the 1911 HCCP had lasted for nearly 25 years, but the prolonged work resulted in a Code which was widely recognized in Europe. The drafter, Sándor Plósz, incorporated elements of German civil procedure and the 1895 Austrian civil procedure in the 1911 HCCP in order to implement an ideal set of procedural laws for social civil action.[10]

The 1911 HCCP turned out to be one of the best European legislations of the era. It provided, through the implementation of modern principles, the possibility of enforcing civil rights under an effective and relatively short procedure, which could prevent undue delay in proceedings caused by *mala fide* litigants. For this purpose, a concentrated procedure was developed. The Code gave effect to the basic principles of procedure that had been in place during the 19th century, including oral hearings, publicity, immediacy and free evaluation of evidence. It also promoted cooperation between the court and the parties by respecting party's control in proceedings while

[7]Harsagi (2012, p. 277).

[8]Magyary and Nizslovszky (1942, p. 23), Novák (1996, p. 155).

[9]For more detail, see Harsági (2012, pp. 277–290).

[10]Kengyel (2000a, p. 233).

putting case management in the hands of the court. It aimed to avoid delay through increasing the powers of the judge.[11]

The prolonged drafting period of the law allowed the legislature to get familiarized with the major European codes of civil procedure in the last decades of the 19th century. The first draft was largely inspired by the German Code of Civil Procedure of 1877 and the French Code of 1806. The influence of Austrian law became visible in the 1890s, and it was used as reference for the 1902 draft.[12] However, as aforementioned, the 1911 HCCP was not a simple transcription of German and Austrian civil procedure. It had incorporated original concepts and many procedural questions which were addressed independently in the Code.[13]

Deviance from German dogmatics was justifiable since the public favoured the ideals of French and English civil procedure. The influence of the Austrian Code of Civil Procedure of 1895 had significantly reshaped the original aspects of the Draft Code in Hungary. Apart from the active role of judges, the extent of *ex officio* powers and the obligation to tell the truth, the social ideals of Austrian civil litigation were also adopted in Hungary.[14]

The 1911 HCCP was replaced in 1952 by a new Act (1952 HCCP) based on the Soviet-Russian Code of Civil Procedure of 1923.[15] The 1952 HCCP was introduced after a surprisingly short preparation time, namely five years before the codification of substantive private law. The 1952 HCCP is still in force, and has gone through 11 major amendments and over 60 minor modifications in the past 70 years.

Procedural legislation during the Socialist period did not blindly copy Soviet law but was largely based on the Hungarian tradition.[16] The 1952 HCCP can be best described as a drastic abridgement of the 1911 HCCP, but the core concepts of the latter were still preserved.[17] István Varga described the 1952 HCCP as ‘breaking with tradition without abandoning it’.[18] The 1952 HCCP had followed the structure and to some extent the content (e.g. the rules on how civil cases should be heard by the court) of the 1911 HCCP. According to Kengyel, ‘structural changes under … Soviet influence (e.g. a two-level system of justice, and one level of appeal) could be fitted into the old structure’. The basic principles were stated at the beginning of the 1952 HCCP, and the significance of special procedures had diminished. Despite the structural similarity between the old and the new HCCP, significant changes were made to the structure of civil proceedings. While the 1911 HCCP divided the civil action into two stages—the pre-trial hearing and the trial on the merits—the 1952 HCCP treated the civil action as an integral process.

---

[11] Kengyel (2003b, p. 234).

[12] Kengyel (2003c, p. 419).

[13] Magyary and Nizslovszky (1942, pp. 14–15).

[14] Kengyel (2003c pp. 420–421), cf. Plósz (1912, pp. 392–398).

[15] See for more details Kengyel (2000c, p. 361).

[16] Horváth (2003, p. 407).

[17] Németh (1998, p. 69).

[18] Varga (2008, p. 278).

The main innovations of the 1952 HCCP include the prevalence of the substantive truth, a redefinition of the principle of party control, the restriction of attorney's activities, the transformation of district courts into courts of first instance with general jurisdiction, the establishment of a two-level justice system with one level of appeal, the unification of the appeal system by abolishing direct appeal to the Supreme Court against court orders, and the elimination of the review system by laying the foundations for 'opposition on legal grounds'. The 1952 HCCP reformed the court and prosecution system in accordance with the Soviet pattern and eliminated the special jurisdiction of the courts. The role of the prosecutor in the civil action was enhanced and a system of lay assessors was introduced.

Soviet influence was best manifested in the basic principles of the 1952 HCCP. With regards to these principles, the Hungarian legislature adopted the text of the Soviet Code of Civil Procedure almost verbatim.[19]

The introduction of a market economy and the rule of law in Hungary since the 1990s resulted in unforeseeable challenges in terms of both quality and quantity. Within a short period of time, the number of litigious and non-litigious cases had multiplied. New types of lawsuits appeared and previous rare case types acquired special significance (e.g. company law and administrative actions). The organizational structure of courts was also radically reformed, where a four-level court system was set up following the establishment of the courts of appeal.[20] In the 1990s, the legislator attempted to renew the 1952 HCCP through repeated amendments with new objectives and principles.[21] Whether this approach was successful is still questionable, but significant innovations have been introduced since 2018.[22]

5 Definition of 'Case Management' in Hungarian Academic Literature

The terminology of 'case management' is not commonly used in Hungarian academic literature. Even if used, its meaning is usually different from that in international legal practice—it is often regarded as an equivalent of 'conducting a case' in Hungary (*Prozessleitung* in German).

[19]Kengyel (2003a, p. 718).
[20]Szabó (2006, p. 5).
[21]Kengyel (2003a).
[22]Cf. Varga (2014, pp. 135–163).

6 Specific Procedural Design

E-justice. Information technology (IT) opens up new possibilities for access to justice. Litigation without legal representation may become easier, forms may be filled in online by electronic support programmes, and a higher level of automation may thus be achieved. The potential use of modern IT in court proceedings is subject to the structure of the system. IT is more useful in simple and routine proceedings where the decision-making process is schematic and standardized.[23] Therefore, in many countries including Hungary, order for payment and company registration procedures have been considered suitable to be conducted electronically. IT also allows communication through the Internet regardless of the geographic location of the court.

However, other types of litigation are still rather resistant to e-justice. The eIDAS Regulation, laying the foundations for electronic identification, was adopted by the European Parliament and the Council in summer 2014. Following this, in May 2015, the Hungarian Government adopted Decision No. 1295/2015 (V. 7.) Korm., which provided that electronic communication should be introduced at certain courts and prosecution services in connection with the codes of administrative and civil procedure.

Preparation. The 2016 HCCP has reintroduced various procedural stages in civil proceedings (which used to be part of the 1911 HCCP by Plósz). According to the Explanatory Memorandum attached to the Draft Bill, it aims to establish a set of procedures which will be more predictable to the parties. The 2016 HCCP clearly states the function and duration of specific stages in civil proceedings, thereby establishing an unambiguous framework for specific procedural actions. This will promote not only the effectiveness but also the predictability of proceedings. Under the 2016 HCCP, first instance proceedings are divided into two stages: the preparatory phase and the main phase. This framework places great emphasis on the preparatory phase, during which the content of the legal dispute will be established. According to the Explanatory Memorandum, the preparatory phase enjoys flexibility, where the court can determine what specific steps to take in this stage and decide on the method of preparation for the case at hand according to its particular characteristics.[24]

The 2016 HCCP also sets a wide range of restrictions. For example, after the closing of the preparatory phase, as a general rule, it is not possible to further modify the claim or defence, or submit any further evidence or motions. The aim of these restrictions—besides to prevent delay in civil proceedings—is to ensure clarity as to the content of the legal dispute such that only evidence needs to be taken.

Evidence. Before 2018, the HCCP only contained a few provisions and violation of these provisions would result in inadmissible evidence. With regard to unlawfully

[23] Kodek (2002, p. 481).

[24] Cf. Köblös (2016, pp. 185–205).

obtained evidence, the HCCP did not contain generally applicable provisions as in the Act on Criminal Procedure. There were prohibitions concerning witness statements and expert opinions, but the lack of general and special prohibitions in other areas resulted in uncertainty,[25] e.g. as regards the theft of documents or unauthorised access to e-mail systems.

Pursuant to Section 269 of the 2016 HCCP, evidence is unlawful and inadmissible in a court action if (i) it is obtained or produced by violating or threatening a person's right to life or physical integrity, (ii) it is obtained in an unlawful manner, (iii) it is produced in an unlawful manner, or (iv) its submission will violate personality rights. The unlawful nature of evidence is to be taken into account by the court *ex officio* and the parties are to be informed accordingly. With the exception of point (i) above, unlawful evidence may exceptionally be taken into account by the court in regard to the nature and extent of its unlawfulness, the legal interests affected by the unlawfulness, the relevance of the evidence in establishing the facts, the availability of any other evidence and all other circumstances of the case.

7 Reforms

The main regulatory objectives of the new Hungarian Code of Civil Procedure as stated in the Draft Bill include:

1. the realization of effective court proceedings;
2. the referral of cases to ADR (mainly mediation);
3. the establishment of procedural rules promoting agreement between the parties;
4. the introduction of various procedural phases;
5. the creation of procedural rules ensuring the concentration of proceedings;
6. the introduction of mandatory legal representation in proceedings before the courts of justice as a guarantee of professional conduct;
7. the creation of domestic rules of collective redress; and
8. the enhancement of the role of IT in civil litigation.

The 2016 HCCP made significant modifications to the rules relating to legal representation, enhanced the role of statements made during the preparatory phase, and laid down stricter requirements regarding parties' statements in civil cases. The court is granted extensive powers to clarify the legal dispute, and expert evidence is given a new statutory basis. There have been significant changes in the rules of the appeal procedure, where access filters at the Curia based on value have been introduced.

[25] Kengyel (2000b, p. A/373).

8 Final Appeals

The 1952 HCCP turned the previous two-instance appellate system into a one-level system. The Act maintained the second instance proceedings characterizing Plósz's 1911 HCCP. After the democratic transition in 1989, reform of Hungarian civil procedure was first driven by a decision of the Constitutional Court in 1992 with the re-introduction of the review procedure before the Curia.

A subsequent problem was the excessive caseload of the courts. Access filters are therefore used to alleviate this problem. The nature of such filters varies,[26] and may be based on value or the exclusion of certain types of cases.

The Basic Law of Hungary provides for an appellate procedure. Problems arise with respect to the admissability of extraordinary appeals. The legislature should clarify the role of the higher courts (especially the Curia) when it comes to extraordinary appeals, as well as the weights to be given to individual legal protection and to providing legal uniformity, respectively.[27]

The 2016 HCCP made the rules on appeal more effective. It aimed at achieving a double goal: to ensure the right to a legal remedy, while simultaneously preventing delay in appellate procedures. Therefore, the Code provides the scope of powers of the second instance court and the content of appeal petitions, while at the same time stating that the second instance court shall adjudicate appeal without a hearing. The Code also regulates the grounds for setting aside a judgment. The gist of the new regulation is that violation of procedural rules which does not warrant mandatory setting aside of a judgment is to be taken into account by the second instance court only at the request of the appellant but not *ex officio*.

The 2016 HCCP also deals with the effect of judgments handed down by the European Court of Human Rights. It has preserved the original rules on the reopening of such cases for revision.

According to the Explanatory Memorandum attached to the Draft Bill, a so-called mixed system has been introduced which treats review as an extraordinary remedy. In certain property cases, the Curia may exceptionally allow review with regard to legal uniformity considerations or any special significance or social importance of the question of law raised in the matter.

9 First Instance

The legislature expected the new rules to significantly promote resolution of cases within a reasonable time. The requirement on detailed content of the statement of claim and the defence, which need to be submitted in written form, was thought to allow proper and expedient preparation of cases. Unfortunately, the results do not meet these expectations. In the first few months following the implementation of

[26] Cf. Kengyel (2002, pp. 270–271).

[27] Cf. Varga (2013, p. 505).

the 2016 HCCP, a considerable number of statements of claim have been dismissed, which has perceivably reduced the willingness of potential claimants to commence litigation.

At the level of district courts, numerous rules have been introduced to facilitate litigation, such as the use of standard forms in civil proceedings and fewer requirements regarding submissions made by the parties. Parties are also supported by the judge in managing their case. According to the Explanatory Memorandum attached to the Draft Bill, this provides a flexible alternative solution in uncomplicated cases, and in cases where weaker parties are involved.

The law in relation to expert evidence has also been reformed—private expert opinions are properly incorporated into the new system. A party may now introduce expert evidence given by: (a) a private expert appointed by the party in the proceedings at hand; (b) an expert appointed in other proceedings; or (c) a court-appointed expert. According to the Explanatory Memorandum of the Draft Bill, these new rules are expected to change the previous practice where private expert opinions were used only to contest or challenge the professional competence of the expert appointed by the court.

The parties' obligation to assist the court in administering justice is also a novelty in the 2016 HCCP. Such obligation may seem problematic at first sight, but it has enhanced the procedural responsibility of the parties, who now play a supportive and active role in civil proceedings.[28] The new rules of procedure have also increased the powers of the court in conducting litigation.[29]

10 Mediation

Following international trends, mediation has been introduced in Hungary. However, the relatively low level of acceptance of mediation has significantly hindered its application in practice.

Article 12 of the EU Mediation Directive requires Member States to bring into force the laws and other regulations necessary to comply with the Directive by 21 May 2011.[30] In Hungary, originally under Act LV of 2002 on Mediation, only out-of-court mediation was possible until court-annexed mediation was introduced in 2012. The Act on Mediation only provides few regulations on the procedure of mediation as it is essentially determined by the parties. Mediation is deemed to be concluded at the end of the fourth month after signing the mediation agreement unless otherwise

[28] Molnár (2017, p. 20).

[29] *Ibidem*, p. 23.

[30] Article 10 of the Directive constitutes an exception, pursuant to which the Commission shall make publicly available, by any appropriate means, information on the competent courts or authorities communicated by the Member States. The deadline for Member States to comply with the obligation under this Article is 21 November 2010.

agreed by the parties.[31] During court proceedings, the parties must be informed about the nature of mediation. At the request of the parties, the court may stay the proceedings if the parties want to attempt mediation. If the parties are able to reach a settlement, they can request the court to approve it. Upon approval, the settlement will have the same effect as a judgment.

In order to encourage out-of-court settlement of cases, the 2016 HCCP has provided an institutional and professional framework for ADR. This is deemed necessary to ensure the enforceability of any potential settlement agreement. The rules combine court-annexed and out-of-court mediation with the summons to attempt settlement under Section 167(2) of 2016 HCCP.

11 Financing the Courts

Statistics compiled during the preparatory work for drafting the 2016 HCCP revealed that the operational costs for the administration of justice were several times the amount of state revenues from procedural duties. This means, that to a large extent, lawsuits are financed by the tax payers instead of the parties.

12 Policy Making and Court Structure

Provisions relating to the internal organization of courts can be found in the Fundamental Law of Hungary and Act CLXI of 2011 on the Organization and Administration of Courts (Jurisdiction Act).

A separate Act shall be adopted by the Parliament for setting up, merging, and terminating courts, and for determining territorial jurisdiction. If there is a change in the administrative boundaries, the corresponding territorial jurisdiction of courts may be modified by an order of the President of the Republic, based on the recommendation of the President of the National Office for the Judiciary (Section 17 of the Jurisdiction Act).

Pursuant to Article 25(5) of the Fundamental Law, the central responsibilities relating to the administration of the courts lie with the President of the National Office for the Judiciary. The National Council of Justice is to supervise the central administration of the courts. The National Council of Justice and other bodies of judicial self-government are to participate in the administration of the courts. Article 25(6) provides that the President of the National Office for the Judiciary is to be elected from among the judges by the National Assembly for nine years on the proposal of the President of the Republic. Meanwhile, the President of the Curia shall be a member of the National Council of Justice, and further members of the Council are to be elected by the judges.

[31] Article 35 of Act LV of 2002 on Mediation.

The President of the National Office for the Judiciary—in observing the constitutional principle of judicial independence—is to perform the central responsibilities of court administration, to exercise management powers on courts under the Budget Act, and to supervise the administrative activities of the presidents of the courts of appeal, and the courts of justice (Section 65 of the Jurisdiction Act).

The judge that is authorized to hear particular cases is the presiding judge who holds relevant competence and jurisdiction that has been assigned to the case according to the pre-defined case distribution schedule. The case distribution schedule is to be drafted by the President of the court. However, the case distribution schedule may be deviated from, based on important reasons affecting the operation or the interests of the court. The case distribution schedule shall specify the composition and number of the chambers operating at the given court (Sections 8–10 of the Jurisdiction Act).

13 Mass Case Processing

The experience in cases relating to environmental pollution and consumer protection in recent years has prompted a reconsideration of the adequacy of the current Hungarian legal regulations on collective redress.[32] The chapter of the 2016 HCCP on collective redress has consolidated existing procedural rules concerning public interest litigation (actio popularis), which had been scattered over separate laws. It also provides new rules aiming to facilitate the enforcement of aggregated private interests. Public interest litigation has to be brought before the courts of justice.

Besides public interest litigation, new rules have also been introduced in relation to mass litigation. The 2016 HCCP covers, amongst others, claims arising from consumer contracts and claims for damages that result from health-related injuries in employment actions.[33] Complicated cases will be heard by a panel of three judges. The action introduced by the 2016 HCCP has provided for an opt-in mechanism based on Commission Recommendation 213/396/EU (of 11 June 2013).

References

Harsági V (2012) Downstream or up the stream–Influence of different legal cultures on Hungarian civil procedure law. In: Maleshin D (ed) Civil procedure in cross-cultural dialogue: Eurasia context. Moscow, pp 277–290

Harsági V (2014) The need for further development of collective redress in Hungary. In: Harsági V, Van Rhee CH (eds) Multi-party redress mechanisms in Europe: Squeaking mice? Cambridge, pp 171–185

---

[32]Cf. Harsági (2014, pp. 171–185), Harsági (2016a, pp. 201–215), Harsági (2016c, pp. 343–355), Harsági (2017).

[33]Harsági (2016b, pp. 751–754).

Harsági V (2016a) Deficiencies of collective redress in Hungary and recommendations for codification. In: Fankhauser R et al (eds) Das Zivilrecht und seine Durchsetzung. Zürich, pp 201–215
Harsági V (2016b) Kollektív igényérvényesítés–Általános indokolás a kollektív igényérvényesítéshez. In: Varga I, Éless T (eds) Szakértői Javaslat az új polgári perrendtartás kodifikációjára. Budapest, pp 751–754
Harsági V (2016c) Quo vadis collective redress? Hungarian aspects. Festschrift für Professor Nikolaos K Klamaris–Essays in Honour of professor Nikolaos K Klamaris. Thessaloniki, Athens, pp 343–355
Harsági V (2017) Combining opt-in and opt-out systems? Expert proposal for the Hungarian regulation of collective redress. ELTE Law journal 2016/2: 25–52. http://eltelawjournal.hu/. Accessed May 2020
Horváth A et al (2003) A perjogok története. In: Mezey B (ed) Magyar jogtörténet. Budapest, pp 357–417
Kengyel M (2000a) A polgári eljárásjog jelene és jövője. In: Benisné Győrffy I (ed) Ötödik magyar jogászgyűlés. Budapest, pp 233–248
Kengyel M (2000b) A bizonyítás. In: Petrik F (ed) Polgári eljárásjog. Kommentár a gyakorlat számára. Budapest, pp A/363–A/406
Kengyel M (2000c) Die Zukunft des ungarischen Zivilprozeßrechts nach der Zivilverfahrens-Novelle 1999. ZZPInt 5:361–374
Kengyel M (2002) Zivilprozessrecht um die Jahrtausendwende. In: Zeitschrift für vergleichende Rechtswissenschaft. pp 260–282
Kengyel M (2003a) Die Entstehungsgeschichte der fünfzigjährigen ungarischen Zivilprozeßordnung. In: Nakamura H et al (eds) Festschrift für Kostas E. Beys dem Rechtdenker in attischer Dialektik, Athens, pp 705–720
Kengyel M (2003b) A bírói hatalom és a felek rendelkezési joga a polgári perben. Budapest
Kengyel M (2003c) Külföldi hatások a 20. század magyar polgári eljárásjogában. In: Kiss D, Varga I (eds) Magister artis et aequi. Studia in honorem Németh János. Budapest, pp 415–438
Kengyel M (2008) Magyar polgári eljárásjog. Budapest
Kengyel M, Harsági V (2013) Hungary–Civil law. In: Eliantionio M et al (eds) Standing up for Your Right(s) in Europe. A Comparative Study on Legal Standing (Locus Standi) before the EU and Member State Courts, Antwerp, pp 322–344
Köblös A (2016) Hungary: Towards more efficient preparatory proceedings. In: Ervo L, Nylund A (eds) Current trends in preparatory proceedings. Cham, pp 185–205
Kodek G (2002) Der Zivilprozeβ und neue Formen der Informationstechnik. Zeitschrift für Zivilprozeß 4:445–490
Magyary G, Nizslovszky E (1942) Magyar polgári perjog. Franklin Társulat Kiadása, Budapest
Molnár T (2017) Az új polgári perrendtartás alapelveinek értékelése, a perjogi kodifikáció hatása a polgári eljárás sajátos alapelveire. Közjegyzők Közlönye 6:13–24
Németh J (1998) Polgári perjogunk a XX. század végén. In: Máthé G (ed) Negyedik magyar jogászgyűlés. Budapest, pp 69–82
Novák I (1996) Első magyar polgári eljárásjogunk–Hommage à 1911.I. tv. Bírák Lapja
Plósz S (1912) Die Prozeßleitung des Gerichts nach der neuen Zivilprozeßordnung. Recht und Wirtschaft: 392–398
Szabó I (2006) Előszó. In: Szabó I (ed) A Polgári perrendtartásról szóló 1952. évi III. törvény magyarázata. I. kötet. Budapest, pp 227–237

Varga I (2008) Foreign influences on the Hungarian civil procedure law. In: Deguchi M, Storme M (eds) The reception and transmission of procedural law in the global society. Antwerp, pp 275–288

Varga I (2013) Perrendi szabályozási igények azonosítása jogösszehasonlító kitekintéssel. In: Varga I (ed) Codificatio processualis civilis. Studia in Honorem Németh János II, Budapest, pp 489–513

Varga I (2014) Identification of civil procedure regulatory needs from a comparative perspective. ELTE Law J 6:135–163

In Search of Efficiency: Court Structure and Case Management in Croatia

Marko Bratković

Abstract In Croatia, a cynic could conclude that it takes a long time for a large number of judges assisted by an equally large number of support staff to handle a large number of court cases. Court backlogs and the length of proceedings are both symptoms of this problem. Such reforms that have been effected to remedy this problem have, so far, failed to do so. The present court structure, procedural rules and administration simply do not allow for the efficient adjudication of civil claims. In order to remedy these problems, the civil justice system should be refocused on citizens as its users i.e., those it is intended to serve.

1 Introduction

Upon hearing that a country's courts handle approximately 1,400,000 civil and commercial cases a year, it might be thought that the country had a large population. It might come as a surprise to hear that the country is Croatia, which is a rather small country with just approximately 4.1 million inhabitants. Furthermore, if Croatia has one of the largest number of courts and judges in Europe relative to its population, a puzzling state of affairs starts coming to light.

Court backlogs and excessively long proceedings have been thought to be the key problem effecting Croatia's judiciary[1] since the 1990s, when it gained its independence from the Socialist Federal Republic of Yugoslavia (SFRY). Despite a number of initiatives and reform attempts, the Croatian judiciary seems to be stuck in a quagmire. A reluctance to examine the roots of the crisis seems to be the main reason for this problem. Backlogs and lengthy proceedings are both no more than symptoms

[1] See usual, commonplace statements in e.g. Vukelić (2014, p. 224).

M. Bratković (✉)
University of Zagreb, Zagreb, Croatia
e-mail: marko.bratkovic@pravo.hr

P. C. H. Chan and C. H. van Rhee (eds.), *Civil Case Management in the Twenty-First Century: Court Structures Still Matter*, Ius Gentium: Comparative Perspectives on Law and Justice 85, https://doi.org/10.1007/978-981-33-4512-6_12

rather than the cause of the problem. So far, however, simply treating those symptoms is the only cure that has been attempted, and then only with a modest degree of success.

In 2016, as many as 68% of Croatian citizens had a negative general opinion on the functioning of the judiciary.[2] In 2019, more than 70% of citizens rated the justice system in Croatia as fairly or very bad in terms of both institutional and individual judicial independence.[3] In that respect, Croatia is ranked at the very bottom of the European Union rankings, along with Bulgaria and Slovakia.[4] This opinion is also shared by Croatian judges. In 2017, only Slovenian, Lithuanian, and Latvian peers had a worse perception than Croatian judges of judicial independence in their respective countries.[5]

Without going deeper into the criteria for evaluating the work outcomes of judges in Croatia—which is an analysis worth carrying out—it is also worth highlighting the fact that 43% of Croatian judges believe that Croatian judges are not appointed based on their ability and experience. Furthermore, 55% of them believe that ability and experience do not constitute the basis for judicial promotion.[6] All this data points to a lack of trust in and amongst the Croatian judiciary. More reliable data is, however, unavailable.

Comparative research has shown that citizens trust the judiciary more when they view the legal system as a function that provides distributive and procedural justice effectively, i.e. when judicial proceedings are organised in an efficient manner, carried out without unreasonable delays and when judgments are enforced effectively.[7] An adequate court structure and proper case management are thus of critical importance for there to be an efficient judiciary that is worthy of public trust. Croatia is, unfortunately, still searching for an efficient judiciary that serves its citizens.

In this contribution, a brief overview of the types of civil and commercial cases[8] that Croatian courts deal with is followed by general observations on Croatia's court structure. This is followed by a particular focus on the way in which those courts handle civil and commercial cases. Given that case management is not a technical term used in Croatian civil procedure, it is taken to cover not only those procedural rules the aim of which is to secure the efficient adjudication of civil cases (similar to German *richterliche Prozessleitung*) but also 'the administration inside the court

[2] Agency Ipsos Plus 2016 research data referred to in a news article: Strengthening the rule of law (2017).

[3] EU Justice Scoreboard (2019, p. 44).

[4] EU Justice Scoreboard (2019, p. 44). In Denmark, by contrast, just under 90% of citizens rated the justice system in their country as (fairly or very) good in terms of the independence of the judiciary.

[5] EU Justice Scoreboard (2018, p. 44). Not surprisingly, among European judges, Danish judges, just like their fellow citizens, have the best opinion on judicial independence in their country.

[6] Supreme Court President Report (2017, pp. 106ff). Responses to the survey refer to 2015 and 2016.

[7] EU Justice Scoreboard (2018, p. 222).

[8] Administrative, criminal and misdemeanour cases are not discussed in this paper, which is focused on civil justice only. However, (some of) the general assessments on the Croatian judiciary presented here are applicable to criminal and administrative justice, as well.

and outside the case', which is sometimes called court management.[9] The contribution concludes by highlighting how the civil justice system should be refocused on citizens as the users of the system: it exists to serve them, or at least that is the way it should be.

2 Civil and Commercial Cases

Its high caseload, which is among the highest in Europe,[10] is often cited as the justification for the Croatian judiciary's lack of efficiency.[11] In 2019, Croatian courts dealt with about 1,400,000 civil and commercial cases, including a backlog of about 380,000 cases from previous years.[12] For a country with just slightly over four million inhabitants, this is an overwhelming number of cases. However, let us look at the structure of these cases (Fig. 1).

Land registry and business registry cases. In 2019, 61% (about 800,000 cases) of all civil and commercial cases filed with Croatia's courts of first instance[13] and court backlogs from previous years were non-litigation cases. These mostly consisted of land registry cases (72% of all non-litigation cases) and business registry cases (18% of all non-litigation cases).[14] Registry cases were dealt with by the courts rather swiftly. In 2019, the disposition time (DT)[15] for land registry cases was 40 days, and

---

[9]Jeuland (2018, p. 108).

[10]See e.g. EU Justice Scoreboard (2019, p. 10), regarding the number of incoming cases at courts of first instance.

[11]For instance, during the accession negotiations with Croatia, the European Union publicly criticized 'the widespread inefficiency of the judicial system', partly because 'too many issues are brought before courts', that therefore suffer from 'serious constraints in their ability to handle the workload'. Opinion on Croatia's application for membership 2004. Uzelac (2010a, p. 89).

[12]The exact number of 1,432,838 civil and commercial cases Croatian courts were dealing with in 2019 is calculated from statistical data reported in the Supreme Court President Report (2018, pp. 48 and 72), and in the Supreme Court President Report (2019, pp. 52, 62, 73, 78 and 88). The total number includes litigation, enforcement, insolvency (including also consumer insolvency cases and pre-bankruptcy settlements), non-litigation (which includes land registry and business registry cases) and court mediation cases filed with the courts of first, second and third instance in 2019, as well as backlogs from previous years.

[13]Unfortunately, separate data for the courts of appeal and for the Supreme Court as regards the number of cases of different types they are dealing with are not available. One could also object to the scarce classification of cases at courts of first instance included in the statistical reports as not (always) appropriate for a more in-depth analysis.

[14]Data derived from Supreme Court President Report (2018, pp. 48 and 72), and Supreme Court President Report (2019, pp. 52, 62, 73, 78 and 88).

[15]The disposition time (DT) is obtained by dividing the number of pending cases at the end of the observed period by the number of resolved cases within the same period multiplied by 365 (days in a year). However, it should be noted that this indicator is not a calculation of the average time needed to process a case but a theoretical estimate of the time needed to process pending cases. CEPEJ (2018, pp. 238 and 239).

Fig. 1 Cases in Croatian courts of first instance in 2019

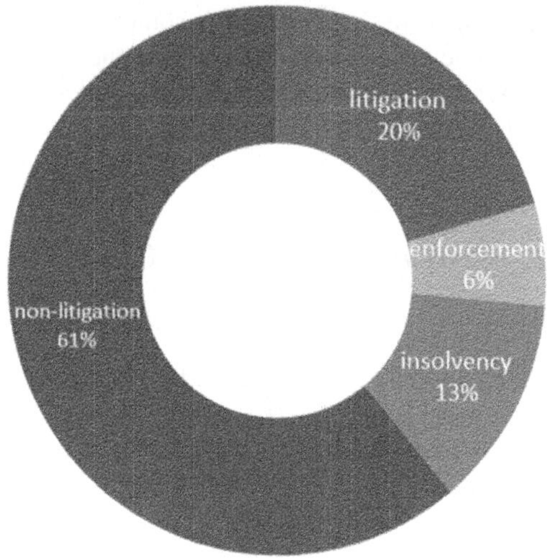

for business registry cases, it was 6 days.[16] It should be noted that land registry cases are mainly dealt with by specially trained non-judicial staff (*zemljišnoknjižni referenti*). Since 2003 non-litigious inheritance cases have been outsourced to notaries public. However, the decrease in the number of these cases at courts did not make a notable contribution to judicial efficiency.

Insolvency cases. The largest part (90%) of all insolvency cases in 2019 (about 165,000 cases) related to consumer insolvency, in particular to simplified consumer insolvency proceedings, which are a new form of proceeding that was introduced into Croatian law at the start of 2019 as a part of measures aimed at helping overly-indebted individuals. The disposition time of 432 days for these cases clearly shows that it takes a considerable amount of time for Croatian courts to get used to this new regulation. Interestingly enough, in statistical reports those circa 150,000 cases are reported separately as if they were not part of the caseload of the courts of first instance.[17] Hopefully, this was not done in order to embellish court statistics but to encourage the judiciary to settle these cases more efficiently in the future.

Enforcement cases. Enforcement cases made up 6% of all civil and commercial court cases (about 40,000 new cases, with a backlog of about 35,000 cases) in 2019. There has been a conspicuously steady decline in the number of incoming enforcement cases over the last two decades (Fig. 2). Since 2006 notaries public have had the power to issue payment orders in the form of enforcement orders based on so-called trustworthy documents, such as invoices, extracts from the creditor's sales register in a bookkeeping system, or bills of exchange. This has resulted in a substantial decrease in the number of enforcement cases coming before the courts. Only those cases where

[16]Supreme Court President Report (2019, pp. 52 and 73).

[17]Supreme Court President Report (2019, pp. 52 and 57).

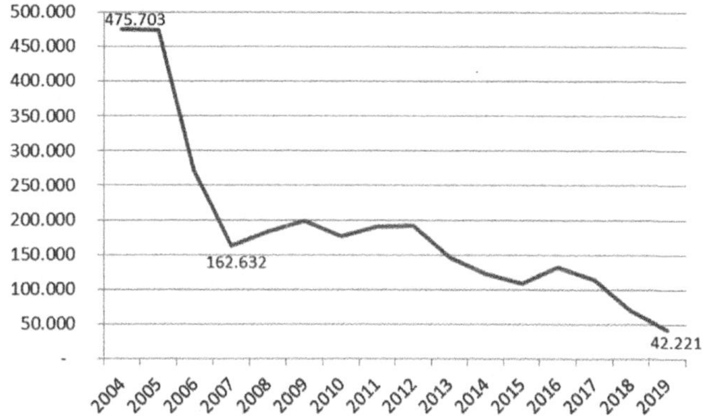

Fig. 2 Incoming enforcement cases in Croatian courts of first instance 2004–2019 (The data presented in the chart are taken from Statistical review 2006–2019 and Supreme Court President Report 2019)

a debtor contests the enforcement order (approximately 6–7%) are transferred to the courts as new (litigation and, afterwards, possibly enforcement) cases.[18]

However, one should bear in mind that notaries public are not entitled to undertake any enforcement action, such as seizure of the debtor's property. They may only issue enforcement orders, i.e. a mere certificate of an uncontested debt.[19] Therefore, although the courts were generally satisfied by the immediate discharge of part of their burden, and notaries public were happy with an additional source of income, it is doubtful whether this idea of 'notarial outsourcing' has really led to an increase in efficiency in the enforcement process. It can also be questioned whether enforcement as such was in fact at all 'outsourced' or just seemingly so.[20]

Interestingly enough, after continued pressure by the EU during Croatia's accession negotiations, private bailiffs, partly modelled on the French *huissiers de justice*, were introduced into Croatian legislation in 2010. Eventually, however, after several suspensions the legislation did not enter into force.[21] A fear of private bailiffs, as well as successful lobbying efforts, appear to have contributed to this.[22]

Either way, outsourcing a number of the enforcement cases, which were previously dealt with by the court and banks, to the Financial Agency (*Fina*) went through smoothly. Since 2011, *Fina* has been given an exclusive power to attach the debtor's bank account. This has resulted in a notable decline in the number of enforcement cases coming before the courts (see Fig. 2). As the central register of bank accounts is held by the same agency, court involvement in bank account attachment has become

[18]Bratković (2015, p. 1036).

[19]See Uzelac and Bratković (2015).

[20]Uzelac (2010a, p. 89).

[21]Uzelac (2010a, p. 90).

[22]See Uzelac (2019, p. 45).

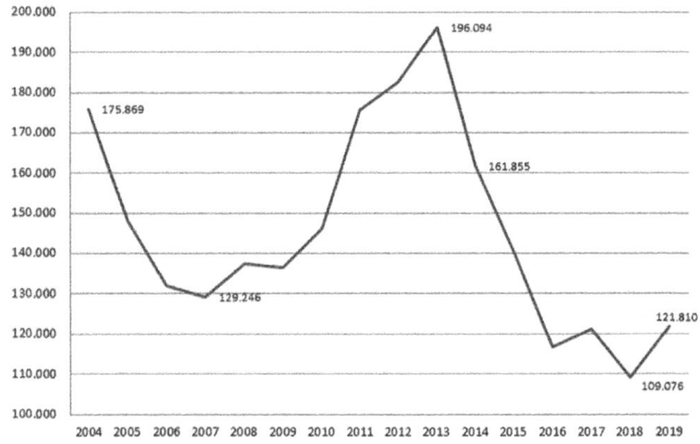

Fig. 3 Incoming litigation cases in Croatian courts of first instance 2004–2019 (Statistical review 2006–2019 and Supreme Court President Report 2019)

unnecessary. That has made bank account attachment very efficient, in some respects perhaps too efficient.[23]

However, the same cannot be said for the system of court enforcement, which is still, despite the lower number of cases, inefficient, 'low in public esteem, poor in financial means, high in bureaucratization and excessive in formalities.'[24] Its 'high level of formalism and rather sophisticated complex formulas of the law have often served as a good excuse for the extended duration of enforcement proceedings.'[25]

Litigation cases. Only a fifth of all civil and commercial cases at Croatian courts in 2019 were litigation cases, which are a core judicial activity. Besides about 120,000 incoming cases, about 145,000 cases were pending or unresolved from previous years.[26] Disposition time (DT) for litigation cases at municipal courts was 544 days (a year and a half). In commercial courts it was 320 days. By comparison, in 2014 DT for litigation cases at municipal courts was 405 days, while in commercial courts it was 343 days.[27] Therefore, despite the reduction in the number of new litigation cases, by about 40,000 cases (see Fig. 3), DT in 2019 did not decrease significantly by comparison with 2014. Moreover, in municipal courts, it even increased by 139 days. Courts handling litigation cases apparently lack specific case and court management skills. Nevertheless, a more accurate conclusion would require more detailed statistical data.

[23] *Ibidem.*

[24] Uzelac (2010a, p. 84), referring to enforcement in all countries of the socialist legal tradition.

[25] Uzelac (2010a, p. 88).

[26] Supreme Court President Report (2018, p. 48); Supreme Court President Report (2019, pp. 52 and 73).

[27] Statistical review (2006–2019, pp. 23 and 29).

What data is available does not provide any insight into the types of litigation cases that courts deal with,[28] such as whether they are difficult and complex, or easy routine claims. Moreover, that data has not been statistically gathered at all. Nevertheless, certain external evidence could support the conclusion that the vast majority of cases are rather routine and relatively straightforward legal matters of modest financial significance.[29] Moreover, it can perhaps be said that around 30% of litigation cases are initiated by contesting a notarial enforcement order based on a so-called trustworthy document.[30] This means that a considerable number of litigation cases relate to unpaid utility and telephone bills, parking tickets and television licence fees.[31] Therefore, it comes as no surprise that, in relation to population, Croatia is at the very top among the European countries in terms of the number of litigation cases dealt with by the courts of first instance, just behind Bosnia and Herzegovina, and ahead of Italy.[32]

3 Court Structure

All civil and commercial cases[33] are handled by municipal (*općinski*) and commercial courts at first instance, county (*županijski*) courts[34] and the High Commercial Court at the appellate level, and the Supreme Court at the apex of the judicial pyramid.

The court structure as a whole is relatively simple (see Fig. 4). It consists of municipal and county courts as courts of general jurisdiction and other specialised commercial, administrative and misdemeanour courts.

As the focus of this contribution is on civil justice, it is sufficient to say that, at first instance, criminal cases are dealt with by municipal and county courts, and administrative cases by four administrative courts, but rarely by the High Administrative Court. Since 2019, misdemeanour cases have been removed from the competence of separate misdemeanour courts and transferred to the competence of municipal courts and newly established municipal misdemeanour courts in the two largest

[28]Bratković (2019, p. 167).

[29]Uzelac (2014b, p. 47).

[30]Bratković (2019, p. 168).

[31]*Ibidem.*

[32]CEPEJ (2018, p. 252).

[33]In Croatia, ADR does not amount to a sizeable decrease in caseload.

[34]In rare civil cases (strikes and lockout bans; annulment of arbitral awards in civil matters) the county courts decide at first instance. In such cases the Supreme Court acts as the regular appellate body.

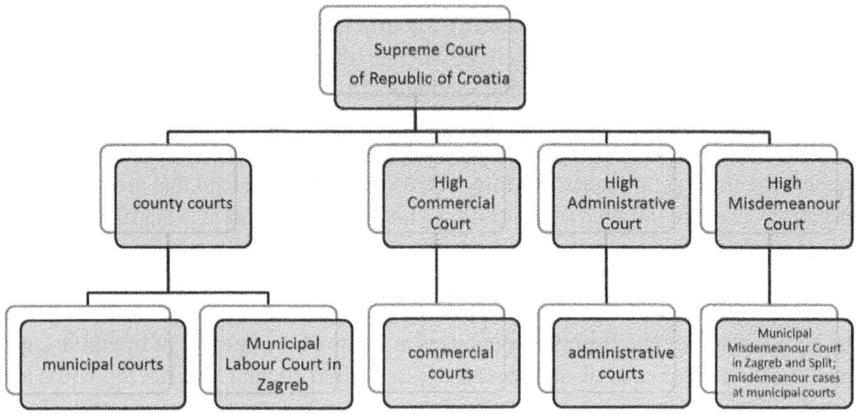

Fig. 4 Court structure in Croatia

cities: Zagreb and Split.[35] At the appellate level, however, all misdemeanour cases are still handled by the High Misdemeanour Court.

'Rationalization' of the court network. Individual courts are weighed down by an uneven amount of cases, which is sometimes a contributing factor to the excessive length of proceedings. Furthermore, the existing court network is financially unstable which is why, for decades on end, its reorganization and rationalization have been part and parcel of every policy developed by the Ministry of Justice.[36] Apart from this, very little has been accomplished in that regard.

Admittedly, the number of municipal courts in Croatia formally decreased from 67[37] in 2012 to 22 in 2016, as was also the case with the specialised courts, the number of which dropped from 74 in 2012 to 36 in 2016. Notwithstanding this reduction, the sheer number of locations in which courts act through 'permanent field offices' has increased.[38] In 2019 courts acted in 251 different locations: 34 municipal courts comprising 70 permanent field offices, as well as 108 land registry offices; 15 county courts, including four permanent field offices; 9 commercial courts, including four permanent field offices; 4 high administrative courts; 4 high specialized courts; and, the Supreme Court.[39] This is too high a number for a country of just over 4 million inhabitants.

[35]Interestingly, the CARDS project back in 2005 came to the conclusion that Croatia has had too many and too small municipal courts, and suggested not only their merger, but also that the perceived necessity of the misdemeanour courts as independent structures be re-examined. In 2007, after an ill-conceived attempt, it was officially announced that the 'merger did not reach the desired results.' Uzelac (2014e, p. 159).

[36]See Review of activities on the reorganization of the judicial system (2019).

[37]Since 2009 the number of municipal courts has been reduced from 108 to 67. Bratković (2019, p. 173).

[38]CEPEJ (2018, p. 208); Bratković (2019, pp. 173ff).

[39]Supreme Court President Report (2019, p. 15).

Judges. Croatia is among the leading countries in Europe regarding the number of appointed judges. In 2019, 1,712 people served in judicial offices of various kinds; 60% of whom were at municipal courts.[40] The greatest number of judges in Europe per 100,000 inhabitants belongs to Slovenia (about 47). This is only outdone by Montenegro, which has 51 judges per 100,000 inhabitants. With 44 judges per 100,000 inhabitants, Croatia regularly comes in second, while Serbia is a steady fourth with 38 judges per 100,000 inhabitants.[41] It comes as no surprise that all four leading countries in this ranking are successor states of the former Yugoslavia.[42]

Non-judicial staff. It is curious that the same four countries also have the greatest number of non-judicial staff in Europe in relation to their population size. In each of them, each court on average has more than 130 non-judicial employees.[43] In 2019, Croatia's courts employed about 6,600 non-judicial staff,[44] the majority of whom were court reporters. In Croatia's courts, a significant number (about 600) of judicial advisers (*sudski savjetnici*)—jurists who have passed the judicial examination—play a rather significant part. In civil and commercial matters, they act as quasi-judges. In litigation cases, they conduct procedures at first instance independently. They also prepare draft decisions, which are signed by their judge mentors if they agree with them. At appellate instances, the role of judicial advisers is quite close to the part played by judges' rapporteurs though they formally do not take part in the decision-making proper.

Taking into account the total number of employees in Croatian courts, it is not surprising that in 2019 80% of the total court budget, approximately 1.3 billion Kuna (about 170 million Euros), related to workforce expenditure.[45]

Municipal and commercial courts. Let us now, however, turn to civil and commercial cases at Croatian courts.[46] As already said, at first instance they are almost exclusively handled by municipal and commercial courts. All cases not explicitly identified as falling within the jurisdiction of commercial courts are in principle handled by municipal courts. Municipal courts are exclusively competent in disputes related to immovables and media disputes.

On the other hand, commercial courts are competent in respect of: disputes between legal persons or sole proprietors; disputes in which one of the parties has gone into company insolvency proceedings; in respect of issues concerning the status of companies, unfair market competition; intellectual property disputes; as well as

---

[40] Supreme Court President Report (2019, p. 20).

[41] CEPEJ (2018, p. 106). Monaco has not been taken into account in the ranking list on account of its size.

[42] Bratković (2019, p. 171).

[43] CEPEJ (2018, p. 163).

[44] Supreme Court President Report (2019, p. 20).

[45] Supreme Court President Report (2019, p. 104).

[46] See above Sect. 2.

maritime and air law disputes.[47] Aside from litigation, commercial courts also handle business registry and corporate bankruptcy proceedings.

The demarcation of competences that pertain to municipal and commercial courts is not always self-evident; often it seems as if the allocation of cases hinges on the momentary caseload of individual courts (as well as on their lobbying power during legislative changes). Such a conclusion may be reached by looking at the effect of the 2019 Amendments to the Code of Civil Procedure (CCP) which has placed disputes relating to unpaid utility and telephone bills, parking tickets, and television licence fees exclusively within the municipal courts' jurisdiction. Before this amendment, jurisdiction was determined by reference to who the parties to proceedings were, in accordance with the general rules on jurisdiction. It is yet to be seen if this change will result in commercial courts actually specializing in real commercial disputes. That has not been the case so far, in part due to the poor state of the economy, and in part due to peculiar rules on jurisdiction.

Individual municipal and commercial courts vary considerably regarding the number of judges acting in their service. In 2019, the largest court in Croatia, the Municipal Civil Court in the capital of Zagreb (*Općinski građanski sud u Zagrebu*), had more than 100 judges who worked solely on civil cases.[48] The remaining municipal courts had an average of 20 judges, including those working on criminal cases. In 2019, the smallest municipal court had 10 judges.[49] The same year, the High Commercial Court in Zagreb had 56 judges, while the other commercial courts had an average of 8 judges. The smallest commercial courts had 4 judges each.[50] However, the number of judges in individual courts often does not match their respective caseload.

In larger courts, judges are appointed to specialised departments according to various legal matters. For instance, the Municipal Civil Court in Zagreb has litigation, enforcement, non-litigation, family law and land registry divisions. For labour cases, only Zagreb has an established specialised Municipal Labour Court. In smaller courts, there is no such specialisation; therefore, each judge handles almost all kinds of cases. In all municipal and commercial courts, single judges adjudicate in all cases before them.

Appellate courts. At the appellate level of the judicial pyramid, in respect of civil and commercial cases, 15 county courts and the High Commercial Court deal, almost exclusively, with appeals from the municipal and commercial courts. Under Croatia's Constitution everyone has a full right to appeal.[51] As a consequence, the right tends to be exercised quite frequently. Appeals are taken from first instance decisions in the overwhelming majority of properly contested cases.[52] Unfortunately, it is impossible

---

[47] Vukelić (2014, p. 227).

[48] Supreme Court President Report (2019, p. 55).

[49] *Ibidem.*

[50] Supreme Court President Report (2019, p. 74).

[51] Criticised by Uzelac (2013).

[52] Uzelac (2014b, p. 48).

to determine in the light of such statistical data as is available what percentage of cases result in an appeal being lodged. However, a single piece of data for 2019 shows that there were about 165,000 new civil litigation and enforcement cases in courts of first instance in comparison with about 95,000 new appeals to the appeal courts.[53]

The information that 148 judges[54] are working in county courts and the High Commercial Court does not allow for a conclusion as to what percentage of them have worked on civil and commercial cases. In appellate proceedings, as a rule, the court adjudicates as a panel of three judges. One of the judges of the panel is appointed as judge rapporteur. Their task is to study the case file, express an opinion on the appeal and report to their fellow judges in the session of the panel.[55] However, through the gradual, but steady, growth of legal exceptions, a single judge may handle certain appeals, e.g. appeals in cases of monetary claims if the amount in dispute is greater than 100,000 kn, which amounts to about 13,000 euros (not a negligible sum), or more than 500,000 kn, which amounts to about 66,000 euros, in cases before commercial courts, as well as in all appeals against procedural orders.

In any event, in 2019 all judges in appeal courts handled about 65,000 civil and commercial cases.[56] In about 60% of the cases they upheld the first instance decision, and in about 15% they quashed it and remitted the case for a re-trial.[57] The relatively high number of courts of second instance and their somewhat conflicting opinions are two of the prime causes of inconsistency in the application of the law.[58]

The Supreme Court. The constitutional role of the Supreme Court is to 'ensure a uniform application of law and equality of all persons in its application'. In civil and commercial cases, the Supreme Court acts as the third and final instance court, deciding second appeals on points of law (*revizija*) from decisions issued by the appeal courts. In 2020, 25 of the total 48 judges decided second appeals on points of law.[59]

The number of second appeal cases in Croatia's Supreme Court is striking. From 2015 onwards, it has handled about 20,000 s appeal cases a year (see Fig. 5). From 2007 to 2016 the number of second appeal cases grew almost eight-fold from about 3,100 to about 24,300 cases.[60]

The sheer scale of second appeal case overload at the Croatian Supreme Court is unambiguously highlighted by the fact that the Italian Supreme Court, a textbook example in comparative literature of an unwieldy and dysfunctional court[61] and

[53] Supreme Court President Report (2019, pp. 52, 62, 73 and 78).

[54] Supreme Court President Report (2019, p. 20).

[55] Uzelac (2014c, p. 246).

[56] Supreme Court President Report (2019, pp. 64 and 79).

[57] *Ibidem.*

[58] Uzelac and Bratković (forthcoming, Sect. 1).

[59] Uzelac and Bratković (forthcoming, Sect. 2).

[60] Uzelac and Bratković (forthcoming, Sect. 4).

[61] The Italian Supreme Court has a total of more than 350 judges serving in various divisions helped by a comparable number of additional staff. In 2015, only in civil matters the Supreme Court made

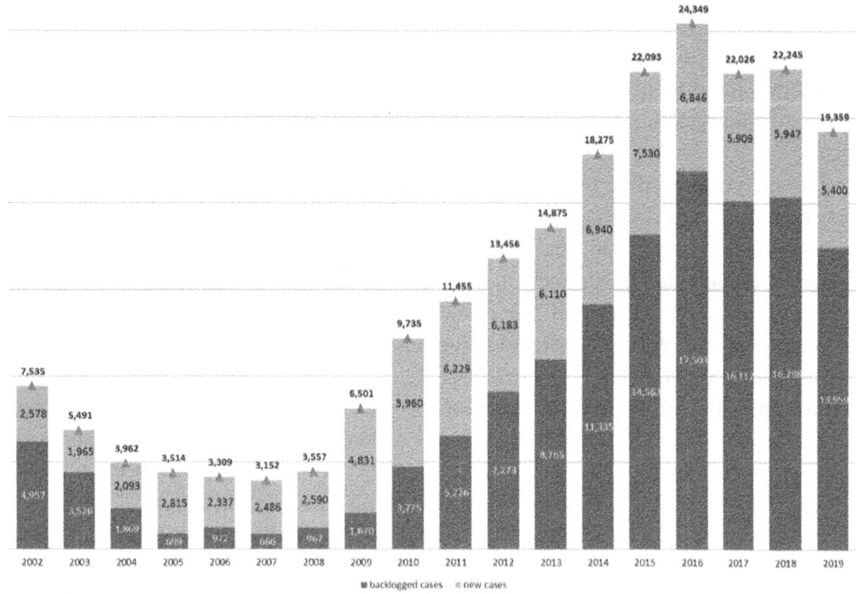

Fig. 5 Second appeal cases before the Croatian Supreme Court (2002–2019) (Uzelac and Bratković forthcoming, Sect. 4)

not exactly a model to be emulated,[62] handles just over 100,000 civil cases a year. Although Italy has a population of almost fifteen times that of Croatia, its number of civil cases is five times that of Croatia. In the United Kingdom, an even larger country than Italy, the Supreme Court decides approximately 70, primarily civil, appeals on the merits per year.[63] In Norway and Finland, the Supreme Courts decide less than 80 civil appeals on the merits per year, while in Denmark, with a comparable population, approximately 200 appeal cases are decided per year.[64]

Interim conclusion. Thus, judging by the overview of Croatia's judicial system given above, one could cynically conclude that it takes a long time for a large number of judges, who are assisted by an equally large number of support staff, to handle a large number of court cases, the outcome of which is difficult to predict. Unfortunately, reforms put in place so far have not solved this issue. Moreover, it appears that no serious reform has ever taken place.

more than 26,000 decisions for whose procedures it took, on average, almost four years. Silvestri (2017, p. 238).

[62]Van Rhee and Fu (2017, p. 11).

[63]Andrews (2017).

[64]Sunde (2017, p. 68).

4 Case Management[65]

What about the micro-perspective? What happens with a particular case when it comes before the court? Let us take the example of a litigation case. Resolving disputes in litigation is the *raison d'être* of courts in the first place. All other tasks that they deal with could be entrusted to other bodies and professionals. It is a political decision whether or not and why this will be done.[66]

Case classification. Each litigation case that comes to court gets a reference number consisting of an abbreviation of the case category name, and its serial number and year, for instance: P-45/2020. Following a cursory examination, a judicial officer in the court registry classifies the case into one of the following categories: family disputes; labour disputes; compensation of damages; contested notarial enforcement orders based on a so-called trustworthy document;[67] and, all other disputes.[68]

This classification is not inconsequential. Each case in a particular category gets a specific, previously defined, weight, the point of which is to ensure an even caseload is assigned to each judge and judicial adviser.[69] However, it is obvious that this is not an entirely appropriate technique because of the varying complexity of particular cases even if they belong to the same category. In any event, each case is assigned to a single judge or judicial adviser. Furthermore, this assignment is executed randomly by a computer programme.

Croatian courts have only recently started to file their records electronically. It is yet to be seen whether or not this will speed up the process of communication between the court registry and the judges' chambers. At present, a considerable amount of time is wasted from the time a claim is filed until a judge starts to work on the case.[70]

When the court file is delivered to the judge, the judge should deal with it in the order of receipt taking due account of the cases the law defines as urgent. Examples of urgent cases are marriage disputes, paternity disputes, child maintenance disputes, labour disputes, copyright disputes, and provisional measures.

Rules of procedure. For all private law disputes the rules of procedure can be found in the Code of Civil Procedure (CCP).[71] Aside from general rules, it contains some

---

[65] Case management as defined above in Sect. 1.

[66] 'Evaluated by the universal standards of due process, as expressed in Article 6 of the ECHR, the residual right to have a contested case dealt with by the *courts* cannot be outsourced; but all other matters and tasks are subject to the discretionary and changeable choice of state authorities.' Uzelac (2014d, p. 13).

[67] See above Sect. 1.

[68] See *Sudski poslovnik*, Official Gazette, 37/14, 49/14, 08/15, 35/15, 123/15, 45/16, 29/17, 33/17, 34/17, 57/17, 101/18, 119/18, 81/19, 128/19, 39/20, 47/20.

[69] By caseload the number of cases a judge is annually expected to resolve is taken into account.

[70] Uzelac (2008a, p. 79).

[71] *Zakon o parničnom postupku*, Official Gazette SFRY, 4/77, 36/77, 36/80, 69/82, 58/84, 74/87, 57/89, 20/90, 27/90, 26/91, 34/91, 35/91; Official Gazette RC, 53/91, 91/92, 112/99, 117/03, 02/07, 84/08, 96/08, 123/08, 57/11, 148/11, 25/13, 89/14, 70/19. CCP was originally enacted in 1976 as a Yugoslav federal law. It continued to be in force as a Croatian law and subject to many amendments.

specific procedural rules, which are partly adjusted to particular types of disputes, such as labour disputes, protection of possession, payment orders, small claims, disputes before commercial courts, and collective claims. There are quite exhaustive specific rules of procedure, in addition to the subsidiary application of general rules of the CCP, contained in the Family Law. A few procedural rules may also be found in substantive laws regulating, for instance, labour, property, anti-discrimination and media law.[72]

Specific rules do not, however, substantially affect the procedural efficiency of the courts in these proceedings. Several specific rules are retained for traditional reasons, e.g. protection of possession or small claims, rather than their ability to effectively boost the resolution of such cases in practice. For instance, the power of judges to disregard new facts and evidence put forward by parties after the pre-trial stage of the proceedings, which was at first foreseen for small claims only, soon became the general rule. Likewise, initially only in family, commercial, and labour disputes, was an appellate court not entitled to quash a first instance judgment in an appeal after the judgment had previously been quashed and sent back for a re-trial.

Length of proceedings. Based on available statistical data, it is not possible to determine how long it takes on average to process a litigation case before Croatian courts.[73] In 2019, for instance, Croatia's commercial courts resolved 80% of 30,000 cases in less than 3 years and 16% of them in less than 7 years. It took more than 7 years to process the rest of the cases. During the same year, commercial courts had about 700 cases on-going for more than 10 years[74] notwithstanding the fact that commercial proceedings are explicitly defined in the CCP as urgent.

It is a certainty that a litigant is pleasantly surprised if a court of first instance reaches a decision in a litigation case of average complexity in less than two years. Proceedings at a court of first instance are conducted inefficiently, through a large number of hearings at long intervals over the course of one, two or more years and are dominated by the exchange of written pleadings by the parties. With some notable exceptions, the impression is often given that neither the judge nor the attorneys representing the parties are suitably prepared to conduct the proceedings. Therefore, adjournments are part of the ordinary course of business both in the pre-trial and trial stages.

In addition, the serving of documents often poses problems. Postal delivery is the most commonly used means of service, but sometimes several months or even

---

[72] Uzelac (2014c, p. 232).

[73] In numerous decisions, the European Court of Human Rights (ECtHR) has confirmed that the Croatian legal system exhibits notable deficiencies as regards reasonable length of proceedings, not only in civil matters. The same court has delivered 412 decisions in cases against Croatia as of the end of 2019. In 109 cases the court determined a violation of the right to a fair trial within a reasonable time. See Violations by Article and by State (2019).

[74] Supreme Court President Report (2019, p. 90).

longer can pass before a document is successfully delivered to a party.[75] Obligatory electronic communication with attorneys has only recently been introduced and is expected to speed up the process of communication.

Pre-trial. After exchange of the statement of claim and defence, the court is almost inevitably bound to hold a preparatory hearing (*pripremno ročište*), which may, according to the rules, be adjourned only once. The hearing usually opens with the claimants' formula that they stand by their 'claim and all its allegations'. If the defendant stands by the defence statement, which is usually the case, the parties do not present their allegations and arguments orally at the hearing. In general, the preparatory hearing comes down to about fifteen minutes of discussion about what evidence is going to be adduced at the main hearing. At all hearings during the proceedings a court reporter is in charge of keeping a court transcript as dictated by the judge.

As a rule, judges allow parties to produce considerable amounts of evidence. Nevertheless, a clear definition of contested matters of fact and law is often missing. The judge will only gain a clearer picture of what issues are in dispute during the main hearing. He will generally only do so, after hearing witnesses, experts, and the parties themselves. At the preparatory hearing future hearings are usually not scheduled, even though they could later be used as a roadmap for subsequent steps in the litigation.[76] Such trial planning is not stipulated by the law. It is not, however, forbidden. An awareness of it is still to be developed among the Croatian judiciary. Recently, intervals between individual hearings have become somewhat shorter. It is only in exceptional cases, however, that they are shorter than several months.

Trial. Similar delays happen at trial hearings. Once again, a trial opens with the claimant's and the defendant's statements that they stand by their allegations and arguments respectively. The hearing usually ends up as no more than a brief meeting between the judge and the parties during which individual witnesses, experts or parties are given a fair hearing. Such hearings are easily adjourned for several months because, for instance, a witness—for whom, *nota bene*, it is unclear what knowledge of the facts at issue he could possess—did not appear at the hearing or because experts did not finish finalising their report or give their evidence in time. During the hearings the judge's intentions are not made clear to the parties. A clear intention to establish only the disputed facts relevant to the case is often missing, so that one fails to see the wood for the trees. Therefore, it is extraordinarily difficult to estimate how long the proceedings will take, as well as what their outcome will be.

Some improvements. All of the above has not changed despite a plethora of changes to the CCP in the last twenty or so years.[77] However, there is some progress. Since amendments made to the CCP in 2003, defendants have submitted their defence

[75] See Uzelac (2014c, p. 242).

[76] See Karolczyk (2013, p. 155), for similar experiences in Poland.

[77] Among the principal goals (and slogans) of the procedural reforms in the 2000s were 'strengthening party discipline' and 'prevention of procedural abuses'. Uzelac (2014a, p. 208).

statements within the time-limit determined by the court because a failure to do so leads to a default judgment (*presuda zbog ogluhe*) if all conditions have been met. This is based on the presumption that a passive defendant admits the claimant's factual allegations.[78] Likewise, in 2003 general bans on certain procedural actions, e.g. general challenges to judges, have been introduced as well as certain limitations of actions, e.g. requests for delegation of jurisdiction, that had previously often been used to prolong the proceedings.[79] However, to this day judges are not particularly keen on imposing fines for 'significant abuses of procedural rights', and if they use them, minimum amounts are preferred.[80]

After 2003, evidence is produced, more or less exclusively, on the initiative of the parties. According to the rules, the court is prohibited from taking any evidence *ex officio* unless it has a legitimate belief that the parties by their own actions would be violating mandatory law or acting against public morality.[81] The parties are thus obliged to submit factual statements that are as complete as possible and to provide evidence in due course.[82]

With the aim of promoting better preparation and a more focused discussion at the trial hearing, from 2013 parties have been allowed to present new statements of facts and evidentiary motions no later than the preparatory hearing. Courts are to disregard delayed submissions unless the parties can prove they were unable to produce them earlier through no fault of their own. From 2013, the law has not permitted parties to modify their claim nor to make a counter-claim at the trial hearing.

Despite these new arrangements having some positive effects, it is fair to say that the imposition of rigorous, statutory limits following which parties are precluded from taking certain procedural actions, hinders procedural flexibility and the court's ability to adjust its treatment to the nature of the case. It can lead to judgments which cannot be considered just. These were the reasons for further amendments to the CCP in 2019, which permit claims to be modified at a trial hearing if the claimants can prove that they were unable to modify them earlier through no fault of their own. In addition, in order to avoid the exchange of written statements not happening until the hearing,[83] in 2019 a rule was introduced that, in principle, written statements must be submitted to the court and the opposing party no later than eight days before the hearing.

Attorneys. Attorneys play a significant part in the way proceedings are conducted. While there is no obligation to be represented by an attorney in Croatia, parties usually make use of their services. Attorneys are, understandably, motivated to be properly remunerated. In accordance with standard attorney's fees, an attorney has a right to be remunerated for nearly every step in the procedure, e.g. for submitting the claim, for

---

[78] Triva and Dika (2004, p. 604ff); Uzelac (2004, Sect. 7.3.4).

[79] See Uzelac (2004, Sect. 7.1).

[80] Uzelac (2004, Sect. 7.3.1).

[81] Uzelac (2004, Sect. 7.2.1).

[82] See Sorabji (2017, p. 192).

[83] See Zelić (2001, p. 109).

reasoned submissions, and for representation at hearings discussing the main issue, depending on the amount in dispute.[84] Thus, attorney's fees increase as a function of the number of steps in the proceedings and of the amount in dispute. Some, hopefully few, attorneys abuse this fact and overcharge for an imperfect service.

Appeal proceedings. The fact that stands out among the reasons for the excessive length of proceedings in Croatia is that only a small part of cases end at first instance. An appeal is an expected part of the litigation process. As already mentioned, the right to appeal is a constitutional right. Not only first instance judgements but also procedural decisions that terminate proceedings and most *interim* court decisions may be subject to an appeal.[85] In reality, the right to appeal is often abused only to delay the proceedings.

In principle, during the pendency of an appeal the initial judgment is not enforced; it is automatically suspended.[86] Exceptionally, in small claims cases an appeal does not suspend the enforcement of the judgment. This rule was introduced in 2019. It will be interesting to see how it will affect the rate of appeals lodged in such cases. In any case, it would be particularly advantageous if separate statistics about it were kept, although this has not been the case to date.

Available statistics do not reveal how long appeal proceedings take. Then again, attorneys are generally pleasantly surprised if a second instance judgment is passed in less than two years. Appellate court panels regularly deliver their judgments at closed sessions, without the participation of the parties and their attorneys.[87] The appellate courts in practice do not hold hearings despite there being a rule which allows for such an option. The usual argument is that appellate courts do not have enough hearing rooms and other logistical facilities to enable them to hold oral hearings.[88]

The legislature tacitly accepted this when it subsequently allowed litigation cases that are subject to an appeal to be assigned to different county courts by random algorithmic allocation. Certainly, this was not in the interest of the parties involved because it does not facilitate access to the hearings at the county courts. Moreover, this has further highlighted the disparities between the case law of Croatian courts. It is not unusual for similar appeals from decisions of the same municipal court to have markedly different outcomes, i.e., some are upheld, while others are dismissed, depending on the county court to which an appeal has been assigned.

It is not rare for first instance judgments to be quashed in the appeal process; in 2019, this happened in about 15% of cases.[89] Thereupon, higher appellate courts refer those cases back to lower courts for a re-trial. This adds to the excessive length

[84] A one-time remuneration for any first instance proceedings regardless of the number of procedural steps taken is given by the standard attorney's fees in, for instance, the case of disputes in which the amount in dispute is less than 1,000 kuna (about 130 euros) as well as in marriage disputes.

[85] Uzelac (2014c, p. 239).

[86] Uzelac (2014b, p. 48).

[87] Uzelac (2004, Sect. 7.2.1).

[88] Uzelac (2014c, p. 245).

[89] See above Sect. 3.

of proceedings. The reasons that the appellate courts frequently give when quashing first instance decisions are that the factual findings were incomplete and, to a lesser extent, that there were procedural errors.

Therefore it remains the case in Croatia today, that it is easy to imagine a scenario in which it takes ten years to handle a case.[90] However, recent trends show a decrease in such cases, partly because since 2013 the appellate courts are no longer allowed to quash first instance judgments more than once. This was introduced in order to incentivise the appellate courts to make their decisions based on the documents from the case file and evidence or, which is rarely the case, by holding a hearing.

Second appeal proceedings. Additionally, the Supreme Court is seen by most litigants and their attorneys as just another opportunity for appeal. Paradoxically, even though the introduction of the 'exceptional' second appeal (*izvanredna revizija*) in 2008 was supposed to facilitate case filtering so that only such cases as are relevant to the uniform application of the law and to the equality of all people in its application should reach the Supreme Court, it led to a flood of cases inundating the Supreme Court.[91]

A second appeal does not automatically suspend enforcement. Despite this, enforcement is commonly suspended by the judge handling the enforcement. It means that the second instance judgment, which is by law *res judicata*, will not be enforced for the following two or three years. That is how long it takes for the Supreme Court to decide a second appeal.[92]

Considering the enormous number of cases dealt with by the Supreme Court, it is not realistic to expect the court's case law to be coherent, well-reasoned and comprehensible.[93] It remains to be seen whether the new model introduced in 2019, which is focused primarily on making the case law uniform, will yield positive changes. According to that model, permission to appeal is subject to separate proceedings in which only admissibility is examined, followed by another set of proceedings on the merits if permission is granted.[94] From the case management perspective, it looks like a reasonable way to sort out important cases relatively fast.

Remnants of the socialist legal tradition. However, one ought not to forget that Croatian legal culture, which may eventually change, embraces an attitude known as *Instanzmentalität* (in German), i.e. a general compulsion in all judicial proceedings to pursue possible legal strategies without a realistic assessment of the prospects for their success.[95] Although this is not exclusive to post-socialist countries, it is partly the result of a socialist attitude, which has its ideological roots in socialist

[90] Uzelac (2014b, p. 48).

[91] See above Sect. 3, in particular Fig. 5. Uzelac and Bratković (forthcoming, Sect. 4).

[92] In 2019, disposition time for civil cases at the Supreme Court was 677 days (somewhat less than two years), much shorter than in 2014, when it was 1,129 days (about three years). Supreme Court President Report (2019, p. 88).

[93] Jolowicz (2000, pp. 332 and 348).

[94] See more Uzelac and Bratković (forthcoming, Sect. 6); Bratković (2020).

[95] Jolowicz (1998, p. 59).

legal theory, particularly in its adherence to the principle of material truth and in understanding that there should be as many levels of 'control' as possible.[96]

Generally, one may claim that the priority of the material truth over efficiency in procedure as well as over legal certainty, as a meta-normative remnant of the socialist legal tradition,[97] continues to contribute, at least in part, to the fact that proceedings before Croatian courts take (too) long. In the period between 1945 and 1991, when Croatia was a constituent part of the SFRY, civil proceedings were primarily aimed at handling only 'secondary' problems, i.e. disputes related to the relics of private property disputes in a society in which collectivist doctrine otherwise dominated.[98] Such an attitude certainly did not spread any awareness among judges of the need for efficient case management.[99]

However, interestingly enough, even during the socialist period, procedural legislation continued to follow the historically preceding model, i.e. the Austrian *Zivilprozessordnung* of Franz Klein of 1895 which had been accepted in the Kingdom of Yugoslavia as the Yugoslav CCP in 1929. However, Klein's model of expeditious, inexpensive and efficient proceedings was never really introduced in Croatia, nor in the wider region.[100] An additional proof that a substantially identical legal text is no guarantee of its identical application nor of equivalent outcomes in practice.

5 Conclusion

Backlogs and excessively lengthy proceedings. Croatia is still in search of an efficient judiciary that properly serves its citizens. Court backlogs and the length of proceedings are both symptoms of its case management problems. In Croatia it takes far too long time for a large number of judges, assisted by an equally large number of support staff, to handle a large number of cases. Despite the court network being subject to 'rationalization', the sheer number of locations in which courts sit has increased.

Proceedings in courts of first instance, whether they concern routine or complex legal issues, are conducted inefficiently. Multiple, usually short, hearings that take place with significant gaps between them over the course of two or more years and which are dominated by a written exchange of party pleadings are the norm. While there are some notable exceptions to this, the general impression given is that neither judges nor attorneys are suitably prepared to conduct proceedings. There is no trial planning and a clear definition of contested matters of fact and law is often absent.

---

[96]Uzelac (2010b, p. 390).

[97]Mańko (2013, pp. 215ff), argues that meta-normative remnants (latently but obstinately) guide today's discourse and practice by framing the working legal thought.

[98]Uzelac (2004, Sect. 4).

[99]*Ibidem*.

[100]*Ibidem*.

It could reasonably be said that the priority of the material truth over procedural efficiency as well as over legal certainty, as a meta-normative remnant of the socialist legal tradition, still affects the way first instance and appeal proceedings are conducted. This continued priority can be seen to contribute to their excessive length. Despite its influence on the text of the Croatian CCP, Klein's 1895 model of expeditious, inexpensive and efficient proceedings never really took effect in practice in Croatia.

Civil justice as a public service. Reliable empirical data about the operation of the civil justice system is, however, is missing. Such information is a necessity. Without it, it will not be possible to properly analyse the current state of affairs, or accurately identify problems, within the system. Nor will it be possible to plan and implement effective reform. Despite a large number of changes in the law, it would appear that no serious attempt at a reform has ever taken place.

The civil justice system should be refocused on citizens as users of the system.[101] It exists to serve them. Individual litigants address the courts in order to have their lawsuit resolved fairly, efficiently, and at reasonable speed. Although courts may be entrusted with other tasks, their core task is adjudicating disputed matters. Therefore, it is paramount for the court to establish a sound classification of claims, not only in relation to their nature but also in respect of their value and complexity. One-size does not fit all.[102] Dealing with a large number of simple cases requires different skills than dealing with juridically complex cases.[103]

Claims are to be managed as a public service. Parties to individual claims should therefore be required to cooperate with the court in managing their claims so as to ensure that no more time and resources than is necessary or proportionate are expended on any case. In this way sufficient time and resources are available for other cases.[104] All judges, whether generalist or specialist, ought to be experts in the art of judging and have a broad knowledge of legal institutions and principles.[105]

It is for the court, in active collaboration with the parties, to determine the intensity and pace of the litigation process and to ensure that it is adapted to the needs of a particular case.[106] Efficiency and expedition are as important as the correctness of the outcome.[107] In trial planning, the court and the parties should together determine how many preparatory briefs the parties should exchange, when the hearings are going to take place, whether there is a need for oral discussion, and so forth. Parties

[101] Uzelac (2008b, p. 425).

[102] Sorabji (2017, p. 33).

[103] Uzelac (2014e, p. 149).

[104] Sorabji (2017, p. 2, 9).

[105] Uzelac (2014e, p. 153).

[106] Active collaboration between the court and the parties is one of the basic principles of the new European Rules of Civil Procedure which have been drafted by ELI and UNIDROIT. It is meant to serve as a model for national reforms of civil procedure. See Uzelac (2017), Van Rhee (2020), and ELI-Unidroit transnational rules of civil procedure (2020).

[107] Zuckerman (2009, p. 49).

that, by their own fault, fail to abide by the trial timetable ought to be precluded from taking specific procedural steps. They ought, also, to be subject to cost penalties for non-compliance.

The court structure, attorney remuneration and the manner in which the work of judges is evaluated should equally be accommodated to the above. Active collaboration between the parties and the court should be focused on final dispute resolution rather than on managing the court files. Hopefully, such an approach would contribute to a reduction in the number of appeals and enable the Supreme Court to secure consistency within the case-law. Undoubtedly, such a new approach to case management would require all lawyers involved to equip themselves with special, managerial, skills, which should be introduced into law schools' curricula, and thereby replace the, current, excessive emphasis that is placed on memorising regulations.

Does this paradigmatic turn seem slightly idealistic? Yes, but one ought to strive for ideals. *Wer immer strebend sich bemüht, den können wir erlösen* (Goethe, Faust II).[108]

References

Andrews N (2017) The Supreme court of the United Kingdom: A selective tribunal with the final say on most matters. In: Van Rhee CH, Fu Y (eds) Supreme courts in transition in China and the West. Adjudication at the service of public goals, Cham, pp 37–51

Bratković M (2015) Reorganizacija ovrhe na temelju vjerodostojne isprave u Sloveniji (Reorganisation of enforcement on the basis of a trustworthy document in Slovenia). Zbornik Pravnog fakulteta Sveučilišta u Rijeci (Collected Papers of the Faculty of Law, University of Rijeka) 36(2):1025–1050

Bratković M (2019) Građansko pravosuđe u službi građana (Civil Justice as a Public Service). In: Barbić J (ed), Europska budućnost hrvatskoga građanskog pravosuđa (European Future of Croatian Civil Justice), Zagreb, pp 161–183

Bratković M (2020) Novine u uređenju revizije u parničnom postupku (Amendments to the regulation of second appeal in civil proceedings). Zakonitost 1(4):16–27

CEPEJ (2018) European judicial systems. Efficiency and quality of justice. 2016 data. https://rm.coe.int/rapport-avec-couv-18-09-2018-en/16808def9c. Accessed June 2020

Communication from the Commission. Opinion on Croatia's application for membership of the European Union. https://eur-lex.europa.eu/legal-content/EN/TXT/?uri=celex%3A52004DC0257. Accessed June 2020

ELI-Unidroit transnational rules of civil procedure (2020) Study LXXVIA. Transnational civil procedure. Formulation of regional rules. https://www.unidroit.org/work-in-progress-eli-unidroit-european-rules. Accessed June 2020

EU Justice Scoreboard 2018. Communication from the Commission to the European Parliament, the Council, the European Central Bank, the European Economic and Social Committee and the Committee of the Regions. https://ec.europa.eu/info/sites/info/files/justice_scoreboard_2018_en.pdf. Accessed June 2020

EU Justice Scoreboard 2019. Communication from the Commission to the European Parliament, the Council, the European Central Bank, the European Economic and Social Committee and the Committee of the Regions. https://ec.europa.eu/info/sites/info/files/justice_scoreboard_2019_en.pdf. Accessed June 2020

[108] *Whoever strives with all his might, that man we can redeem.*

Jeuland E (2018) Towards a new court management? Peking Univ Law J 6(1):105–177
Jolowicz JA (1998) The role of the supreme courts at the national and international level. In: Yessiou-Faltsi P (ed) The role of the supreme courts at the national and international level. Reports for the Thessaloniki International Colloquium, Thessaloniki, pp 37–63
Jolowicz JA (2000) On civil procedure. Cambridge
Karolczyk B (2013) Pretrial as a part of judicial case management in Poland in comparative perspective. Comparative Law Review 15:151–188
Mańko R (2013) Weeds in the gardens of justice? The survival of hyperpositivism in Polish legal culture as a symptom/sinthome. J Law Lit C 7(2):207–233
Review of activities on the reorganization of the judicial system (2019). https://pravosudje.gov.hr/istaknute-teme/reorganizacija-8688/pregled-aktivnosti-na-reorganizaciji-pravosudnog-sustava/6179. Accessed June 2020
Silvestri E (2017) The Italian supreme court of cassation: Of misnomers and unaccomplished missions. In: Van Rhee CH, Fu Y (eds) Supreme courts in transition in China and the West. Adjudication at the service of public goals, Cham, pp 229–245
Sorabji J (2017) Managing claims. Peking Univ Law J 6(1):179–235
Statistical review (2006–2019). https://pravosudje.gov.hr/pristup-informacijama-6341/strategije-planovi-i-izvjesca/statisticki-pregled/6719. Accessed June 2020
Strengthening the rule of law: 68% of citizens think badly about justice, 11 December 2017. http://www.glas-slavonije.hr/350719/1/Lose-o-pravosudju-misli-68—gradjana. Accessed June 2020
Sunde J (2017) From courts of appeal to courts of precedent. Access to the highest courts in the Nordic countries. In: Van Rhee CH, Fu Y (eds) Supreme courts in transition in China and the West. Adjudication at the service of public goals, Cham, pp 53–76
Supreme Court President Report on the State of the Judiciary (2017). http://www.vsrh.hr/CustomPages/Static/HRV/Files/2018dok/izvjesce_predsjednikaVSRH_o_stanju_sudbene_vlasti_2017.pdf. Accessed June 2020
Supreme Court President Report on the State of the Judiciary (2018). http://www.vsrh.hr/custompages/static/HRV/files/Izvjesca/Izvjesce_predsjednika_VSRH_2018.pdf. Accessed June 2020
Supreme Court President Report on the State of the Judiciary (2019). http://www.vsrh.hr/custompages/static/HRV/files/Izvjesca/Statisticko_izvjesce_2019_%20stanje_sudbene_vlasti.pdf. Accessed June 2020
Triva S, Dika M (2004) Građansko parnično procesno pravo (The Law of Civil Litigation). Zagreb
Uzelac A (2004) Accelerating civil proceedings in Croatia. A history of attempts to improve the efficiency of civil litigation. In: Van Rhee CH (ed) The law's delay. Essays on undue delay in civil litigation. Antwerp, pp 283–313
Uzelac A (2008a) Reforming Mediterranean civil procedure: Is there a need for shock therapy? In: Van Rhee CH, Uzelac A (eds) Civil justice between efficiency and quality: From ius commune to the CEPEJ. Antwerp, Oxford, Portland, pp 71–99
Uzelac A (2008b) Turning civil procedure upside down: From judges' law to users' law. In: Van Rhee CH, Heirbaut D, Storme M (eds) The French code of civil procedure (1806) after 200 years. The civil procedure tradition in France and abroad, Kluwer Belgium, pp 413–427
Uzelac A (2010a) Privatization of enforcement services. A step forward for countries in transition? In: Van Rhee CH, Uzelac A (eds) Enforcement and enforceability. Tradition and reform. Antwerp, Oxford Portland, pp 83–101
Uzelac A (2010b) Survival of the third legal tradition. Supreme Court Law Rev 49(2d):377–396
Uzelac A (2013) Ustavno pravo na žalbu u građanskim stvarima: jamstvo ispravnog pravosuđenja ili relikt prošlosti? (The constitutional right to appeal in civil matters: A guarantee to a fair trial or a relic of the past?) In: Uzelac A, Garašić J, Maganić A (eds) Djelotvorna pravna zaštita u pravničnom postupku. Izazovi pravosudnih transformacija na jugu Europe. Liber amicorum Mihajlo Dika. Pravni fakultet Sveučilišta u Zagrebu, pp 219–243
Uzelac A (2014a) Croatia: Omnipotent judges as the cause of procedural inefficiency and impotence. In: Van Rhee CH, Fu Y (eds) Civil litigation in China and Europe. Essays on the role of the judge and the parties, Dordrecht, pp 197–221

Uzelac A (2014b) Delays and backlogs in civil procedure. A (south) east European perspective. Revista de Processo 39(238):39–64
Uzelac A (2014c) Features and shortcomings of appellate review in civil and administrative cases in Croatia. In: Uzelac A, Van Rhee CH (eds) Nobody's perfect. Comparative essays on appeals and other means of recourse against judicial decisions in civil matters, Antwerp, Oxford, Portland, pp 229–258
Uzelac A (2014d) Goals of civil justice and civil procedure in the contemporary world. Global developments. Towards harmonisation (and back). In: Uzelac A (ed) Goals of civil justice and civil procedure in contemporary judicial systems. Cham, pp 3–31
Uzelac A (2014e) Mixed blessing of judicial specialisation: The devil is in the detail. Russ Law J 4:146–164
Uzelac A (2017) Towards European rules of civil procedure: Rethinking procedural obligations. Hung J Legal Stud 58(1):3–18
Uzelac A (2019) Hrvatsko građansko pravosuđe između Strasbourga, Luxembourga i Zagreba ili O europeizaciji ovršnog prava na primjeru ovrhe na nekretnini (Croatian Civil Justice Between Strasbourg and Luxembourg. On Europeanization of Civil Enforcement: The Example of Enforcement on Immovables). In: Barbić J (ed) Europska budućnost hrvatskoga građanskog pravosuđa (European Future of Croatian Civil Justice). Zagreb, pp 39–66
Uzelac A, Bratković M (2015) Certificiranje nespornih tražbina u domaćem i poredbenom pravu (Certification of Uncontested Debt in National and Comparative Law). In: Rijavec V et al (eds) Aktualnosti građanskog procesnog prava (Novelties in civil procedure). Pravni fakultet Sveučilišta u Splitu, Split, pp 81–116
Uzelac A, Bratković M (forthcoming) Croatia: Supreme court between individual justice and system management. In: Bravo-Hurtado P, Van Rhee CH (eds) Supreme Courts under pressure: Controlling caseload in the administration of civil justice
Van Rhee CH (2020) Towards harmonised European rules of civil procedure: Obligations of the judge, the parties and their lawyers. Access Justice East Eur 1(6):6–33
Van Rhee CH, Fu Y (2017) Introduction. In: Van Rhee CH, Fu Y (eds) Supreme courts in transition in China and the West. Adjudication at the service of public goals, Cham, pp 1–12
Violations by Article and by State (2019). https://www.echr.coe.int/Documents/Stats_violation_1959_2019_ENG.pdf. Accessed June 2020
Vukelić M (2014) Commercial courts in Croatia and case management. In: Van Rhee CH, Fu Y (eds) Civil litigation in China and Europe. Essays on the role of the judge and the parties, Dordrecht, pp 223–232
Zelić I (2001) Ne dopustimo da se parnični postupak pretvori u neformalno 'druženje' stranaka sa sudom (Why litigation should not turn into an informal meeting between the parties and the court). Hrvatska pravna revija 1(5):102–109
Zuckerman AA (2009) The challenge of civil justice reform: Effective court management of litigation. City Univ Hong Kong Law Rev 1(1):69–71

Special Themes

A Brief Note on the Application of Information and Communication Technology in Civil Judicial Case Management

Fuhua Wang

Abstract The application of information and communication technology in court enhances case management efficiency. This brief note discusses the experience with e-courts in China. The experience has been predominantly positive. The important step going forward is to integrate state-of-the-art technology with best practices so that the use of technology becomes a driving force for judicial reform in China.

1 Introduction

Electronic communication, data processing and data transmission have made considerable impact on how court proceedings are conducted in China. The development of instant electronic communication and payment systems has propelled e-commerce and online business transactions. The intensification of online commercial activities inevitably creates a need for a technologically-advanced dispute resolution infrastructure. This is the backdrop of the rise of e-justice in China (which began in 2000),[1] in particular, the use of information and communication technology (ICT) in judicial case management with the view to reduce costs and increase efficiency. With the promulgation of the *Five-Year Plan for Information Construction at People's Courts* (2016–2020),[2] the application of ICT in litigation and the establishment of e-courts have been formalized. Many courts in China are now equipped with electronic service systems and video trial systems, among other technological capabilities. With parties'

[1] Kengyel and Nemessányi (2012).

[2] Adopted by the Supreme People's Court in February 2016.

F. Wang (✉)
Shanghai Jiao Tong University, Shanghai, People's Republic of China
e-mail: wangfuhua@sjtu.edu.cn

P. C. H. Chan and C. H. van Rhee (eds.), *Civil Case Management in the Twenty-First Century: Court Structures Still Matter*, Ius Gentium: Comparative Perspectives on Law and Justice 85, https://doi.org/10.1007/978-981-33-4512-6_13

agreement, the court can hear a case by videoconferencing. Witnesses and experts can testify using audiovisual transmission technology or a synchronized video test room.[3]

2 e-Courts and Case Management

The development of e-courts is an important milestone for case management in China. The use of ICT not only improved case-flow management, but also facilitated communication between the judge and the parties. Court automation and computerization have made enforcement of judgments more efficient.[4] Some courts are completely 'virtual' (also known as 'external e-courts'), while others are still 'physical courts' with internal ICT capabilities (also known as 'internal e-courts').

In January 2011, the Supreme People's Court[5] proposed to establish a case information management system and apply information technology to trial scheduling, trial quality assessment, case-flow management, casefile management, performance appraisal, and court human resources management. This marks the beginning of a technological revolution in China's judicial management. Electronic systems in the court are designed to manage the entire litigation process and not just some aspects of it.

In February 2017, the National Unified Electronic Service Platform for Courts (全国法院统一送达平台)[6] was given a test run in Fengman District People's Court in Jilin Province, Huadian City People's Court in Jilin Province, Hangzhou Railway Transport Court and Yuhuan People's Court in Zhejiang Province. It supports the service of litigation documents through Sina Weibo, Sina Email, Alipay and other platforms. The possibility to serve and receive court documents on social media is particularly important in promoting efficiency, given the popularity of social media in China.

3 External e-Courts

External e-courts have been widely established in China, for example, the Jilin Provincial Electronic Court and the Hangzhou Yuhang, West Lake and Binjiang District Electronic Court. External e-courts are equipped with electronic service systems, virtual trial platforms and other electronic procedural systems. The

---

[3]This approach has proven to be especially effective under the massive lockdown in China due to COVID-19.

[4]World Bank (2019).

[5]Notice of the Supreme People's Court on Issuing Several Opinions on Strengthening the Administration of Trials by the People's Courts, No. 2 [2011] of the Supreme People's Court, issued on 1 June 2011, effective on 1 June 2011, revised by Notice by the Supreme People's Court of Amending or Repealing Certain Regulatory Documents (issued on 3 May 2020; effective on 3 May 2020).

[6]National court uniform service platform (2020).

Hangzhou Internet Court conducts all its procedures online, from case filing to enforcement of judgments.

Many external e-courts have special subject-matter jurisdiction. For instance, the Hangzhou Internet Court has a special jurisdiction over internet-related disputes,[7] e.g. disputes relating to internet commerce, online microfinancing, internet copyright infringement, and internet domain name disputes. The jurisdiction of the Hangzhou Internet Court is very broad, covering civil as well as administrative disputes. In the first three years since its establishment, the civil judgments issued by the Hangzhou Internet Court have reached more than 4,600, most of which were contractual and tort disputes.[8]

4 Internal e-Courts

Automation is an important component of the internal e-court. It is particularly important in China, as automation can reduce the possibility of interference with adjudication. Before the introduction of ICT systems, case deliberation was done behind closed doors. No records were made of these discussions. It was rather easy for someone senior in the court to influence the decision of the adjudicators. However, when ICT systems are installed, communications among adjudicators are recorded. While the records are unavailable to the public, a 'paper trail' is retained. This can serve as a deterrent to external interference with the deliberation process.

Informatization is another key component of the internal e-court. The court's information network in effect becomes the platform that allows the parties and the judge to keep in touch and interact with each other. The judge, in a way, becomes more 'accessible' to the parties. The court also becomes more transparent.

The internal e-court is changing the organizational fabric of the judicial institution. In the past, the judicial hierarchy was very 'vertical' in that court leaders and the higher-level court exerted immense influence over the judge in adjudication. But with the e-court, owing to the sharing of information and increased transparency, the court organization is less vertical, which in turn enhances adjudicatory independence.

The internal e-court promotes case management through the digitization of court documents. Electronic files break through geographical barriers and allow multiple individuals to use the files at the same time. The information becomes non-exclusive. Prior to digitization, the public had to go to the courthouse to check the files. Information disclosure is another important feature of the internal e-court. Judicial data, when widely shared, can facilitate better case preparation.

---

[7]On 26 June 2017, the Central Leading Group for Comprehensively Deepening the Reform (中央全面深化改革领导小组) decided to set up the Hangzhou Internet Court (杭州互联网法院) to play a pivotal role in e-commerce dispute resolution.

[8]A search was conducted on China Judgments Online, with 'Hangzhou Internet Court' (杭州互联网法院) set as the designated court and 'Judgment' (判决书) set as the document type.

5 Conclusion

The application of information and communication technology in court no doubt enhances case management efficiency. The experience with e-courts in China has been predominantly positive. The important step going forward is to integrate state-of-the-art technology with best practices so that the use of technology becomes a driving force for judicial reform in China.

References

China Judgements Online. https://wenshu.court.gov.cn/website/wenshu/181217BMTKHNT2W0/index.html?pageId=112b49bdaecfd1333ed5048dc5de832c&s2=%E6%9D%AD%E5%B7%9E%E4%BA%92%E8%81%94%E7%BD%91%E6%B3%95%E9%99%A2&s8=01&s6=01. Accessed 27 June 2020

Kengyel M, Nemessányi Z (eds) (2012) Electronic technology and civil procedure: New paths to justice from around the world. Dordrecht

National court uniform service platform (2020). https://songda.court.gov.cn/. Accessed on 27 June 2020

Worldbank (2019) Enforcing contracts. https://www.doingbusiness.org/en/data/exploretopics/enforcing-contracts/good-practices#Court%20automation. Accessed on 27 June 2020

A Prospective Court-Connected Mandatory Mediation Regime in Macau: A Brief Note

Hugo Luz dos Santos

Abstract This brief note discusses the prospective court-connected mandatory mediation regime in Macau. The model will benefit from Macau's legal culture while implementing a high-quality mediation regime.

1 Introduction

Justice in Macau is an advocate-controlled, lengthy procedure that is exceptionally expensive. It is underpinned by an outdated adversarial[1] model[2] that drives hostility[3] between the disputants.[4] Moreover, Macau has failed to fulfil the promise of affording a fundamental right to its residents: effective access to justice (Art. 36(1) Macau Basic Law). This situation is worrisome. Change is needed. Macau must embrace a court-connected mandatory mediation regime in order to alleviate existing problems. This Note explores two issues, firstly, determining the role of mediation in the context of Macau's legal culture. Secondly, the suitability of court-connected mandatory mediation for Macau.

[1]For Spain, Cortina (2007, pp. 18ff) (hailing the benefits of cordial relations for building robust citizenship).

[2]See Nolan-Haley (2012, p. 61).

[3]This trend has been pointed out earlier by several scholars such as Kovach (2005, pp. 60–61) (arguing that the vanishing trial will lead to mediation becoming like arbitration).

[4]For this very reason, doctrine is advocating for a paradigm shift in the realms of justice, in which ADR (especially Mediation) will play a role of paramount importance; for Italy, Taruffo (2007 pp. 319–331); for Portugal, Costa e Silva (2008, pp. 735–736); for Germany, Gottwald (2001, pp. 137–155).

H. L. dos Santos (✉)
University of Macau, Macau, People's Republic of China
e-mail: yb87211@um.edu.mo

P. C. H. Chan and C. H. van Rhee (eds.), *Civil Case Management in the Twenty-First Century: Court Structures Still Matter*, Ius Gentium: Comparative Perspectives on Law and Justice 85, https://doi.org/10.1007/978-981-33-4512-6_14

2 Macau's Legal Culture and Mediation

Courts in Macau are overburdened by a high number of cases. Macau's legal system needs to assemble an alternative dispute resolution mechanism that is capable of solving the burden on the courts. In Macau's case,[5] mediation can be used to alleviate this problem. Through its Confucian cultural background, Macau can promote the implementation of mediation.[6] Scholars have demonstrated the positive impact this cultural background could have when solving disputes in Macau.[7]

Moreover, the use of mediation as a tool for building trust between interested parties would aid in enhancing trust in Macau's judicial system. There is the growing issue of a loss of trust in the judiciary worldwide, whereby this loss of trust[8] has to be corrected by efficient justice systems. Mediation is an instrument that can build relationships and encourage trust.

A court-connected mandatory mediation regime is needed in Macau because disputants lack a system of alternative dispute resolution. The lack of awareness of mediation in Macau needs to be corrected in order to allow disputants to make informed[9] dispute resolution choices with regard to mediation.[10] However, both laypeople and disputants have no in-depth knowledge of mediation. Voluntary mediation may not be beneficial to Macau if the standard of education and training is not of the highest quality.[11] Evidently, mediation would otherwise benefit Macau's judicial system.[12]

---

[5]One should not forget that Macau is 'predominantly a Chinese society'. Tong (2015, pp. 1–80).

[6]'China has maintained a negative bias against litigation and the social disharmony that accompanies it. This cultural tradition carried over to the sphere of international commerce and trade.' Huang (2017, p. 423).

[7]Shiga (1988, pp. 18–26).

[8]This phenomenon has a perverse effect: the erosion of the *trust theory* (*Vertrauenstheorie*) which pervades Macau's legal system in a holistic sense. In general, about the importance of trust in contractual relationships, Von Jhering (1881, pp. 327–425). For Italy, Marasco (2006, p. 18ff). The same relationship (Justice as a *public service*; *trustworthiness* and *trust* perceived by the *service users*. i.e. citizens who access the Judicial System on a regular basis) has been described in French doctrine; see Severin (2011, p. 54ff). The relationship between justice and trustworthiness was shown to be reciprocal; see Colquitt and Rodell (2011, p. 1183).

[9]Nolan-Haley (2018, pp. 386–392) (discusses the interplay between party autonomy, informed dispute resolution choices and informed consent in mediation).

[10]Fogel and Strong (2016, pp. 260–279) (highlighting, with the benefit of hindsight, the importance of dispute resolution education in mediation and litigation).

[11]Sander (2007, p. 16) (contending that mandatory mediation is a 'kind of temporary expedient').

[12]Dos Santos (2019, pp. 14–15).

3 Blueprint for Prospective Court-Connected Mandatory Mediation

A court-connected mandatory mediation regime in Macau would achieve two objectives. Firstly, it would enable Macau residents to reconnect with their traditional legal culture of resolving disputes in an amicable manner. Secondly, it would foster their dispute resolution education as the disputants would become acquainted with mediation.

However, lawyers can negatively affect mediation due to their adversarial mindset and, sometimes, self-interested values.[13] For these reasons alone, the prospective Macau lawmaker should seriously contemplate the possibility to remove lawyers from both mediation sessions and caucuses.[14]

Lawmakers have to make use of incentives,[15] specifically those incentives aimed at encouraging disputants to partake in mediation in good faith.[16] Disputants should not face an unnecessary expense when opting-out from court-connected mandatory mediation, if they had previously participated in mediation sessions in good faith.[17] This would protect the principle of party autonomy. Additionally, this would aid in aligning the private interests of the disputants[18] with the public interest, to make Macau's system of justice efficient.

Furthermore, lawmakers also need to examine Macau's main societal issues.[19] The societal issues are the problems that have increasingly needed disputes resolved in court and are negatively affecting the caseload before the court. To that end, empirical research needs to be conducted to capture the main issues within the litigation cases in Macau. Upon completion, the legislator should use these issues to adapt the law to the real issues of Macau. Gaming law contracts and gaming concessions should be

---

[13]Nolan-Haley (2013, p. 157) (notes that 'in fact, some lawyers are so familiar with the process that they have become skilled in mediation tricks–spinning the mediator, using mediation for discovery purposes, lying and transforming mediation into a legal process that fits more with their adversarial inclination').

[14]Martins (2016, p. 256).

[15]Sunstein (2015, p. 415) (noting that if 'we believe that the social ordering (including those forms for which government is responsible) is to promote social welfare ..., we will favour welfare-promoting nudges'). Thaler and Sunstein (2009, *passim*) (by steering (better said: nudging) disputants in the direction they see procedurally fit, like mediation).

[16]Woolf (1995) (highlighting the importance of a costs rationale: 'The court... will take into account whether the parties have unreasonably refused to try ADR or behaved unreasonably in the course of ADR').

[17]*Dunnet v Railtrack* (2002) EWCA (Civ) 2003 (Eng.) (in which the Court applied Part 44 of the Civil Procedure Rules and refused the disputant's legal costs due to the fact that he had refused to contemplate mediation in good faith prior to the appeal).

[18]Rampall and Feehily (2018, p. 354) (alluding to party autonomy as a guiding principle of dispute resolution).

[19]Eberle (2009, p. 452) (noting that 'we need to excavate the underlying structure to understand better what the law really is and how it really functions within a society').

included, for example, given their importance to Macau's economy. The same goes for matters related to child support, child custody, and alimony.

The accreditation of mediators and their training within the mediation regime plays a pivotal role in building credibility to Macau's forthcoming court-connected mandatory mediation regime. To cater to that, an Independent Committee of Mediation of Macau is to be created. The Independent Committee of Mediation is to be prescribed the task of providing appropriate training to prospective mediators. The prospective mediators must become acquainted with the various styles of mediation. The most important styles of mediation range from transformative mediation,[20] narrative mediation,[21] evaluative mediation,[22] directive mediation,[23] and insight mediation.[24]

Correspondingly, the Independent Committee of Mediation is to also hold the responsibility for overseeing the accreditation of mediators and handling any complaints lodged against mediators or mediators-arbitrators, on the grounds of mediator's misconduct. This includes exerting coercion in mediation,[25] failing to display impartiality throughout joint mediation sessions or caucuses, or threatening behaviour.[26] Subsequently, it produces the pressing need to create codes of conduct that prevent misconduct. To ensure only high-quality mediators within the mediation regime in Macau, robust standards of quality should be implemented as well.[27] Additionally, this also means that the ethics of mediation need to be of a high standard.[28]

The binding nature and enforcement of the agreement arising from mediation[29] is the central element of a mediation regime. To fulfil the long-held desire of becoming a dispute resolution hub in Asia, Macau must outline a streamlined procedure to

---

[20]Bush and Folger (2004, pp. 1–304) (on transformative mediation and the quest for party empowerment).

[21]Winslade and Monk (2008, pp. 1–341) ('The narrative mediation approach encourages the conflicting parties to tell their personal 'story' of the conflict and reach resolution through a profound understanding of the context of their individual stories').

[22]Riskin (1996, pp. 7–49) (evaluative mediation assesses the weaknesses and strengths of the case or legal position thereby predicting the likelihood of success – or the lack thereof – of the latter and directing 'some or all of the outcomes of the mediation').

[23]Riskin (2003, p. 79ff) (in which Riskin revises his old grid, and deals with, the harsh criticism that it sparked in the dispute resolution field).

[24]Picard (2016, pp. 1–200) ('Cheryl A. Picard, co-founder of insight mediation, explains how the theory of cognition presented in Bernard Lonergan's *Insight* can be used as the basis for a learning-centred approach to conflict resolution').

[25]Sander et al. (1996, pp. 885–887) (on the seminal distinction between coercion into mediation and coercion in mediation).

[26]Welsh (2001, p. 47) (contending that threats amount to coercion in mediation).

[27]Tantamount to the European Code of Conduct for Mediators Providers (2018) (stating that 'this code of conduct sets out a number of principles to which mediation centres, institutes or other mediation providers may voluntarily decide to commit themselves').

[28]Menkel-Meadow and Abramson (2011, pp. 305–338).

[29]Pound (1908, pp. 605–618) (on the paramount importance of enforcement in a given system of administration of justice).

enforce domestic mediated settlement agreements. The application of the Singapore Convention on Mediation should be extended to Macau (Art. 13(1) Singapore Convention on Mediation),[30] thereby allowing the enforcement of international[31] and cross-border mediated settlement agreements in Macau.

4 Conclusion

This brief note introduced the reasoning for certain elements within the prospective court-connected mandatory mediation regime in Macau. The model will benefit from Macau's legal culture while implementing a high-quality mediation regime.

References

Bush RAB, Folger JP (2004) The promise of mediation: The transformative approach to conflict. San Francisco

Colquitt JA, Rodell JB (2011) Justice, trust, and trustworthiness: A longitudinal analysis integrating three theoretical perspectives. Acad Manag J 54:1183–1206

Cortina A (2007) Ética de la razón cordial: Educar en la ciudadanía en el siglo XXI. Ovied

Costa e Silva P (2008) De minimis non curat praetor. O acesso ao sistema judicial e os meios alternativos de resolução de controversias. O Direito 140:735–736

Dos Santos HL (2019) Mixing honey and milk: Mediation and gaming in Macau. Canadian Gaming Lawyer Magazine, Fall/Winter, pp 14–15

Eberle EJ (2009) The method and role of comparative law. Wash Univ Global Stud Law Rev 8(3):451–486

European code of conduct for mediation providers (2018) European commission for the efficiency of justice. Mediation development toolkit ensuring implementation of the CEPEJ Guidelines on mediation: European code of conduct for mediation providers. https://rm.coe.int/cepej-2018-24-en-mediation-development-toolkit-european-code-of-conduc/1680901dc6. Accessed on 14 June 2020

Fogel J, Strong SI (2016) Introduction: judicial education, dispute resolution, and the life of a judge: A conversation with judge Jeremy Fogel, director of the federal judicial center. J Dispute Resolut 2(3):260–279

Gottwald P (2001) Mediation und gerichtlicher Vergleich: Unterschiede und Gemeinsamkeiten. In: Luke G, Mikami T, Prutting H (eds) Festschrift fur Akira Ishikawa zum 70 Geburtstag. Berlin, New York, pp 137–155

Huang JL (2017) One country, two systems: Hong Kong's unique status and the development and growth of arbitration in China. Cardozo J Conflict Resolut 18(2):423–455

[30] Article 13 of the Singapore Convention on Mediation reads as follows: 'If a Party to the Convention has two or more territorial units in which different systems of law are applicable in relation to the matters dealt with in this Convention, it may, at the time of signature, ratification, acceptance, approval or accession, declare that this Convention is to extend to all its territorial units or only to one or more of them, and may amend its declaration by submitting another declaration at any time.'

[31] Sussman (2018, p. 40ff) (brings forth an intriguing account of the objectives undergirding the Singapore Convention on Mediation).

Kovach KK (2005) The vanishing trial: Land mine on the mediation landscape or opportunity for evolution: Ruminations on the future of mediation practice. Cardozo J Conflict Resolut 7:27–75
Marasco G (2006) La rinegoziazione del contrato–Strumenti legali e convenzionali a tutela dell'equilibrio negozionale. Padua
Martins RA (2016) Uma história da defensoria pública. In: Antunes MJ, Santos CC, Amaral CDP (eds) Os novos atores da justiça penal. Coimbra, pp 256–257
Menkel-Meadow C, Abramson HI (2011) Mediating multiculturally: Culture and the ethical mediator. In: Waldman E (ed) Mediation ethics: Cases and commentaries. San Francisco, pp 305–338
Nolan-Haley J (2012) Mediation: The new arbitration. Harvard Negot Law Rev 17:61–95
Nolan-Haley J (2013) Judicial review of mediated settlement agreements: Improving mediation with consent. Yearbook Arbitr Mediat 5:157–169
Nolan-Haley J (2018) Does ADR's access to justice come at the expense of meaningful consent. Ohio State J Dispute Resolut 33:386–392
Picard CA (2016) Practising insight mediation. Ontario
Pound R (1908) Mechanical jurisprudence. Columbia Law Rev 8(8):605–623
Rampall YD, Feehily R (2018) The sanctity of party autonomy and the powers of arbitrators to determine the applicable law: The quest for an arbitral equilibrium. Harvard Negotiation Law Rev 23:345–403
Riskin LL (1996) Understanding mediator orientations, strategies and techniques: A grid for the perplexed. Harvard Negot Law Rev 1:7–49
Riskin LL (2003) Decision-making in mediation: The new old grid and the new grid system. Notre Dame Law Rev 79(1):1–54
Sander FEA (2007) Another view of mandatory mediation. Dispute Resolut Mag 13(2):16–20
Sander FEA, Allen HW, Hensler D (1996) Judicial (mis)use of ADR? A debate. Univ Toledo Law Rev 27:885–896
Severin E (2011) Comment l'espirit du management est venu à l'administration de la justice. La Nouveau Management de la Justice et l'indépendance des juges, Paris
Shiga S (1988) A study of Chinese legal culture focusing on the litigation landscape. J Comp Law (Bijiao Fa Yanjiu) 3:18–26 (in Chinese)
Sunstein CR (2015) The ethics of nudging. Yale J Regul 32(2):413–445
Sussman E (2018) The Singapore Convention: Promoting the enforcement and recognition of international mediated settlement agreements. ICC Dispute Resolut Bull 3:42–54
Taruffo M (2007) Un'alternativa alle alternative: Modeli di risoluzione dei confliti. Revista De Processo 152:319–331
Thaler RH, Sunstein CR (2009) Nudge: Improving decisions about health, wealth, and happiness. London
Tong IC (2015) The road towards a sustainable legal order: In search of the rule of law for 'one country, two systems.' Acad Sinica Law J 17:1–80
Von Jhering R (1881) Culpa in contrahendo: oder Schadensersatz bei nichtigen oder nicht zur Perfection gelangten Verträgen. Gesammelte Ausfsätze aus den Jahrbüchern für die Dogmatik des heutigen römischen und deutschen Privatrechts, vol 1, Jena, pp 327–425
Welsh NA (2001) The thinning vision of self-determination in court-connected mediation: The inevitable price of institutionalization? Harvard Negot Law Rev 6(1):1–96
Winslade J, Monk G (2008) Practising narrative mediation: A new approach to conflict resolution. San Francisco
Woolf H (1995) Access to justice: Interim report to the lord chancellor on the civil justice in England and Wales, London

The manufacturer's authorised representative in the EU is Springer Nature Customer Service Centre GmbH, Europaplatz 3, 69115 Heidelberg, Germany. If you have any concerns regarding our products, please contact ProductSafety@springernature.com

Printed and bound by CPI Group (UK) Ltd, Croydon, CR0 4YY
30/09/2026
02225290-0004